Collins
New Primary Maths

Enriching Maths 4

A problem-solving, cross-curricular programme for children working above end-of-year expectations

Peter Clarke

William Collins' dream of knowledge for all began with the publication of his first book in 1819. A self-educated mill worker, he not only enriched millions of lives, but also founded a flourishing publishing house. Today, staying true to this spirit, Collins books are packed with inspiration, innovation and practical expertise. They place you at the centre of a world of possibility and give you exactly what you need to explore it.

Collins. Freedom to teach.

Published by Collins
An imprint of HarperCollins*Publishers*
77–85 Fulham Palace Road
Hammersmith
London
W6 8JB

Browse the complete Collins Education catalogue at
www.collinseducation.com

10 9 8 7 6 5 4 3 2

ISBN 978-0-00-743116-8

British Library Cataloguing in Publication Data
A Catalogue record for this publication is available from the British Library

Cover design by Neil Adams
Series design by Steve Evans and Mark Walker
Cover artwork by Jonatronix Ltd.
Internal design by Steve Evans and Mark Walker Design
Illustrations by Steve Evans, Bethan Matthews and Lisa Williams
Edited by Amanda Dickson
Proofread by Ros and Chris Davies

Acknowledgements
Peter Clarke wishes to thank Brian Molyneaux for his valuable contribution to this publication.

Printed and bound by Martins the Printers.

Contents

Quick reference guide to *Enriching Maths 4*

Introduction

Enriching Maths aims to provide support in meeting the needs of those children who are exceeding age-related expectations by providing a range of problem-solving and cross-curricular activities designed to enrich children's mathematical knowledge, skills and understanding.

The series has been designed to provide:

- a flexible 'dip-in' resource that can be easily adapted to meet the needs of individual children, and different classroom and school organisational arrangements
- extension and enrichment activities that require children to use and apply their mathematical knowledge, skills and understanding
- mathematical activities linked to the entire primary curriculum, thereby ensuring a range of cross-curricular contexts
- an easy-to-use bank of activities to save teachers time in thinking up new extension and enrichment activities
- an interesting, unique and consistent approach to presenting extension and enrichment activities to children.

The *Enriching Maths* series consists of six Resource Packs, each with an accompanying CD-ROM, one for each year group from Year 1 to Year 6.

Resource Pack

Containing:

- Pupil activity booklets (Issues)
- Teacher's notes
- Resource copymasters (RCMs)

CD-ROM

Containing editable:

- Pupil activity booklets (Issues)
- Teacher's notes
- Resource copymasters (RCMs)

It is envisaged that the activities in *Enriching Maths* will be used by either individuals or pairs of children. However, given the flexible nature of the resource, if appropriate, children can work in groups. The activities are intended to be used as:

- an alternative to the work that the rest of the class is given
- additional work to be done once children have finished other set work
- in-depth work that is to be undertaken over a prolonged period of time, such as during the course of several lessons, a week or a particular unit of work
- a resource for gifted classes, promoting independent thinking and learning
- springboards for further investigations into mathematics based on the children's suggestions.

The National Curriculum (2000) outlines the thinking skills that complement the key knowledge, skills and understanding which are embedded in the primary curriculum.

Enriching Maths aims to develop in children these key thinking skills.

Information processing skills

- locate and collect relevant information
- sort, classify, sequence, compare and analyse part and / or whole relationships

Reasoning skills

- give reasons for opinions and actions
- draw inferences and make deductions
- use precise language to explain what they think
- make judgements and decisions informed by reason or evidence

Enquiry skills

- ask relevant questions
- pose and define problems
- plan what to do and how to research
- predict outcomes and anticipate conclusions
- test conclusions and improve ideas

Creative thinking skills

- generate and extend ideas
- suggest hypotheses
- apply imagination
- look for alternative innovative outcomes

Evaluative skills

- evaluate information
- judge the value of what they read, hear or do
- develop criteria for judging the value of their own and others' work or ideas
- have confidence in their judgement

The activities in *Enriching Maths* also aim to develop children's middle and higher order thinking skills by providing a range of suitable extension and enrichment activities.

Bloom's Building Blocks to Thinking

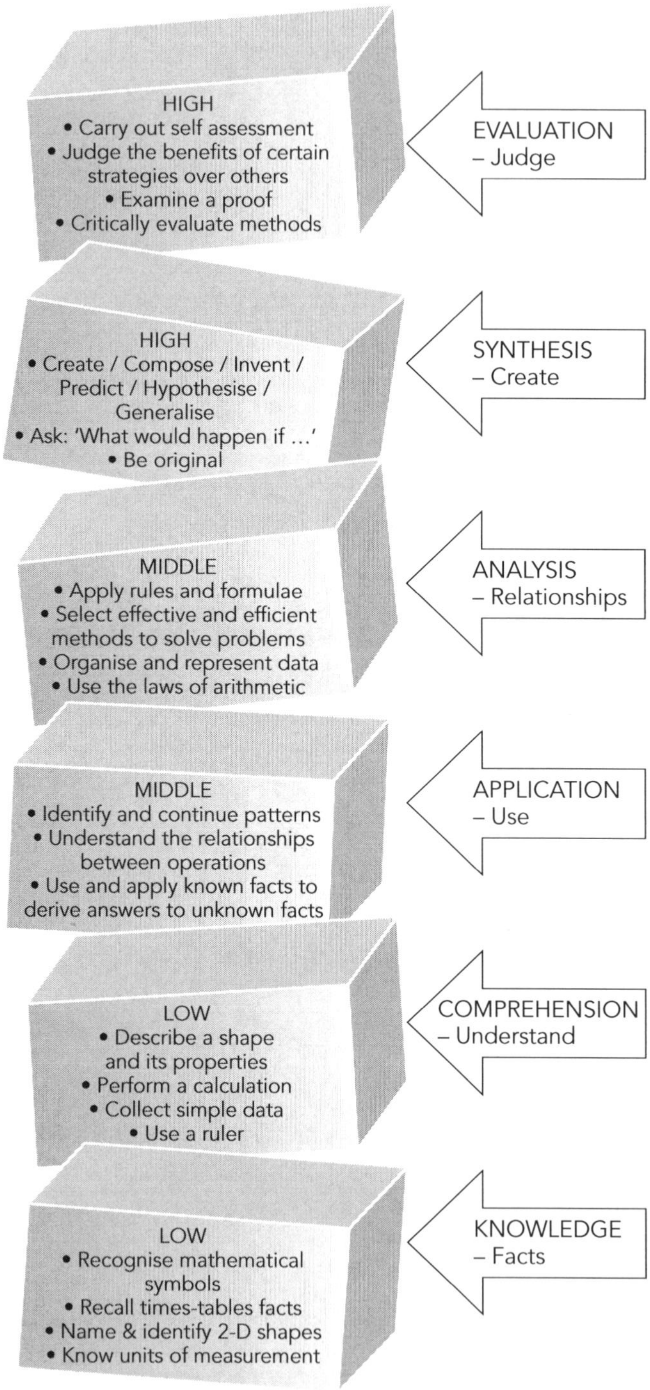

Source: Bloom

Mathematically gifted children

Some characteristics of gifted children

The following characteristics are not necessarily proof of high mathematical ability. However, they may provide an indication of a pupil's level of ability.

Mathematically gifted children may:

- be inquisitive and ask searching questions
- grasp new concepts quickly
- be imaginative
- be logical
- show unusual and original responses
- have an ability to work things out in their head very quickly
- approach problems from different perspectives
- be persistent
- make generalisations
- easily identify patterns and relationships
- use mathematical symbols confidently
- develop concise logical arguments
- have good memories
- be quick thinkers
- be very articulate for their age
- give quick verbal responses
- prefer verbal to written activities
- communicate well with adults – often better than with their peer group
- have a wide general knowledge
- be interested in topics which one might associate with an older child
- have a range of interests, some of which are almost obsessions
- be self-taught in their own interest areas
- have strong views and opinions
- have a lively and original imagination / sense of humour
- be very sensitive and aware
- focus on their own interests rather than on what is being taught
- be easily bored by what they perceive as routine tasks
- show a strong sense of leadership
- not necessarily be well-behaved or well-liked by others.

The identification of gifted children

Research suggests that up to 20% of pupils can be identified as being either more or exceptionally able. Before effective provision can be made for these children the identification of such children needs to be undertaken.

Schools have the discretion to decide how best to identify gifted children, but are likely to obtain the best results by drawing on a wide range of sources, including both qualitative and quantitative information.

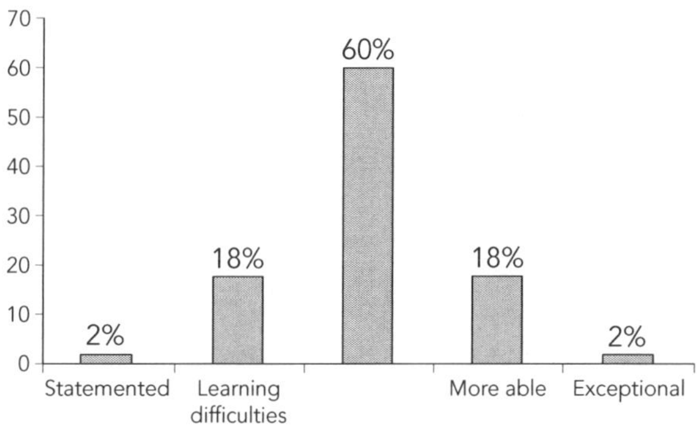

Source: OFSTED

A range of popular methods for identification include:

- teacher nomination
- checklists
- testing
- assessment of children's work
- peer or self nomination
- parental information
- discussions with children
- community resources, e.g. educational psychologists.

The key principles of identification are that it is:

- a continuous process
- a systematic whole-school approach
- based on a portfolio approach, using a range of qualitative and quantitative measures
- to be vigilant for the 'hidden gifted', such as underachievers, EAL children, those with specific learning or physical disabilities, those from different cultural or disadvantaged socio-economic groups
- a process that involves all educators, pupils and parents / carers.

Providing provision for gifted children

The most important aspect of meeting the needs of gifted children is the day-to-day experience in the classroom. This can be achieved through a combination of the following:

- incorporating breadth across the whole curriculum
- increasing depth within the subject
- accelerating the pace of learning
- promoting independence in thinking and learning
- providing opportunities for autonomous learning
- encouraging high expectations in both educators and children
- creating an appropriate, challenging and supportive environment where all children can achieve their full potential.

Source: DfES

The features of *Enriching Maths*

Pupil activity booklets (Issues)

- Each of the 36 issues in *Enriching Maths 4* consists of a four-page A5 pupil activity booklet (to be printed double sided onto one sheet of A4 paper).
- The 36 issues cover the different attainment targets, strands and topics of the primary mathematics curriculum (see pages 15 to 22).
- The issues have been designed to resemble a newspaper, with each of the issues consisting of between four and twelve different activities, all related to the same mathematical topic.
- The terms 'Issue' and 'Volume' have been used rather than 'Unit' and 'Year group' because they are in keeping with the newspaper theme, and means that an issue can be used in whichever year group needed, rather than being confined to one particular year group.

Types of activities

- All of the activities in the *Enriching Maths* series are designed to enhance children's use and application of mathematics. There are four different types of 'using and applying' activities in the series:

  What's the Problem? The Puzzler

  Looking for Patterns Let's Investigate

- Alongside developing children's problem-solving skills, the series also provides activities with cross-curricular links to other subjects in the primary curriculum. The following shows the *Enriching Maths* features and its corresponding primary curriculum subject.

Curriculum subject	***Enriching Maths* feature**
English	The Language of Maths
Science	Focus on Science
ICT	Technology Today
Geography	Around the World
History	In the Past
	Famous Mathematicians
Art and Music	The Arts Roundup
Design and Technology	Construct
Physical Education	Sports Update

- As well as the features mentioned above, other regular features in *Enriching Maths* include:

  Money Matters At Home (home–school link activities).

- A chart showing the link between the issues, the *Enriching Maths* features and cross-curricular links can be found on pages 23 and 24.
- Please note the following symbols that occur beside an activity when appropriate.

  Denotes that children are likely to need access to a computer.

  Denotes that children are likely to need access to a computer with internet access.

- Enriching Maths Uncovered (EMU) is a recurring feature of the series. In each issue there is an emu holding a mathematical word or symbol. Children locate the emu and write about the meaning of the word or symbol.

Teacher's notes

Each of the 36 issues includes a two-page set of teacher's notes, including answers.

Issue number

Mathematics topic

Prerequisites for learning

Lists the prerequisites for learning that children need to have acquired prior to this issue.

Lists the associated knowledge and skills that contribute to understanding the issue topic.

Resources

To aid preparation, the resources needed for the issue are listed.

Teaching Support

Provides teaching points for each of the activities in the issue. These may be helpful when introducing the issue to the children, or when children experience difficulty whilst working on a particular activity.

Almost all of the activities in *Enriching Maths* can be undertaken either individually or in pairs (or sometimes in small groups). Where an activity is particularly suitable for pairs to work on, this is denoted by [pairs icon].

When children are likely to need access to a computer, this is denoted by [computer icon].

When children are likely to need access to a computer with internet access, this is denoted by [www icon].

Simplifications

Where appropriate, offers suggestions for supporting children who may be experiencing difficulties understanding the main mathematical ideas.

Extensions

Where appropriate, offers suggestions for extending children's understanding if you feel they are developing a good understanding of the main mathematical ideas.

Assessment for learning

Each issue includes a list of questions specifically designed to assist in assessing pupils' understanding of the issue topic.

Answers

These are provided where appropriate.

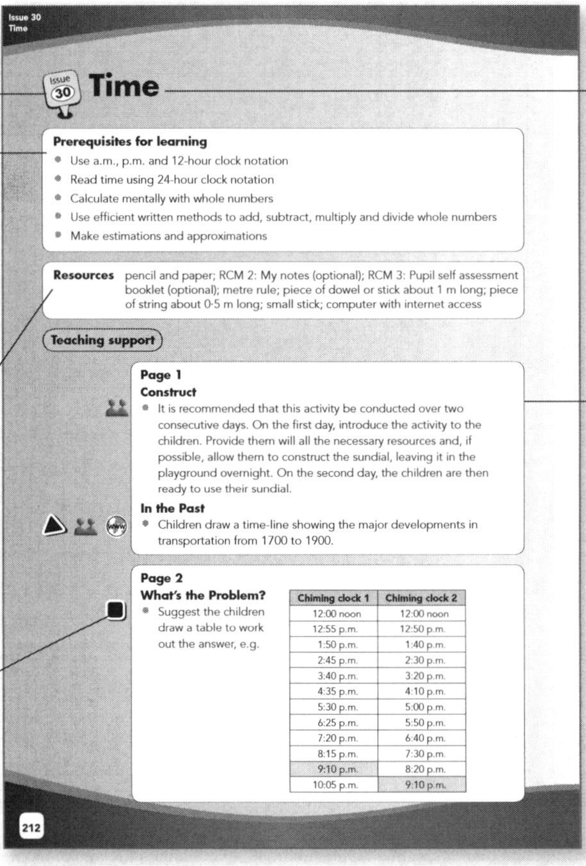

Issue 30
Time

Issue 30 **Time**

Prerequisites for learning

- Use a.m., p.m. and 12-hour clock notation
- Read time using 24-hour clock notation
- Calculate mentally with whole numbers
- Use efficient written methods to add, subtract, multiply and divide whole numbers
- Make estimations and approximations

Resources pencil and paper; RCM 2: My notes (optional); RCM 3: Pupil self assessment booklet (optional); metre rule; piece of dowel or stick about 1 m long; piece of string about 0·5 m long; small stick; computer with internet access

Teaching support

Page 1
Construct
- It is recommended that this activity be conducted over two consecutive days. On the first day, introduce the activity to the children. Provide them will all the necessary resources and, if possible, allow them to construct the sundial, leaving it in the playground overnight. On the second day, the children are then ready to use their sundial.

In the Past
- Children draw a time-line showing the major developments in transportation from 1700 to 1900.

Page 2
What's the Problem?
- Suggest the children draw a table to work out the answer, e.g.

Chiming clock 1	Chiming clock 2
12:00 noon	12:00 noon
12:55 p.m.	12:50 p.m.
1:50 p.m.	1:40 p.m.
2:45 p.m.	2:30 p.m.
3:40 p.m.	3:20 p.m.
4:35 p.m.	4:10 p.m.
5:30 p.m.	5:00 p.m.
6:25 p.m.	5:50 p.m.
7:20 p.m.	6:40 p.m.
8:15 p.m.	7:30 p.m.
9:10 p.m.	8:20 p.m.
10:05 p.m.	9:10 p.m.

212

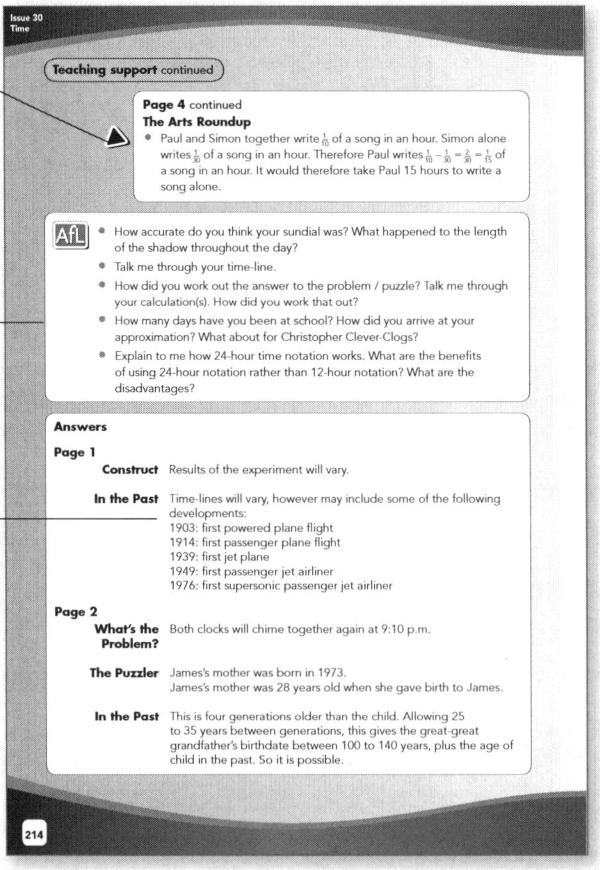

Issue 30
Time

Teaching support continued

Page 4 continued
The Arts Roundup
- Paul and Simon together write $\frac{1}{10}$ of a song in an hour. Simon alone writes $\frac{1}{30}$ of a song in an hour. Therefore Paul writes $\frac{1}{10} - \frac{1}{30} = \frac{2}{30} = \frac{1}{15}$ of a song in an hour. It would therefore take Paul 15 hours to write a song alone.

AfL
- How accurate do you think your sundial was? What happened to the length of the shadow throughout the day?
- Talk me through your time-line.
- How did you work out the answer to the problem / puzzle? Talk me through your calculation(s). How did you work that out?
- How many days have you been at school? How did you arrive at your approximation? What about for Christopher Clever-Clogs?
- Explain to me how 24-hour time notation works. What are the benefits of using 24-hour notation rather than 12-hour notation? What are the disadvantages?

Answers

Page 1

Construct Results of the experiment will vary.

In the Past Time-lines will vary, however may include some of the following developments:
1903: first powered plane flight
1914: first passenger plane flight
1939: first jet plane
1949: first passenger jet airliner
1976: first supersonic passenger jet airliner

Page 2

What's the Problem? Both clocks will chime together again at 9:10 p.m.

The Puzzler James's mother was born in 1973.
James's mother was 28 years old when she gave birth to James.

In the Past This is four generations older than the child. Allowing 25 to 35 years between generations, this gives the great-great grandfather's birthdate between 100 to 140 years, plus the age of child in the past. So it is possible.

214

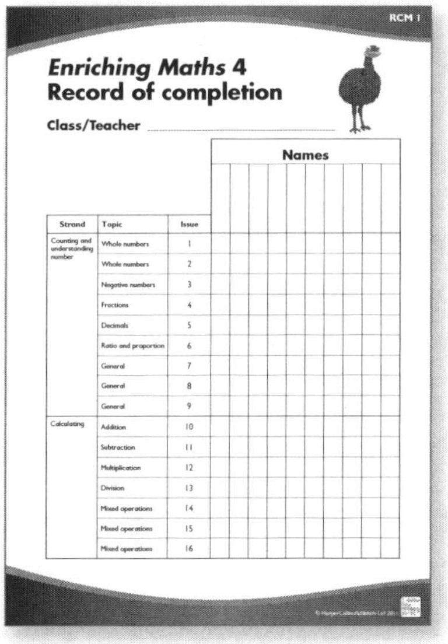

RCM 1

Enriching Maths 4
Record of completion

Class/Teacher

Strand	Topic	Issue	Names
Counting and understanding number	Whole numbers	1	
	Whole numbers	2	
	Negative numbers	3	
	Fractions	4	
	Decimals	5	
	Ratio and proportion	6	
	General	7	
	General	8	
	General	9	
Calculating	Addition	10	
	Subtraction	11	
	Multiplication	12	
	Division	13	
	Mixed operations	14	
	Mixed operations	15	
	Mixed operations	16	

Record of completion

To assist in keeping a record of which issues children have completed.

Once a child has completed an issue you could either put a tick or write the date in the corresponding box.

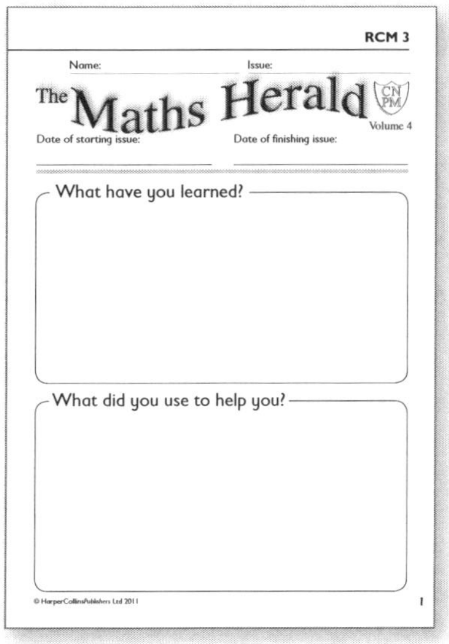

RCM 3

Name: Issue:

The Maths Herald Volume 4

Date of starting issue: Date of finishing issue:

What have you learned?

What did you use to help you?

© HarperCollinsPublishers Ltd 2011

Pupil self assessment booklet

Each Resource Pack in the *Enriching Maths* series includes an age-appropriate pupil self assessment A5 booklet (to be printed double sided onto one sheet of A4 paper).

This booklet is a generic sheet that can be used for any, or all, of the 36 issues in the Resource Pack.

The booklet is designed to provide children with an opportunity to undertake some form of self assessment once they have completed the issue.

After the children have completed the booklet, discuss with them what they have written.

This can then be kept, together with the child's copy of the issue and their working out and answers, including, if appropriate, 'My notes'.

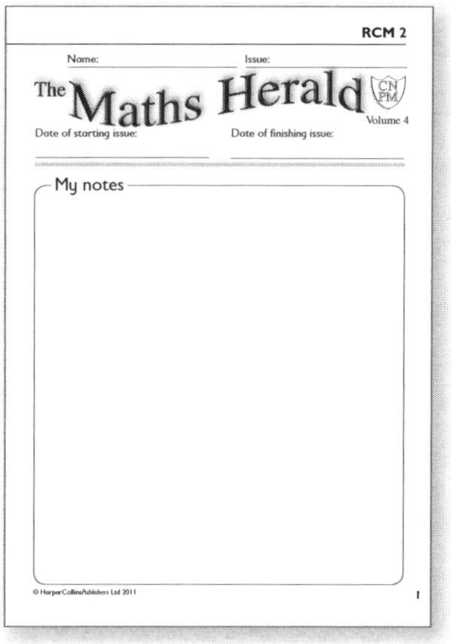

RCM 2

Name: Issue:

The Maths Herald Volume 4

Date of starting issue: Date of finishing issue:

My notes

© HarperCollinsPublishers Ltd 2011

My notes

The pupil activity booklets have been designed to resemble a newspaper. This means that there is insufficient space in the booklets for children to show their working and answers.

You may decide to simply provide children with pencil and paper to record their work. Alternatively, you could provide them with a copy of the A5 booklet: 'My notes' (to be printed double sided onto one sheet of A4 paper). This can then be kept, together with the child's copy of the issue and, if appropriate, their 'Pupil self assessment booklet'. Whichever method you choose for the children to record their working and answers, i.e. on sheets of paper, using a 'My notes' booklet, in an exercise book, or any other method, children need to be clear and systematic in their recording. For ease of marking and discussion of their work at a later stage, it is recommended that you instruct the children to write the issue page number and *Enriching Maths* feature, for each activity, clearly beside their working and answer.

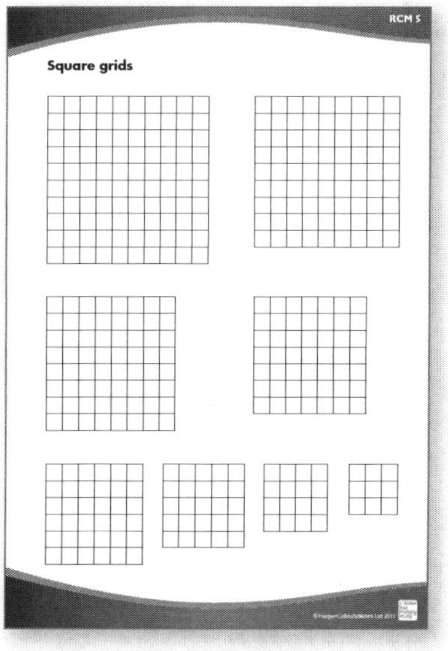

Other resource copymasters (RCMs)

For some of the activities, children are required to use a resource copymaster (RCM).

These are included both in the back of this Resource Pack and on the CD-ROM.

A possible *Enriching Maths* teaching and learning sequence

As the diagram on the right illustrates, the process of learning about mathematics can be thought of as the interrelationship between knowledge, understanding and application.

A suggested teaching sequence for working with children based on this model and using the activities in *Enriching Maths* is given below.

A complete sequence may occur during a particular lesson if the activity given is designed to be completed during the course of the lesson. Alternatively, the teaching and learning sequence may extend for a longer period of time if the activities are to be completed over the course of several lessons, a week or during a particular unit of work.

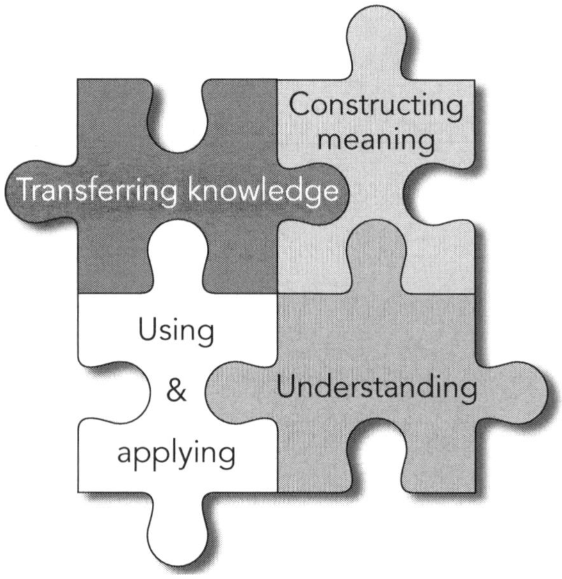

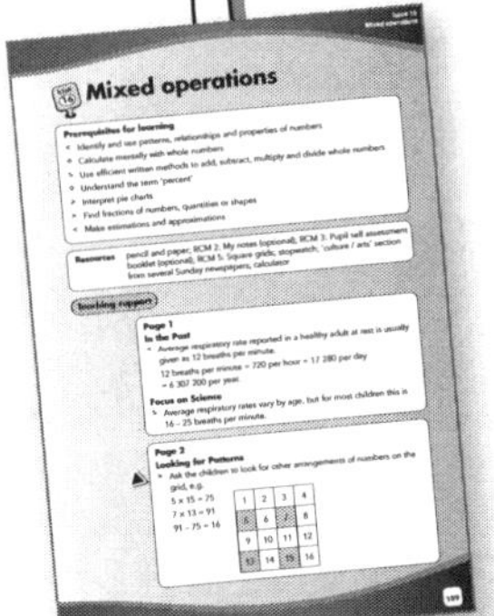

Briefing

The teacher:

- introduces the topic
- checks prerequisites for learning
- introduces the activity
- checks for understanding
- clarifies any misconceptions
- ensures there is easy access to any necessary resources.

Working

- Children work individually, in pairs, or if appropriate, in groups.
- Teacher acts only as a 'guide-on-the-side'.

De-briefing

The child / children:

- reports back to others
- reflects on their learning
- identifies the 'next step'.

The teacher evaluates learning.

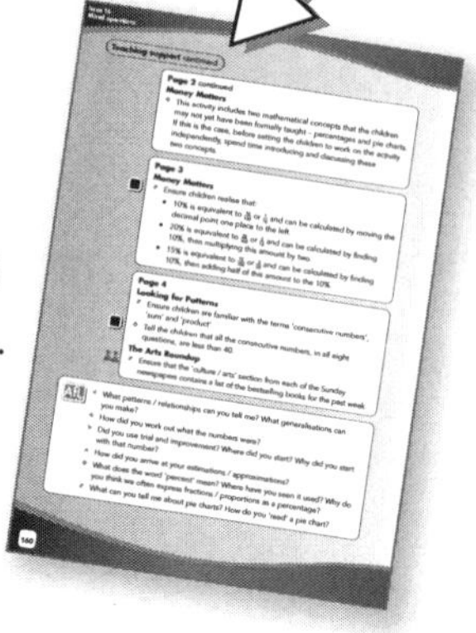

Enriching Maths 4 and Assessing Pupils' Progress (APP)

Assessing Pupils' Progress (APP) is a structured approach to periodically assessing mathematics so teachers can:

- track pupils' progress
- use diagnostic information about pupils' strengths and weaknesses.

Using APP materials, teachers can make National Curriculum (NC) level judgements for each of the following Mathematics Attainment Targets (ATs):

- using and applying mathematics
- number and algebra
- shape, space and measures
- handling data.

APP identifies particular Assessment Focuses (AFs) which are based on the National Curriculum programmes of study and level descriptions.

Using AFs helps teachers to:

- see how pupils' work on a small number of teaching objectives can contribute to the bigger picture of their progress and attainment
- give more precise feedback to pupils
- refine learning targets for individual children and groups within the class
- identify gaps in teaching and learning and adjust planning accordingly
- plan next steps based on the diagnostic information that emerges.

Overall, the information gained from the APP approach:

- provides diagnostic information on pupils' strengths and weaknesses
- enables forward planning based on group and individual pupil needs
- makes the most of pupils' learning experiences across the whole curriculum.

Part of the *Collins NEW Primary Maths* series is an *Assessment Pack* for each year group. Each *CNPM Assessment Pack* consists of:

- Adult Directed Tasks
- Pupil Self assessments
- Tests or Individual Assessment Sheets.

All three of these components can assist teachers when making periodic teacher assessment judgements using the APP approach.

The Adult Directed Tasks from the *CNPM Assessment Packs* can also be used as a diagnostic assessment tool to assist with identifying individual pupil's strengths and weaknesses, and when making the decision to provide extension work to individuals or groups of children using *Enriching Maths.*

The following chart shows the links between the 2006 Primary *Framework* strands, the NC Attainment Targets, the APP AFs for mathematics and the issues within *Enriching Maths 4*. This chart, along with the NC referencing charts on the following pages, will help formalise your assessments of pupils' mathematics into level judgements.

2006 Primary *Framework* Strands	**National Curriculum (NC) Attainment Targets**	**Assessing Pupils' Progress (APP) Assessment Focuses (AFs) for Mathematics**	***Enriching Maths 4***
Using and applying mathematics →	Ma1 Using and applying mathematics →	Problem solving →	*Incorporated within each issue.*
		Communicating →	
		Reasoning →	
Counting and understanding number →	Ma2 Number and algebra →	Numbers and the number system →	Issues 1 & 2: Whole numbers Issue 3: Negative numbers Issues 7–9: Counting and understanding number – General
		Fractions, decimals, percentages and ratio →	Issue 4: Fractions Issue 5: Decimals Issue 6: Ratio and proportion Issues 7–9: Counting and understanding number – General Issue 17: Calculating with fractions
Knowing and using number facts →		Operations and the relationships between them →	Issue 10: Addition Issue 11: Subtraction Issue 12: Multiplication Issue 13: Division Issues 14–16: Mixed operations Issue 17: Calculating with fractions Issues 18 & 19: Calculating – General
		Mental methods →	
Calculating →		Solving numerical problems →	
		Written and calculator methods →	
Understanding shape →	Ma3 Shape, space and measures →	Shape →	Issue 20: 2-D shapes Issue 21: 3-D solids Issue 22: Symmetry and reflection Issues 25 & 26: Understanding shape – General
		Position and movement →	Issue 23: Position and direction Issue 24: Movement and angle Issues 25 & 26: Understanding shape – General
Measuring →		Measures →	Issue 27: Length Issue 28: Weight Issue 29: Capacity Issue 30: Time Issue 31: Area Issue 32: Perimeter Issues 33 & 34: Measuring – General
Handling data →	Ma4 Handling data →	Processing and representing data →	Issues 35 & 36: Organising and interpreting data
		Interpreting data →	

Links to the Mathematics National Curriculum (2000) Attainment Targets and Levels, and the Primary National Strategy (2006) *Framework* objectives and strands for Year 4

	Enriching Maths Issue																																			
National Curriculum Attainment Target: Ma1 – Using and applying mathematics **Primary National Strategy Strand:** Using and applying mathematics	1	2	3	4	5	6	7	8	9	10	11	12	13	14	15	16	17	18	19	20	21	22	23	24	25	26	27	28	29	30	31	32	33	34	35	36
• Solve one-step and two-step problems involving numbers, money or measures, including time; choose and carry out appropriate calculations, using calculator methods where appropriate (NC Level 3)		•	•	•	•	•			•		•	•	•		•		•	•	•				•				•	•	•	•		•		•		
• Represent a puzzle or problem using number sentences, statements or diagrams; use these to solve the problem; present and interpret the solution in the context of the problem (NC Level 3)	•	•	•	•	•	•	•	•	•	•	•	•		•	•				•	•	•		•	•	•	•	•	•	•		•	•		•		
• Suggest a line of enquiry and the strategy needed to follow it; collect, organise and interpret selected information to find answers (NC Level 3)							•	•												•		•											•		•	•
• Identify and use patterns, relationships and properties of numbers or shapes; investigate a statement involving numbers and test it with examples (NC Level 3)	•	•	•		•	•	•	•	•	•	•	•	•	•	•	•	•	•	•	•	•	•	•	•	•	•	•	•	•	•	•	•	•			
• Report solutions to puzzles and problems, giving explanations and reasoning orally and in writing, using diagrams and symbols (NC Level 3)	•	•	•	•	•	•	•	•	•	•	•	•	•	•	•	•	•	•	•	•	•	•	•	•	•	•	•	•	•	•	•	•	•	•	•	•

	Enriching Maths Issue																																			
National Curriculum Attainment Target: Ma2 – Number and algebra **Primary National Strategy Strand:** Counting and understanding number	1	2	3	4	5	6	7	8	9	10	11	12	13	14	15	16	17	18	19	20	21	22	23	24	25	26	27	28	29	30	31	32	33	34	35	36
• Recognise and continue number sequences formed by counting on or back in steps of constant size (NC Level 3)	●	●	●				●	●	●																											
• Partition, round and order four-digit whole numbers; use positive and negative numbers in context and position them on a number line; state inequalities using the symbols < and >, e.g. $^-3 > {}^-5$, $^-1 < {}^+1$ (NC Level 3)	●	●	●				●	●	●																		●									
• Use decimal notation for tenths and hundredths and partition decimals; relate the notation to money and measurement; position one-place and two-place decimals on a number line (NC Level 3)		●	●		●									●					●										●							
• Recognise the equivalence between decimal and fraction forms of one half, quarters, tenths and hundredths (NC Level 4)					●																								●							
• **Use diagrams to identify equivalent fractions, e.g. $\frac{6}{8}$ and $\frac{3}{4}$, or $\frac{70}{100}$ and $\frac{7}{10}$; interpret mixed numbers and position them on a number line, e.g. $3\frac{1}{2}$** (NC Level 3)				●													●																			
• Use the vocabulary of ratio and proportion to describe the relationship between two quantities, e.g. there are 2 red beads to every 3 blue beads, or 2 beads in every 5 beads are red; estimate a proportion, e.g. 'about one quarter of the apples in the box are green' (NC Level 3)						●			●																											

National Curriculum Attainment Target: Ma2 – Number and algebra **Primary National Strategy Strand:** Knowing and using number facts	1	2	3	4	5	6	7	8	9	10	11	12	13	14	15	16	17	18	19	20	21	22	23	24	25	26	27	28	29	30	31	32	33	34	35	36
• Use knowledge of addition and subtraction facts and place value to derive sums and differences of pairs of multiples of 10, 100 or 1000 (NC Level 3)	●	●	●	●			●	●		●	●			●	●	●		●	●				●					●						●		
• Identify the doubles of two-digit numbers; use these to calculate doubles of multiples of 10 and 100 and derive the corresponding halves (NC Level 3)												●		●	●																					
• **Derive and recall multiplication facts up to 10 × 10, the corresponding division facts and multiples of numbers to 10 up to the tenth multiple** (NC Level 4)	●	●					●	●				●	●	●		●		●	●									●						●		
• Use knowledge of rounding, number operations and inverses to estimate and check calculations (NC Level 3)	●								●	●					●	●			●																	
• Identify pairs of fractions that total 1 (NC Level 3)																																				

NOTE: Key objectives are in **bold**.

	Enriching Maths Issue																																			
National Curriculum Attainment Target: Ma2 – Number and algebra **Primary National Strategy Strand:** Calculating	1	2	3	4	5	6	7	8	9	10	11	12	13	14	15	16	17	18	19	20	21	22	23	24	25	26	27	28	29	30	31	32	33	34	35	36
• **Add or subtract mentally pairs of two-digit whole numbers, e.g. 47 + 58, 91 – 35** (NC Level 3)	●	●	●							●	●			●	●	●		●	●				●					●	●				●	●		
• Refine and use efficient written methods to add and subtract two- and three-digit whole numbers and £.p (NC Level 3)	●		●		●					●	●			●		●		●	●								●		●					●		
• Multiply and divide numbers to 1000 by 10 and then 100 (whole-number answers), understanding the effect; relate to scaling up or down (NC Level 4)		●			●							●					●	●											●							
• **Develop and use written methods to record, support and explain multiplication and division of two-digit numbers by a one-digit number, including division with remainders, e.g. 15 × 9, 98 ÷ 6** (NC Level 4)	●					●						●	●	●		●		●	●								●		●				●	●		
• Find fractions of numbers, quantities or shapes, e.g. $\frac{1}{5}$ of 30 plums, $\frac{3}{8}$ of a 6 by 4 rectangle (NC Level 3)									●							●	●	●																		
• Use a calculator to carry out one- and two-step calculations involving all four operations; recognise negative numbers in the display, correct mistaken entries and interpret the display correctly in the context of money (NC Level 3)			●		●						●			●																						

National Curriculum Attainment Target: Ma3 – Shape, space and measures **Primary National Strategy Strand:** Understanding shape	1	2	3	4	5	6	7	8	9	10	11	12	13	14	15	16	17	18	19	20	21	22	23	24	25	26	27	28	29	30	31	32	33	34	35	36
• Draw polygons and classify them by identifying their properties, including their line symmetry (NC Level 3)																				●		●			●	●						●				
• Visualise 3-D objects from 2-D drawings and make nets of common solids (NC Level 3)																					●				●	●										
• Recognise horizontal and vertical lines; use the eight compass points to describe direction; describe and identify the position of a square on a grid of squares (NC Level 3)																							●	●	●											
• **Know that angles are measured in degrees and that one whole turn is 360°; compare and order angles less than 180°** (NC Level 3)																								●	●	●						●				

NOTE: Key objectives are in **bold**.

	Enriching Maths Issue																																			
National Curriculum Attainment Target: Ma3 – Shape, space and measures **Primary National Strategy Strand:** Measuring	1	2	3	4	5	6	7	8	9	10	11	12	13	14	15	16	17	18	19	20	21	22	23	24	25	26	27	28	29	30	31	32	33	34	35	36
• **Choose and use standard metric units and their abbreviations when estimating, measuring and recording length, weight and capacity; know the meaning of 'kilo', 'centi' and 'milli' and, where appropriate, use decimal notation to record measurements, e.g. 1·3 m or 0·6 kg** (NC Level 3)																	●	●									●	●	●				●	●		
• Interpret intervals and divisions on partially numbered scales and record readings accurately, where appropriate to the nearest tenth of a unit (NC Level 3)																											●							●		
• Draw rectangles and measure and calculate their perimeters; find the area of rectilinear shapes drawn on a square grid by counting squares (NC Level 3)																															●	●	●			
• Read time to the nearest minute; use a.m., p.m. and 12-hour clock notation; choose units of time to measure time intervals; calculate time intervals from clocks and timetables (NC Level 3)																														●			●	●		
National Curriculum Attainment Target: Ma4 – Handling data **Primary National Strategy Strand:** Handling data																																				
• **Answer a question by identifying what data to collect; organise, present, analyse and interpret the data in tables, diagrams, tally charts, pictograms and bar charts, using ICT where appropriate** (NC Level 3)			●																														●		●	●
• Compare the impact of representations where scales have intervals of differing step size (NC Level 3)			●																																	●

NOTE: Key objectives are in **bold**.

Links to the Mathematics National Curriculum (2000) Attainment Targets and Levels, and the Primary National Strategy (2006) *Framework* objectives and strands for Year 5

	Enriching Maths Issue																																			
National Curriculum Attainment Target: Ma1 – Using and applying mathematics **Primary National Strategy Strand:** Using and applying mathematics	1	2	3	4	5	6	7	8	9	10	11	12	13	14	15	16	17	18	19	20	21	22	23	24	25	26	27	28	29	30	31	32	33	34	35	36
• Solve one-step and two-step problems involving whole numbers and decimals and all four operations, choosing and using appropriate calculation strategies, including calculator use (NC Level 4)		●	●	●	●	●			●		●	●	●		●		●	●	●				●				●	●	●	●		●		●		
• Represent a puzzle or problem by identifying and recording the information or calculations needed to solve it; find possible solutions and confirm them in the context of the problem (NC Level 4)	●	●	●	●	●	●	●	●	●	●	●	●		●	●				●	●	●		●	●	●	●	●	●	●		●	●		●		
• Plan and pursue an enquiry; present evidence by collecting, organising and interpreting information; suggest extensions to the enquiry (NC Level 4)		●			●																					●			●				●	●	●	●
• Explore patterns, properties and relationships and propose a general statement involving numbers or shapes; identify examples for which the statement is true or false (NC Level 4)	●	●	●		●	●	●	●	●	●	●	●	●	●	●	●	●	●	●	●	●	●	●	●	●	●	●	●	●	●	●	●	●			
• Explain reasoning using diagrams, graphs and text; refine ways of recording using images and symbols (NC Level 4)	●	●	●	●	●	●	●	●	●	●	●	●	●	●	●	●	●	●	●	●	●	●	●	●	●	●	●	●	●	●	●	●	●	●	●	●

National Curriculum Attainment Target: Ma2 – Number and algebra / Primary National Strategy Strand: Counting and understanding number	1	2	3	4	5	6	7	8	9	10	11	12	13	14	15	16	17	18	19	20	21	22	23	24	25	26	27	28	29	30	31	32	33	34	35	36
• Count from any given number in whole-number and decimal steps, extending beyond zero when counting backwards; relate the numbers to their position on a number line (NC Level 4)	●	●	●				●	●	●																											
• **Explain what each digit represents in whole numbers and decimals with up to two places, and partition, round and order these numbers** (NC Level 4)	●	●	●		●		●	●	●					●					●								●		●							
• Express a smaller whole number as a fraction of a larger one, e.g. recognise that 5 out of 8 is $\frac{5}{8}$; find equivalent fractions, e.g. $\frac{7}{10} = \frac{14}{20}$, or $\frac{19}{10} = 1\frac{9}{10}$; relate fractions to their decimal representations (NC Level 4)				●	●												●												●							
• Understand percentage as the number of parts in every 100 and express tenths and hundredths as percentages (NC Level 4)																●																				
• Use sequences to scale numbers up or down; solve problems involving proportions of quantities, e.g. decrease quantities in a recipe designed to feed six people (NC Level 4)						●			●																											

Enriching Maths Issue

National Curriculum Attainment Target: Ma2 – Number and algebra / Primary National Strategy Strand: Knowing and using number facts	1	2	3	4	5	6	7	8	9	10	11	12	13	14	15	16	17	18	19	20	21	22	23	24	25	26	27	28	29	30	31	32	33	34	35	36
• **Use knowledge of place value and addition and subtraction of two-digit numbers to derive sums and differences, doubles and halves of decimals, e.g. 6·5 + 2·7, halve 5·6, double 0·34** (NC Level 4)	●	●	●	●			●	●		●	●	●		●	●	●		●	●				●					●						●		
• Recall quickly multiplication facts up to 10 × 10 and use them to multiply pairs of multiples of 10 and 100; derive quickly corresponding division facts (NC Level 4)	●	●					●	●				●	●	●	●	●		●	●									●						●		
• Identify pairs of factors of two-digit whole numbers and find common multiples, e.g. for 6 and 9 (NC Level 4)												●	●																							
• Use knowledge of rounding, place value, number facts and inverse operations to estimate and check calculations (NC Level 4)	●									●	●				●		●		●																	

NOTE: Key objectives are in **bold**.

Enriching Maths Issue

National Curriculum Attainment Target: Ma2 – Number and algebra **Primary National Strategy Strand:** Calculating	1	2	3	4	5	6	7	8	9	10	11	12	13	14	15	16	17	18	19	20	21	22	23	24	25	26	27	28	29	30	31	32	33	34	35	36
• Extend mental methods for whole-number calculations, e.g. to multiply a two-digit by a one-digit number (e.g. 12 × 9), to multiply by 25 (e.g. 16 × 25), to subtract one near multiple of 1000 from another (e.g. 6070 – 4097) (NC Level 4)	●	●	●			●						●		●		●		●	●								●	●	●				●	●		
• **Use efficient written methods to add and subtract whole numbers and decimals with up to two places** (NC Level 4)	●		●		●					●	●			●	●	●		●	●										●				●	●		
• Use understanding of place value to multiply and divide whole numbers and decimals by 10, 100 or 1000 (NC Level 5)		●			●							●					●	●											●							
• Refine and use efficient written methods to multiply and divide HTU × U, TU × TU, U·t × U, and HTU ÷ U (NC Level 4)	●											●	●	●		●		●	●								●		●					●		
• Find fractions using division, e.g. $\frac{1}{100}$ of 5 kg, and percentages of numbers and quantities, e.g. 10%, 5% and 15% of £80 (NC Level 4)									●							●	●	●																		
• Use a calculator to solve problems, including those involving decimals or fractions, e.g. to find $\frac{3}{4}$ of 150 g; interpret the display correctly in the context of measurement (NC Level 4)			●		●						●			●																						
National Curriculum Attainment Target: Ma3 – Shape, space and measures **Primary National Strategy Strand:** Understanding shape																																				
• Identify, visualise and describe properties of rectangles, triangles, regular polygons and 3-D solids; use knowledge of properties to draw 2-D shapes and identify and draw nets of 3-D shapes (NC Level 4)																				●	●				●	●						●				
• **Read and plot coordinates in the first quadrant; recognise parallel and perpendicular lines in grids and shapes; use a set-square and ruler to draw shapes with perpendicular or parallel sides** (NC Level 4)																							●	●												
• Complete patterns with up to two lines of symmetry and draw the position of a shape after a reflection or translation (NC Level 4)																						●				●										
• Estimate, draw and measure acute and obtuse angles using an angle measurer or protractor to a suitable degree of accuracy; calculate angles in a straight line (NC Level 4)																								●	●	●						●				

NOTE: Key objectives are in **bold**.

	Enriching Maths Issue																																			
National Curriculum Attainment Target: Ma3 – Shape, space and measures **Primary National Strategy Strand:** Measuring	1	2	3	4	5	6	7	8	9	10	11	12	13	14	15	16	17	18	19	20	21	22	23	24	25	26	27	28	29	30	31	32	33	34	35	36
• Read, choose, use and record standard metric units to estimate and measure length, weight and capacity to a suitable degree of accuracy, e.g. the nearest centimetre; convert larger to smaller units using decimals to one place, e.g. change 2·6 kg to 2600 g (NC Level 4)																	●	●									●	●	●				●	●		
• Interpret a reading that lies between two unnumbered divisions on a scale (NC Level 4)																											●							●		
• **Draw and measure lines to the nearest millimetre; measure and calculate the perimeter of regular and irregular polygons; use the formula for the area of a rectangle to calculate its area** (NC Level 4)																															●	●	●			
• Read timetables and time using 24-hour clock notation; use a calendar to calculate time intervals (NC Level 4)																														●			●	●		

National Curriculum Attainment Target: Ma4 – Handling data **Primary National Strategy Strand:** Handling data	1	2	3	4	5	6	7	8	9	10	11	12	13	14	15	16	17	18	19	20	21	22	23	24	25	26	27	28	29	30	31	32	33	34	35	36
• Describe the occurrence of familiar events using the language of chance or likelihood (NC Level 4)																																			●	
• Answer a set of related questions by collecting, selecting and organising relevant data; draw conclusions, using ICT to present features, and identify further questions to ask (NC Level 4)			●																														●		●	●
• **Construct frequency tables, pictograms and bar and line graphs to represent the frequencies of events and changes over time** (NC Level 4)			●																														●		●	●
• Find and interpret the mode of a set of data (NC Level 4)																																				

NOTE: Key objectives are in **bold**.

Cross-curricular links to the Primary National Curriculum (2000)

Strand	Topic	Issue	Cross-curricular link and *Enriching Maths* feature													
			Mathematics				English	Science	ICT	Geography	History	Art and Music	Design and Technology	Physical Education	Links to money	Links with home
			What's the Problem?	Looking for Patterns	The Puzzler	Let's Investigate	The Language of Maths	Focus on Science	Technology Today	Around the World	In the Past / Famous Mathematicians	The Arts Roundup	Construct	Sports Update	Money Matters	At Home
Counting and understanding number	Whole numbers	1		•	•	•		•			•					
	Whole numbers	2		•	•	•		•			•					
	Negative numbers	3		•	•			•		•	•					
	Fractions	4	•	•	•	•	•						•			
	Decimals	5	•	•			•	•		•						
	Ratio and proportion	6	•	•		•	•			•					•	
	General	7	•	•	•				•						•	
	General	8		•	•		•				•				•	
	General	9	•		•			•			•	•				
Calculating	Addition	10		•	•	•		•						•		•
	Subtraction	11	•	•	•	•										
	Multiplication	12		•		•		•	•		•				•	
	Division	13	•	•		•				•		•				
	Mixed operations	14		•	•	•			•	•					•	
	Mixed operations	15	•		•	•		•	•						•	
	Mixed operations	16		•				•			•	•			•	
	Calculating with fractions	17	•			•		•							•	
	General	18			•	•	•	•							•	•
	General	19	•	•		•		•			•	•			•	

			Cross-curricular link and *Enriching Maths* feature													
			Mathematics				English	Science	ICT	Geography	History	Art and Music	Design and Technology	Physical Education	Links to money	Links with home
Strand	**Topic**	**Issue**	What's the Problem?	Looking for Patterns	The Puzzler	Let's Investigate	The Language of Maths	Focus on Science	Technology Today	Around the World	In the Past / Famous Mathematicians	The Arts Roundup	Construct	Sports Update	Money Matters	At Home
Understanding shape	2-D shapes	20		●		●						●	●			
	3-D solids	21		●	●								●			
	Symmetry and reflection	22		●		●		●		●			●			
	Position and direction	23								●			●			
	Movement and angle	24		●				●		●	●					●
	General	25		●	●	●	●						●			
	General	26		●		●	●				●		●			
Measuring	Length	27								●	●				●	
	Weight	28	●		●			●			●					●
	Capacity	29	●				●	●		●					●	
	Time	30	●		●		●				●	●	●			
	Area	31	●	●		●				●			●	●		
	Perimeter	32	●		●	●							●			
	General	33						●		●			●	●		●
	General	34	●		●	●		●		●	●		●	●		
Handling data	Organising and interpreting data	35				●	●			●	●			●		●
	Organising and interpreting data	36				●	●	●			●			●	●	

Resources used in *Enriching Maths 4*

A fundamental skill of mathematics is knowing what resources to use and when it is appropriate to use them. It is for this reason that many of the activities in *Enriching Maths* give no indication to the children as to which resources to use. Although the teacher's notes that accompany each activity include a list of resources, children should be encouraged to work out for themselves what they will need to use to successfully complete an activity.

It is assumed that for each activity children will have ready access to pencil and paper, and any other resources that are specifically mentioned in an activity, for example, computers or other RCMs. However, all other equipment should be left for the children to locate and use as and when they see is appropriate.

A list of all the resources children are likely to need in *Enriching Maths 4* is given below.

	***Enriching Maths* Issue**																	
Resource	**1**	**2**	**3**	**4**	**5**	**6**	**7**	**8**	**9**	**10**	**11**	**12**	**13**	**14**	**15**	**16**	**17**	**18**
pencil and paper	●	●	●	●	●	●	●	●	●	●	●	●	●	●	●	●	●	●
RCMs	2, 3	2, 3	2,3, 12	2, 3, 10, 11, 13	2, 3	2, 3	2, 3	2, 3, 11	2, 3, 10	2, 3	2, 3	2, 3, 4, 5	2, 3	2, 3, 6	2, 3	2, 3, 5	2, 3	2, 3
computer with internet access	●	●	●			●	●	●		●		●	●	●	●			●
data handling software														●	●			
ruler			●	●				●	●									
calculator	●	●	●	●	●	●					●	●	●	●	●	●	●	●
lemon, banana, pear, pepper, cucumber, tomato		●																
knife and plate		●																
1, 2, 3, 1, 2, 3 digit cards		●																
scissors				●								●						
tape measure				●														
red, blue and green counters				●														
paper clips				●														
coloured pencils					●													
child's reading book						●												
1, 2, 3, 1, 2, 3, dice						●												
selection of tariffs for different mobile phone providers							●											
set of dominoes								●		●					●			
selection of supermarket advertisements / catalogues / flyers										●								
selection of supermarket till receipts										●								
material for making a poster										●								
pack of playing cards											●							
selection of travel/holiday brochures														●				
school's electricity bill															●			
data handling software															●			
culture / arts section from several Sunday newspapers																●		

	Enriching Maths Issue																	
Resource	**19**	**20**	**21**	**22**	**23**	**24**	**25**	**26**	**27**	**28**	**29**	**30**	**31**	**32**	**33**	**34**	**35**	**36**
pencil and paper	●	●	●	●	●	●	●	●	●	●	●	●	●	●	●	●	●	●
RCMs	2, 3	2, 3, 7, 8, 10, 11, 12	2, 3, 10, 11, 14	2, 3, 9, 10	2, 3, 10, 11	2, 3, 13	2, 3, 10, 11, 14	2, 3, 11	2, 3, 10, 11	2, 3	2, 3	2, 3	2, 3, 10, 13	2, 3, 10, 13	2, 3, 10, 12	2, 3	2, 3, 10, 12	2, 3, 10, 11, 12
computer	●																	●
computer with internet access		●		●	●				●	●	●	●	●		●	●	●	
data handling software																	●	●
ruler		●	●	●		●	●		●	●			●	●	●		●	●
calculator	●										●						●	
stopwatch	●														●	●		
several different bank statements	●																	
scissors		●	●	●				●		●				●	●	●		
paper squares		●		●														
A4 paper		●	●	●				●							●			
geostrips and fasteners		●																
large sheets of paper			●											●				
cellotape			●					●						●	●	●		
glue			●					●						●	●	●		
Centicubes or interlocking cubes			●															
pair of compasses			●															
coloured pencils				●									●					
selection of different fruit				●														
knife				●														
paper clips				●														
tape recorder (or similar)					●													
road map or street directory that shows distances					●													
compass					●		●											
analogue watch					●													
protractor						●												
tape measure							●						●	●	●	●		●
interlocking cubes							●							●				
cardboard								●										
labels from a collection of supermarket fruit and vegetables showing country of origin									●									
atlas with a scale									●									
road map									●									
5p and 10p coins									●									
collection of different sized weights up to a total of 5 kg, including 1 kg, 500 g and 100 g weights										●								
spring balance										●								
different types of fabric and material										●								
scale balance										●								
metre rule												●			●			
piece of dowel or stick about 1 m long												●						
piece of string about 0·5 m long												●						
small stick												●						
matchsticks														●				
selection of commercially produced paper bags														●				
10p coins and £2 coins														●				
selection of newspapers															●	●		
modelling clay or similar																●		
string or wool																●		
different material and fabric, including plastic and tissue paper																●		
business section of a newspaper for 10 days																		●
child's skipping rope																		●

Looking for Patterns

Look at the number of pairs in the table in the Famous Mathematicians activity on page 3.

What pattern do you notice?

This pattern is referred to as the *Fibonacci sequence*.

Apply the rule to write the first 20 numbers of the Fibonacci sequence.

Let's Investigate

Approximately how much paper do you use in a day?

Approximately how much paper does your class use in a day?

What about in:

- a week?
- a term?
- throughout the entire school year?

Write about how you arrived at your approximations.

Be prepared to justify your approximations.

Focus on Science

Investigate how much paper is produced from one tree.

How does this compare with how much paper you and your class use in:

- a day?
- week?
- term?
- throughout the entire school year?

Name:

The Maths Herald

Volume 4

Date:

Famous Mathematicians

Pythagoras was a Greek philosopher (569–500 BC). He made many important discoveries in mathematics, particularly in geometry.

Pythagoras also showed how whole numbers could be represented as geometric shapes.

A *square number* can be represented by dots in a square pattern.

These are the first four *square numbers*:

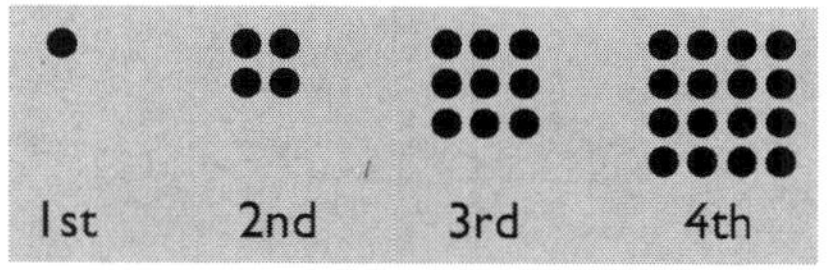

A *triangular number* can be represented by dots in a triangular pattern.

These are the first four *triangular numbers*:

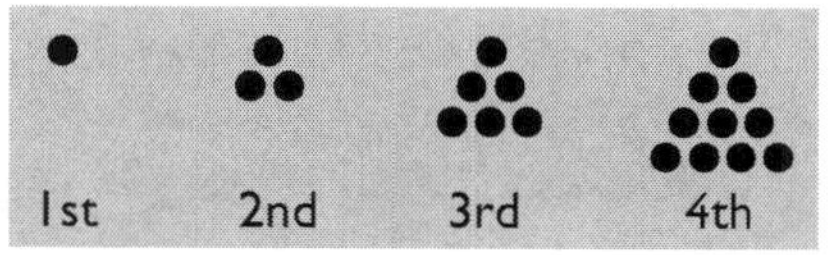

An *oblong number* can be represented by dots in a rectangular pattern, where one side is longer than the other.

These are the first four *oblong numbers*:

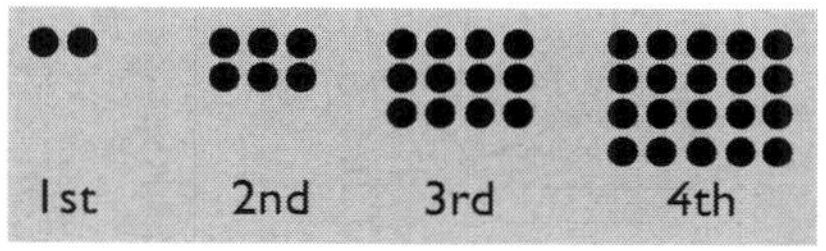

Can you work out what the 5th to 10th square, triangular and oblong numbers are?

What about the 50th square, triangular and oblong numbers?

Can you work out a rule for finding any square, triangular or oblong number?

The Puzzler

The display on the calculator uses seven light bars to create each of the digits from 0 to 9.

The four-digit number below uses 12 light bars.

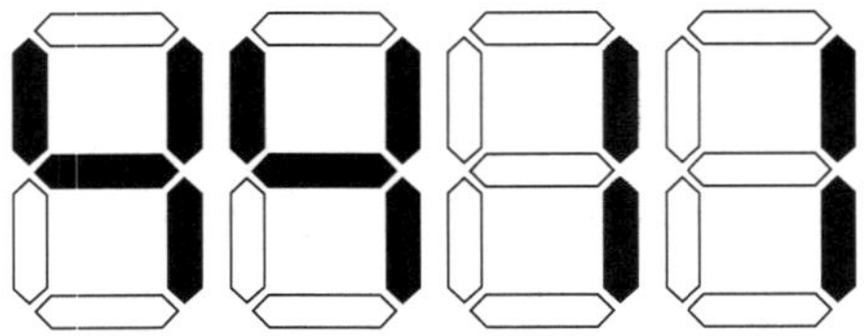

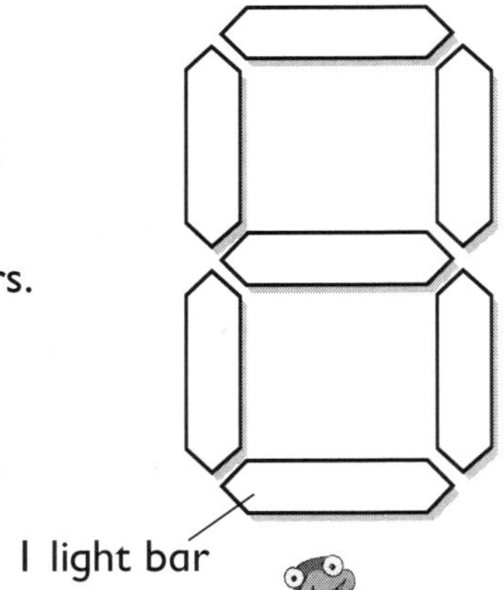

Using exactly 12 light bars, what is the smallest number you can show?

Using exactly 12 light bars, what is the largest number you can show?

Famous Mathematicians

Pythagoras was able to show many different number relationships using shapes.

Draw dot arrays to show these relationships.

The sum of two consecutive triangular numbers is a square number.

Two times a triangular number is an oblong number.

Eight times a triangular number plus one is a square number.

The sum of two odd numbers equals an even number.

The sum of two even numbers equals an even number.

The sum of an even number and an odd number equals an odd number.

Famous Mathematicians

Leonardo Pisano Bogollo was born in Pisa in Italy around 1170 AD. He was also known as Leonardo of Pisa and more commonly was called Fibonacci. He is said to have been the greatest European mathematician of the Middle Ages.

Fibonacci was interested in how numbers occur in patterns in nature.

One of his most famous problems involved rabbits. Fibonacci assumed that:

- a male (M) and a female (F) rabbit can start reproducing at one month old
- a pair of rabbits will create another pair of rabbits every month: one male and one female.

He wanted to know how many pairs of rabbits there would be at the end of the year.

Fibonacci knew that in real life this problem would probably not happen. However, he was interested in the numbers and the patterns that occurred.

The following table shows what Fibonacci discovered.

Month	Rabbits	Pairs	
1	MF^1	1	First pair of rabbits. They are not yet a month old and therefore are too young to reproduce.
2	MF^1	1	First pair of rabbits are now a month old and are therefore able to reproduce.
3	MF^1 ↓ MF^2	2	Pair MF^1 reproduce pair: MF^2
4	MF^1 ↙ ↘ MF^2 MF^3	3	Pair MF^1 reproduce another pair: MF^3 Pair MF^2 are too young to reproduce.
5	MF^1 ↙ ↓ ↘ MF^2 MF^3 MF^4; MF^2 ↓ MF^5	5	Pair MF^1 reproduce another pair: MF^4 Pair MF^2 reproduce pair: MF^5 Pair MF^3 are too young to reproduce.
6	MF^1 ↙ ↓ ↓ ↘ MF^2 MF^3 MF^4 MF^6; MF^2 ↙ ↘ MF^5 MF^7; MF^3 ↓ MF^8	8	Pair MF^1 reproduce another pair: MF^6 Pair MF^2 reproduce another pair: MF^7 Pair MF^3 reproduce pair: MF^8 Pairs MF^4 and MF^5 are too young to reproduce.

Using the information in the table, can you work out how many rabbits there would be at the end of the year?

Looking for Patterns

Complete the sequences and write in the rules.

9 →(×3) 27 →(−4) 23 →(×3) ☐ →(−4) ☐ →(×3) ☐ →(−4) ☐ →(×3) ☐

600 →(÷2) 300 →(×5) 1500 →(÷2) ☐ → ☐ → ☐ → ☐ → ☐

42 →(+5) 47 → 45 →(+5) 50 → ☐ → ☐ → ☐ → ☐

8 → 32 → 33 → 132 → 133 → 532 → 533 → 2132

4000 → 400 → 406 → 40·6 → ☐ → ☐ → ☐ → ☐

Make some up for a friend to complete.

Let's Investigate

Imagine you have 33 beads.

You have to make a four-digit number on the abacus.

You must use all 33 beads for each number you make.

How many different four-digit numbers can you make?

Write them in order.

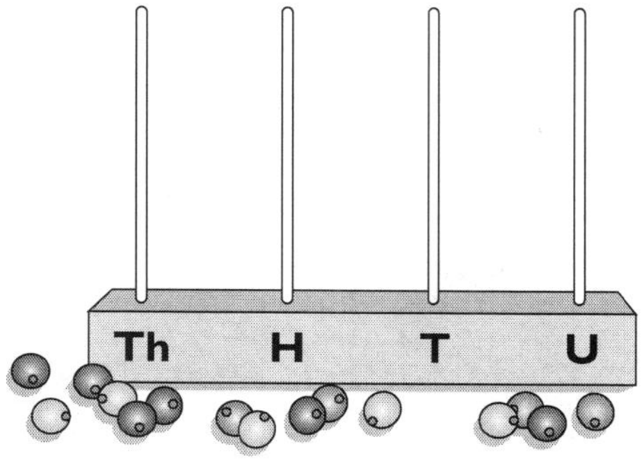

Name:

The Maths Herald

Volume 4

Date:

Famous Mathematicians

Carl Gauss was a German mathematician who lived from 1777 to 1855. He was particularly interested in the theory of numbers.

Gauss found a *formula* for finding the total of any set of *consecutive* counting numbers starting from 1.

Look at the table on the right to help you discover the formula.

Can you use the letter '*n*' to help you write your formula?

Look at the numbers in the third column. What do you notice about them?

Use your formula to work out the total of the first 100 numbers:

1 + 2 + 3 + 4 + 5 … + 100 =?

Counting numbers	Number in set (*n*)	Total
1	1	1
1 + 2	2	3
1 + 2 + 3	3	6
1 + 2 + 3 + 4	4	10
1 + 2 + 3 + 4 + 5		
1 + 2 + 3 + 4 + 5 + 6		
1 + 2 + 3 + 4 + 5 + 6 + 7		
1 + 2 + 3 + 4 + 5 + 6 + 7 + 8		
1 + 2 + 3 + 4 + 5 + 6 + 7 + 8 + 9		
1 + 2 + 3 + 4 + 5 + 6 + 7 + 8 + 9 + 10		

In the Past

Twelve knights met up for a tournament.

Before it started, each knight shook hands with each of the other knights.

How many times did the knights shake hands altogether?

Looking for Patterns

The number pattern on the right is a special sequence of numbers.

What name do we give to this sequence?

What is the rule?

What are the next ten numbers in this sequence? Write the numbers in the circles.

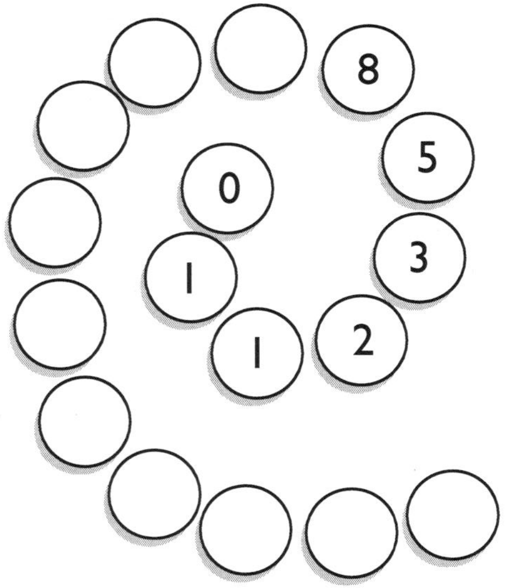

Mathematicians and scientists believe that most plants grow in this pattern. It enables new leaves to get sunlight and water without being blocked by older leaves.

Investigate which plants show numbers from this sequence.

Can you find any examples in the school grounds?

Focus on Science

Referring to the sequence of numbers in the Looking for Patterns activity above, investigate how each of these foods show a number in the sequence.

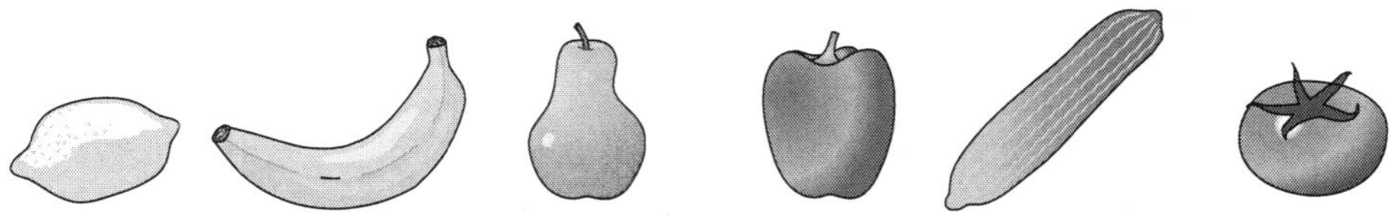

lemon banana pear pepper cucumber tomato

The Puzzler

Rearrange all the digits in each of the black boxes to make a different number. Write this number in the white boxes to the right ➤ and / or below ▼. Two have been done for you.

			73 ▼	516 ▼	5204 ▼			54 ▼	026 ▼	118 ▼	
	5632 ➤ ▼					1466 ➤ ▼					5497 ▼
		1407 ➤ ▼	7	1	0	4	5098 ➤ ▼				
42 ➤		4	9512 ➤ ▼					172 ➤ ▼			
103 ➤		0		6204 ➤					5413 ▼	5 ➤	
759 ➤		7		45 102 ▼	1536 ➤					45 132 ▼	
	3512 ➤ ▼	1				1784 ➤					9325 ▼
		620 ➤ ▼				367 ▼	208 ▼	552 ➤			
32 ➤			1748 ➤					321 ➤			
01 ➤			75 160 ➤						95 ➤		
62 ➤			3521 ➤					438 ➤			

The Puzzler

1 1 2 2 3 3

Arrange these digits to make a six-digit number where:

- each of the 1 digits is separated by one digit
- each of the 2 digits is separated by two digits
- each of the 3 digits is separated by three digits.

Focus on Science

The table below shows the depth of a submarine as it dives and makes a journey underwater.

Time (min)	0	10	20	30	40	50	60	70	80	90	100	120	130	140	150	160	170	180	190	200
Depth (m)	0	10	25	40	60	80	100	120	140	160	160	150	140	140	140	110	80	50	20	0

Then using 0·5 squared paper, copy the graph on the right.

Then use the information in the table to draw a line graph of the submarine's journey.

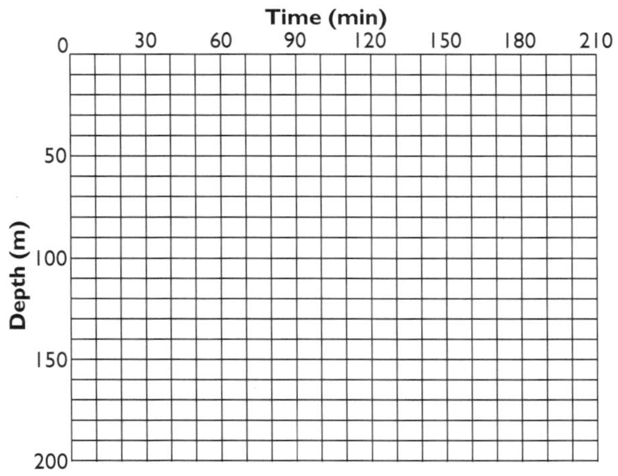

The Puzzler

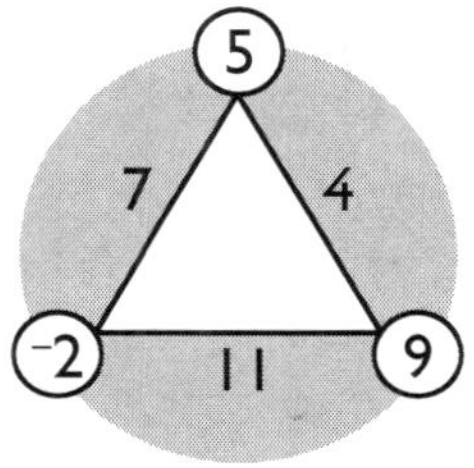

In the triangle on the right, the number in the middle of each line is the difference between the numbers at the points of the triangle.

Work out the missing numbers in the triangles below.

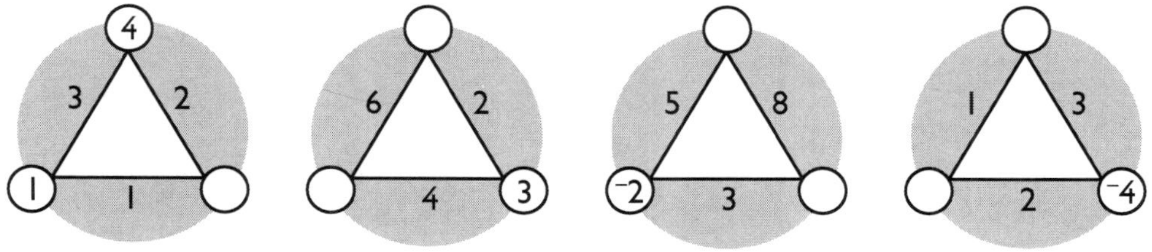

Name:

The Maths Herald

Volume 4

Date:

Around the World

Most weather forecasts give the expected daily high (maximum) and low (minimum) temperature readings.

The difference between the maximum and minimum temperature readings is referred to as the *temperature range*.

Search the internet for the weather forecast in different parts of the world. Try and locate places where it is wintertime.

Write down the following:

- Name of city or town
- Forecast maximum temperature
- Forecast minimum temperature
- Temperature range

Remember!

To calculate the temperature range you find the difference between the maximum and minimum temperatures.

In the Past BC and AD

In the UK, years are numbered by the length of time after the birth of Jesus Christ. So, if you were born in the year 2003, it means you were born 2003 years after the birth of Christ, or 2003 AD (from the Latin *Anno Domini*). The time before the birth of Christ is numbered in years BC (Before Christ). So, if something happened 130 years before the birth of Christ, it happened in 130 BC.

Calculate how many years passed between each of these pairs of events.

- The Roman Emperor Claudius was born in 10 BC. He died in 54 AD. How old was he when he died?

- The Romans invaded Britain in 54 BC. Hadrian's Wall was completed in 130 AD. How long after they invaded Britain did the Romans complete Hadrian's Wall?
- The Romans invaded Britain in 54 BC. They left Britain in 409 AD. How long after they invaded did the Romans leave?
- Rome was founded in 753 BC. It was conquered by barbarians in 410 AD. How long after it was founded was Rome conquered by barbarians?
- There were Roman Emperors from 27 BC until 1453 AD. For how many years were there Roman Emperors?

Focus on Science

An iceberg is a large piece of freshwater ice that floats in open water.

Only one-ninth of the volume of an iceberg is above the water level, the rest is below. So, an iceberg with the top 2 m above sea level, or sea level + 2 m, and the bottom 16 m below sea level, or sea level – 16 m, is 18 m tall.

How tall are each of the following icebergs:

- Sea level + 3·5 m to sea level – 23·7 m
- Sea level + 2·72 m to sea level – 15·47 m
- Sea level + 4·89 m to sea level – 17·59 m
- Sea level + 1·87 m to sea level – 8·63 m
- Sea level + 23·19 m to sea level – 87·82 m

Focus on Science

The temperatures of the planets in our solar system vary a lot, not only from planet to planet, but also on each planet as well.

The temperature depends on a variety of factors including distance from the Sun, whether the planet has an atmosphere to insulate it (like the Earth and Venus), how much heat is generated in the centre of the planet, and how much heat it loses into space.

The table below shows the temperature ranges for the four closest planets to the Sun, and also for the Moon.

Planet	Maximum Temperature	Minimum Temperature
Mercury	450 °C	⁻184 °C
Venus	460 °C	440 °C
Earth	50 °C	⁻85 °C
Moon	110 °C	⁻182 °C
Mars	36 °C	⁻140 °C

- Which planet gets the hottest?
- Which planet gets the coldest?
- Which planet has the greatest temperature difference and what is it?
- Which planet has the least temperature difference and what is it?

Investigate why the planet with the greatest temperature difference is like this.

Investigate why the planet with the least temperature difference is like this.

Looking for Patterns

Write the missing numbers in each of these number sequences.

⁻7, ☐, ⁻3, ⁻1, 1, ☐, ☐

⁻13, ☐, ⁻7, ⁻4, ⁻1, ☐, ☐

11, 7, 3, ⁻1, ☐, ☐, ☐

☐, ⁻25, ⁻18, ⁻11, ☐, ☐, 10

19, 14, 9, 4, ☐, ☐, ☐

20, ☐, ☐, ⁻7, ⁻16, ☐, ⁻34

Name:

The Maths Herald

Volume 4

Date:

Construct

$$\frac{1}{2} \text{ of } \frac{1}{4} = \frac{1}{4} \text{ of } \frac{1}{2}$$

Draw a diagram to show that $\frac{1}{2}$ of $\frac{1}{4}$ and $\frac{1}{4}$ of $\frac{1}{2}$ is the same.

Can you show this in more than one way?

Let's Investigate

Approximately what fraction of the walls of your classroom is made of glass?

Write about what you did to find out.

The Language of Maths

Write statements involving fractions that describe how much of the day you spend doing different things.

What's the Problem?

Twelve friends go out for a meal to Giovanni's Pizzeria.

They order seven pizzas and cut some of them into thirds and some into quarters. They all have the same amount of pizza.

How is this possible?

The Puzzler

If five is added to both the numerator and denominator of a fraction, it triples in value.

What is the fraction?

The Puzzler

$$\frac{abc}{a + b + c}$$

a, b and c each represents a different 1 to 9 digit.

For example, $\frac{123}{1 + 2 + 3} = \frac{123}{6} = 20{\cdot}5$

What is the largest number that you can make with this fraction?

Looking for Patterns

Using squared dot paper, draw a 6 × 8 rectangle.

Draw a cross in the top left corner.

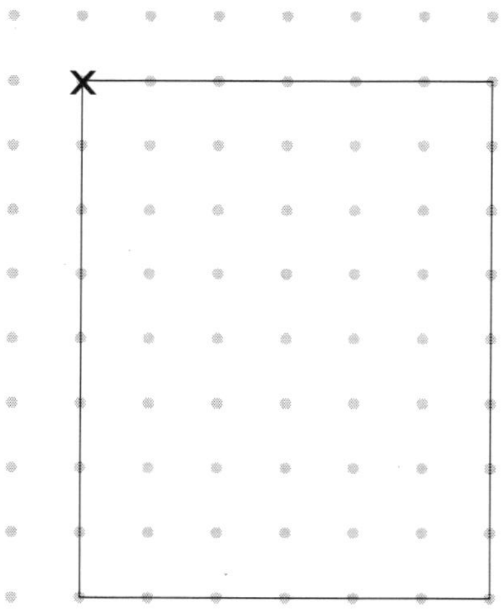

Can you draw a route around $\frac{1}{6}$ of the squares and back to your cross?

Once you have started on your route you cannot take your pencil off the paper and you cannot go over the same line twice.

Draw another 6 × 8 rectangle with a cross in the top left corner.

Can you draw a route around $\frac{1}{4}$ of the squares and back to your cross?

Now draw a third 6 × 8 rectangle with a cross in the top left corner.

Can you draw a route around $\frac{7}{16}$ of the squares and back to your cross?

The Puzzler

What fraction of each of the three squares below is shaded?

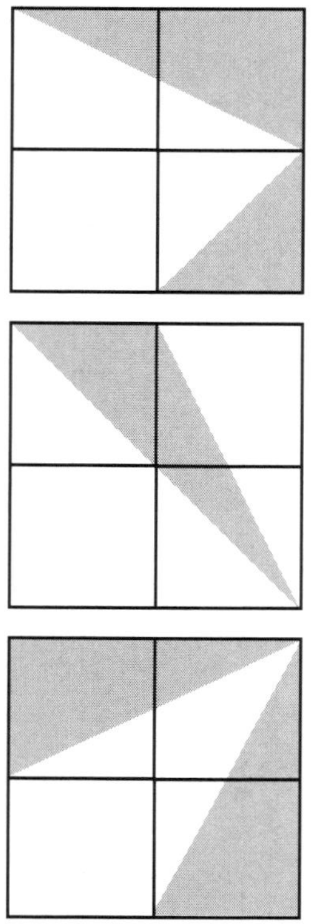

Using squared paper, draw a 2 × 2 square. Then use a ruler to draw two lines both from the same point to two other points. Shade sections of the square.

Describe what fraction you have shaded.

Let's Investigate

You need:

- pencil and paper clip (for the spinner)
- red, blue, green counters

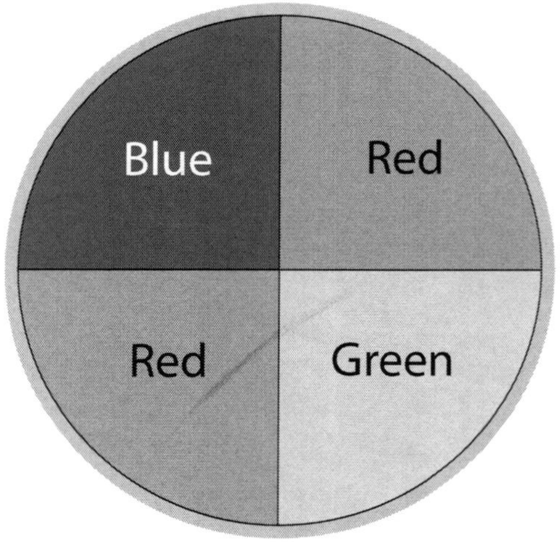

What fraction of the circle has 'Red' written in it?

What fractions of the circle have 'Blue' and 'Green' written on them?

Make a spinner by putting the point of the pencil through the paper clip, and putting the point of the pencil on the centre of the circle.

If you spin the paper clip 20 times, how many times do you think it will land on 'Red', how many times on 'Blue' and how many times on 'Green'?

Make a prediction. Be sure to explain your thinking.

Now flick the paper clip to spin it. If it lands on:

- 'Red' – take a red counter
- 'Blue' – take a blue counter
- 'Green' – take a green counter.

Do this for a total of 20 times.

How many of each colour counter do you have?

Is this what you expected?

What's the Problem?

A frog falls down a well that is 2·45 m deep.

With each jump the frog can jump 1m up the side of the well, but after each jump it has to rest. It then slides back down 0·4 times its height up the side of the well.

So, on the first jump, the frog jumps 1 m up the side of the well, but then slides back down 0·4 × 1 m. It ends up 0·6 m above the water.

On the second jump it gets 1 m + 0·6 m above the water and then slips back 0·4 × 1·6 m = 0·64 m. So it ends up 0·96 m above the water.

Does the frog ever get out of the well?

If so, how many jumps does it take?

Write about how you worked out the answer.

The Language of Maths

True or false?

0·35 is less than $\frac{1}{3}$

$\frac{1}{4}$ is less than 0·3

$\frac{2}{3}$ is more than 0·65

$\frac{8}{9}$ is more than 0·9

0·6 is less than $\frac{5}{8}$

$\frac{1}{4}$ is more than 0·25

$\frac{5}{16}$ is more than 0·3

$\frac{7}{9}$ is less than 0·75

Name:

The Maths Herald

CN PM

Volume 4

Date:

Focus on Science

The atmosphere of the Earth, as decimals, is approximately 0·781 nitrogen, 0·21 oxygen and 0·009 argon.

Out of every 1000 parts of the atmosphere, how many parts are nitrogen?

How many parts are oxygen?

How many parts are argon?

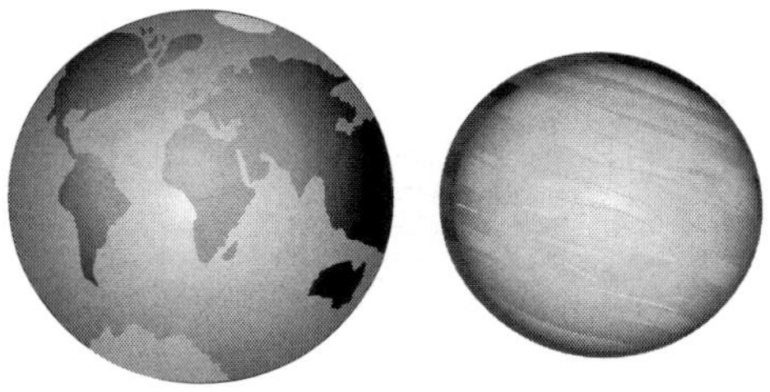

On Mars, out of every 1000 parts of atmosphere, 290 parts are sodium, 220 parts are hydrogen, 420 parts are oxygen, 60 parts are helium and 5 parts are potassium.

Write these parts as decimals of the whole atmosphere.

Looking for Patterns

Starting at the cross, can you draw a route around 0·2 of the triangles in this decagon and back to the cross?

Once you have started on your route you cannot take your pencil off the paper and you cannot go over the same line twice.

Using a different coloured pencil, can you draw a route around 0·5 of the triangles?

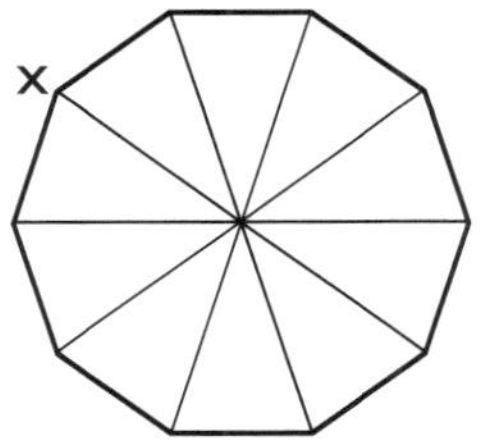

Starting at the cross, can you draw a route around 0·375 of the triangles in this octagon and back to the cross again?

Can you draw a route around 0·625 of the triangles and back again?

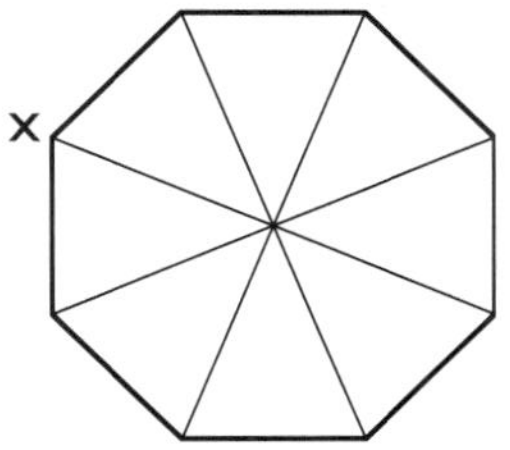

Around the World

In a town in Wales, 0·1 of the population speaks Welsh and 0·96 of the population speaks English.

If the population of the town is 150, how many people speak both Welsh and English?

Focus on Science

The purity of gold is traditionally measured in *carats*. However, it is becoming more popular nowadays to use the *millesimal fineness* system. This marks the purity of the metal in parts of pure gold per thousand parts of metal.

So, a piece of gold jewellery marked '750' means that it contains 750 g of pure gold in every 1000 g. That is, 0·75 of the weight of the piece of jewellery is pure gold.

If a piece of jewellery weighed 100 g, there would be 0·75 × 100 g = 75 g of pure gold in it.

Calculate how much pure gold there is in each of the following pieces of jewellery:

- A gold pin, marked 750, weighing 80 g
- A pair of gold earrings, marked 500, weighing 338 g
- A gold necklace, marked 750, weighing 276 g
- A gold bracelet, marked 875, weighing 176 g
- A gold box, marked 585, weighing 1·6 kg

Around the World

When you buy a cup of coffee in a café or coffee shop, only a very small part of the price is the cost of the coffee itself. In fact it is the smallest part of the cost.

This is how the price of a £2.50 cup of coffee is made up:

Milk	0·06
Coffee	0·02
Labour	0·18
Rent	0·12
Administration	0·25
Cup / sugar / lid	0·04
VAT	0·20
Profit	0·13
TOTAL	1·00 unit = £2.50

Work out how many pence each of these categories contribute to the cost.

What's the Problem?

Samuel and Taylor are shovelling sand into sacks.

Samuel can bag up 1·38 tonnes of sand in a day, and Taylor can bag up 0·74 tonnes a day.

Samuel works by himself for one-third of the time and then Taylor joins him.

The pile of sand they are bagging up weighs between 11 and 12 tonnes and they both work for whole numbers of days to finish bagging it.

How many days do they take to bag up the sand?

Write about how you worked out the answer.

Looking for Patterns

Write the missing numbers in the boxes to complete these number sentences.

0·5 + 0·35 + ☐ = 1

☐ + 0·74 + 2·6 = 4

3·2 – 1·58 – 0·63 = ☐

2·75 + 0·8 – ☐ = 2·12

0·2 – 3·67 + ☐ = 1·58

6·24 – 3·79 – ☐ = 0·32

Let's Investigate

If you roll a pair of 1, 2, 3, 1, 2, 3 dice, the sum of the two dice can be 2, 3, 4, 5 or 6.

Roll a pair of 1, 2, 3, 1, 2, 3 dice 45 times and note how many times you get each total.

What is the most frequent total?

What is the least frequent total?

What is the approximate ratio of the most frequent total to the least frequent total?

Money Matters

I have £5.60 in coins.

These are the ratios of the coins I have:

- For every 50p I have two 10p.
- For every two 5p I have a 50p.
- For every two 10p I have three 20p.

What coins do I have?

Looking for Patterns

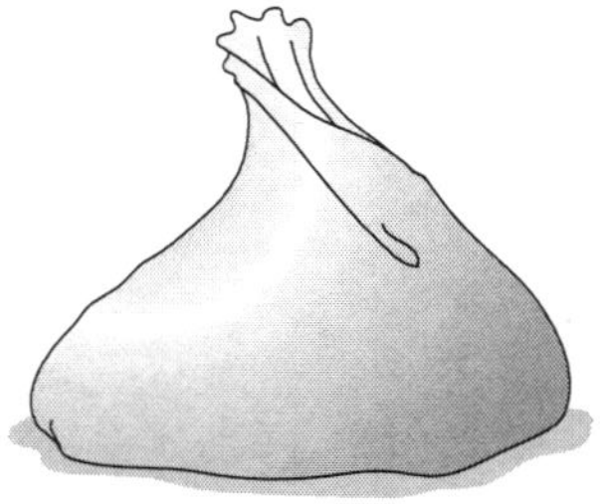

A bag has red, green, blue and yellow counters in it.

The ratio of red counters to green counters is 6 : 5.

The ratio of green counters to blue counters is 5 : 4.

The ratio of blue counters to yellow counters is 8 : 5.

There are between 40 and 80 counters in the bag.

How many of each colour of counter is in the bag?

Name:

The Maths Herald

Volume 4

Date:

Around the World

The pyramids at Giza, in Egypt, were built approximately 4500 years ago. For over 4000 years the Great Pyramid, the largest of the three, was the tallest monument in the world. It is still the largest stone monument ever built.

All three pyramids are the shape of a square-based pyramid.

When they were built, the ratio of the bases of the pyramids to their heights was 8 : 5.

The Great Pyramid of Khufu	Width of base 230 m
The Pyramid of Khafre	Width of base 214 m
The Pyramid of Menkare	Width of base 105 m

Work out the heights of each of the pyramids.

Money Matters

If you go on holiday to the USA you will need to change some UK pounds (£) into US dollars ($) to spend while you are there.

The ratio between the pound and the US dollar varies from day to day, but is approximately 5 : 8.

In other words £5 will buy you $8.

Work out how many dollars each of these people got when they changed their pounds into dollars.

- Peter changed £100.
- Aslan changed £50.
- Silvia changed £140.
- Tommi changed £175.
- Rada changed £320.

Some of them didn't spend all of their dollars while they were in America.

- Silvia returned with $72.
- Tommi returned with $116.
- Rada returned with $162.

When they returned they changed their dollars back into pounds.

How many pounds did they get?

What's the Problem?

What is the ratio of starfish to shells in the bucket?

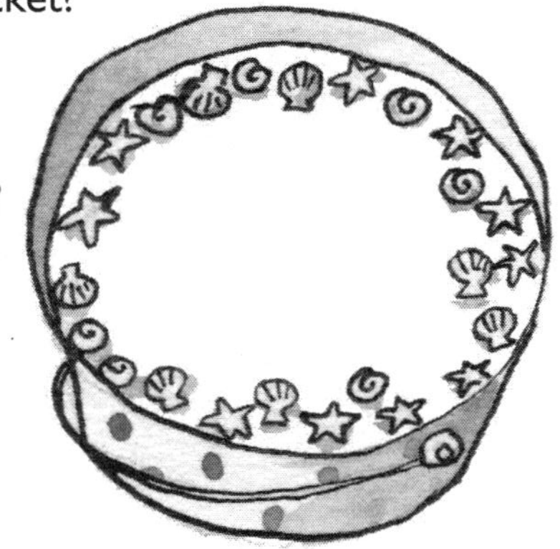

What fraction of the contents of the bucket are shells?

What proportion of the contents are starfish?

Now draw six fish in the bucket.

What is the ratio of fish to starfish to shells?

What proportion of the contents of the bucket are starfish now?

Let's Investigate

There are eight main planets in our *Solar System*. They all *orbit* around the Sun. Generally, the farther a planet is from the Sun the longer it takes to orbit it. The Earth is the third planet from the Sun and takes 365 days to orbit it.

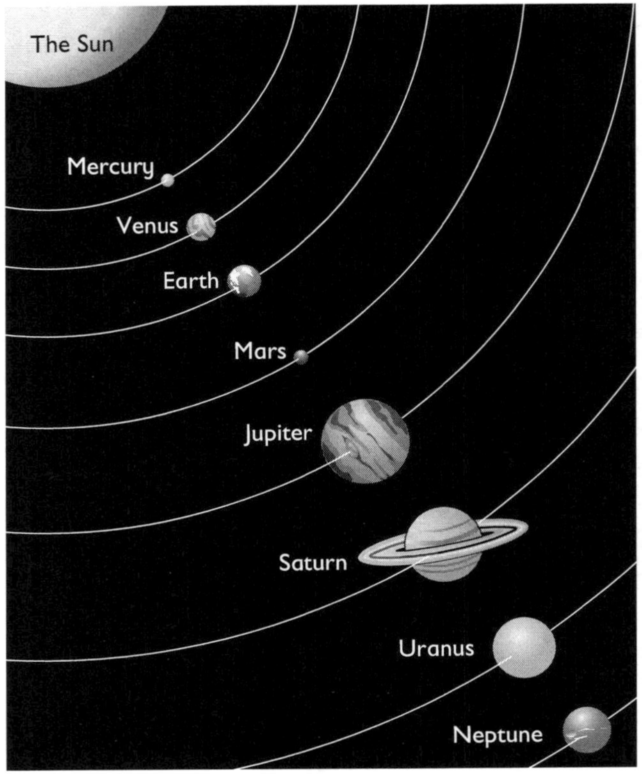

Investigate how long the other planets in our Solar System take to orbit the Sun.

What is the approximate ratio of the time that each planet takes to orbit the Sun, to the time the Earth takes?

The Language of Maths

The letter 'e' is the most frequently used letter in the English language.

Open your favourite book on any page that is full of text.

Count the number of letter 'e's on it.

Now count the number of letter 'd's there are.

What is the approximate ratio of 'e's to 'd's?

If you opened your book at another page and did the same thing, would you expect the ratio to be the same?

Why or why not?

Try this out and see if you are right.

Technology Today

Imagine you work in a shop that sells mobile phone contracts.

The following people come into your shop. They are not happy with the mobile phone tariff they are on at the moment, and want some advice on what tariff they should change to.

Consulting a range of tariffs for different mobile phone providers, what would be your recommendations?

Looking for Patterns

In each pair of columns there is a rule that relates the number on the left to the number on the right.

Find the rule and write the last two numbers in each pair of columns.

3	9	4	9	2	7	5	28	14	6	19	6	9	5
4	12	5	11	4	15	7	38	18	8	25	8	13	7
6	18	7	15	6	23	8	43	26	12	34	11	19	10
9	27	8	17	7	27	11	58	30	14	40	13	27	14
11		12		9		15		38		49		37	
13		15		11		20		50		61		47	

Name:

The Maths Herald

Volume 4

Date:

Technology Today

Memory size in a computer is measured in *bytes*.

How much is a byte?

What about:

- a kilobyte?
- a megabyte?
- a gigabyte?
- a terabyte?

Money Matters

When sending a letter from within the United Kingdom to someone who is also in the United Kingdom, the charge is referred to as a *national* charge.

When sending a letter from within the United Kingdom to someone in another country, the charge is referred to as an *international* charge.

- Compared with the United Kingdom, in which countries in Europe is it cheaper to send a letter within the country (nationally)?
- What about sending a letter to another country (internationally)?
- In which countries in Europe is it more expensive to send a letter nationally?
- What about internationally?

Display your results in a table.

What's the Problem?

The Roach family consists of Mr and Mrs Roach, Tamsin Roach, Lisa Roach and William Roach.

The family are having their photo taken.

Mr and Mrs Roach want to stand next to each other.

How many different ways can all five members of the Roach family stand in a line to have their picture taken?

The Puzzler

Trevor, Steven and Nigel are brothers. Their ages are 7, 9 and 10.

The name of each brother and their age do not begin with the same letter.

Steven is not the eldest brother.

How old is each brother?

The Puzzler

A magician has eight apprentices.

All the apprentices stand in a row as the magician walks down the row handing out spells.

When he gets to the end of the row, he walks back to the beginning and starts again, handing out the ninth spell to the first apprentice and the tenth spell to the second apprentice.

He continues like this until he has handed out 100 spells.

Which apprentice gets the last spell?

How many spells does each apprentice receive?

Money Matters

Is it cheaper to buy things over the internet or in person in a shop?

Choose a range of different types of goods to investigate. For example, television, washing machine, book, computer game, clothing and a selection of groceries.

Are some things cheaper to buy over the internet while other things are more expensive, and vice versa?

What conclusions can you make? Be sure to justify your conclusions with examples.

The Puzzler

Anil, Bob, Cath, Des, Ellie and Firoza go for a ride at the circus.

Who sits in which seat?

- Anil and Bob are separated by two seats.
- Firoza sits three seats and five seats, in one direction or the other, from Ellie and Cath.
- Des sits in a seat numbered 5 more than Anil's.

In the Past

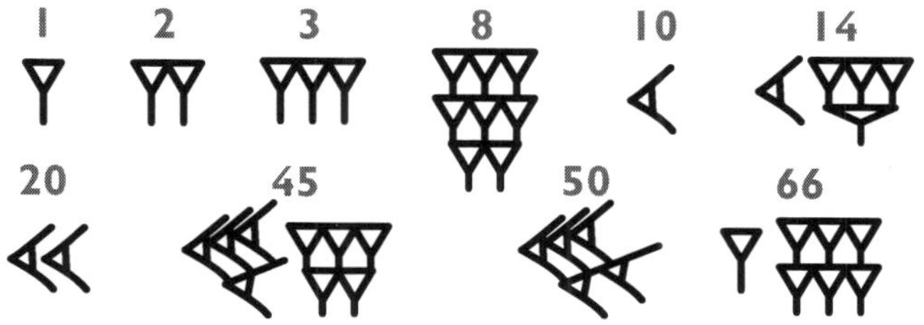

Throughout history, different civilisations have used symbols to represent numbers. These symbols are called *numerals*. The numeral system we use is called the *Hindu-Arabic* system.

The system above is the *Ancient Babylonian numeral* system.

Notice that the numeral for 1 and for 60 is the same. However, the numeral 60 is separated from the units by a gap.

Use the Ancient Babylonian numeral system to write:

- your age
- the day of the month you were born
- this month.

Choose 10 different two-digit numbers and write them using the Ancient Babylonian numeral system.

Name:

The Maths Herald

Volume 4

Date:

Money Matters

When you fly a long distance, most airlines offer three or four different classes of travel. The amount of space you have, and the level of service you are offered, depends on the type of class you travel in.

These different classes may be called the following, although some airlines use other terms to describe them.

- First
- Business
- Premium Economy
- Economy

Investigate the price of travelling from London to Sydney in each of the different classes.

By comparing the different prices and what you get for your money, which class of travel do you think offers the best value for money?

Write a statement justifying your decisions.

Looking for Patterns

Fourteen people sat down to dinner around a table. Each person clinked glasses with the people on either side of them. How many times were glasses clinked?

The Puzzler

The diagram on the right has been made using ten different dominoes from a set of normal double-six dominoes.

However, it does not show how the dominoes were arranged.

Draw in the lines to show how the 10 dominoes were arranged.

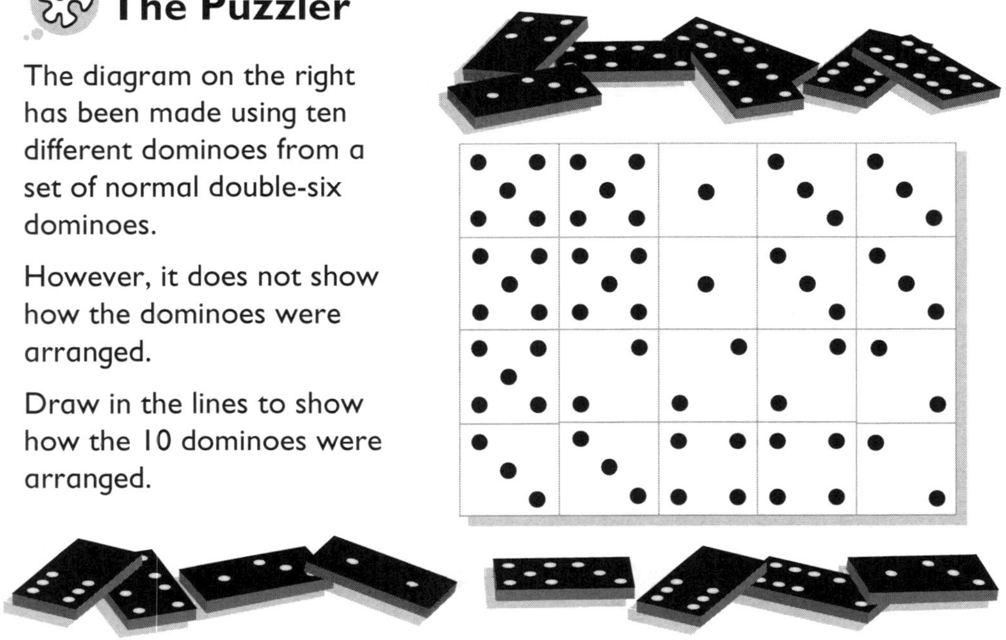

Looking for Patterns

Follow the pattern to work out the next three numbers in each sequence.

4, 7, 10, 13, . . .

3, 5, 9, 17, . . .

5, 8, 12, 17, . . .

128, 64, 32, . . .

2, 4, 8, 14, . . .

7, 11, 19, 31, . . .

What is the rule for each sequence?

Looking for Patterns

The diagram below is part of a 1–100 number square. However, the numbers are not in the order of an ordinary number square.

Use the pattern in the number square below to fill in the squares on the right.

91	92	93	94	95	96	97	98	99	100
90	89	88	87	86	85	84	83	82	81
71	72	73	74	75	76	77	78	79	80
70	69	68	67	66	65	64	63	62	61
51	52	53	54	55	56	57	58	59	60

The Language of Maths

Haiku is a form of Japanese poetry with 17 syllables in three non-rhyming lines.

The first line has exactly five syllables, the second line has exactly seven syllables and the third line has five syllables.

Haiku poems generally describe nature or the seasons.

Write a different Haiku poem for each of the four seasons.

Spring fresh blooms abound
Sun climbs to help nature grow
The earth is awake

Focus on Science

The ratio of the number of teeth on the big wheel to the small wheel is 12 : 6 or 2 : 1.

Each time the big wheel turns once, the small wheel will turn twice.

So the ratio of the number of turns of the big wheel to the small wheel is 1 : 2.

What is the ratio of the number of teeth on the big wheel to the small wheel?

Each time the big wheel turns once, how many times will the small wheel turn?

What is the ratio of the number of turns of the big wheel to the small wheel?

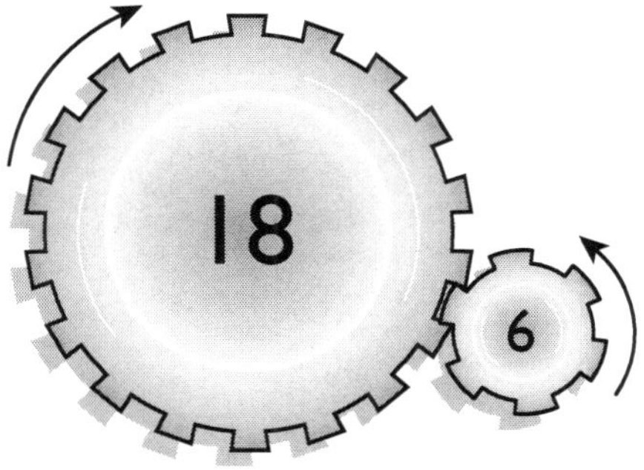

What is the ratio of the number of teeth on wheel A to wheel B to wheel C?

What is the ratio of the number of turns of wheel A to wheel B to wheel C?

What is the ratio of the number of teeth on wheel A to wheel B to wheel C?

What is the ratio of the number of turns of wheel A to wheel B to wheel C?

Name:

The Maths Herald

Volume 4

Date:

Focus on Science

Leonardo Pisano Bogollo, also known as Leonardo of Pisa was born in Pisa in Italy around 1170 AD. He was more commonly known as Fibonacci and is said to have been the greatest European mathematician of the Middle Ages.

In The Maths Herald Volume 4 Issue 1 you discovered what the *Fibonacci sequence* was.

Here is part of the sequence.
Write the next five terms.

0, 1, 1, 2, 3, 5, 8, 13 ☐, ☐, ☐, ☐, ☐

Fibonacci was interested in how numbers occur in patterns in nature.

How does the spiral of the chambered nautilus shell represent numbers in the Fibonacci sequence?

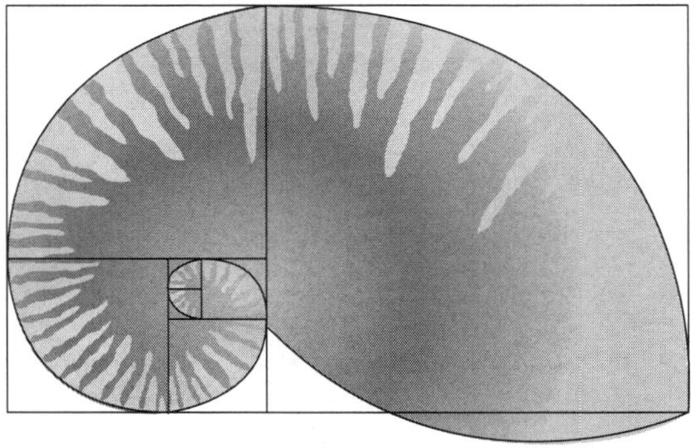

The Arts Roundup

How do the keys on a piano represent numbers in the Fibonacci sequence?

The Puzzler

What two-digit number becomes nine times larger if you put a 2 before it.

In the Past

Throughout history, different civilisations have used symbols to represent numbers. These symbols are called *numerals*. The numeral system we use today is called the *Hindu-Arabic* system.

The system below is the numeral system of the *Central American Mayans*.

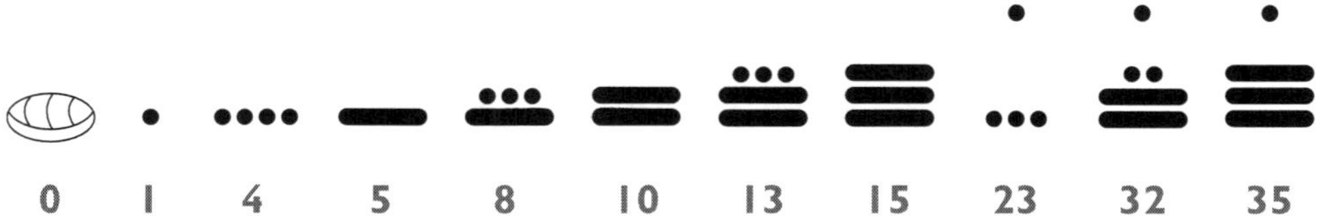

Notice that when the symbol • is raised up, it stands for 20.

Numbers more than 19 were written vertically in powers of twenty. So 32 is written as one dot above two dots, which are in turn above two lines. The top dot represents one twenty or 1×20, which is added to two dots and two bars, or 12. Therefore, $(1 \times 20) + 12 = 32$.

Use the Mayan numeral system to write:

- your age
- the day of the month you were born
- this month.

Choose ten different two-digit numbers and write them using the Mayan numeral system.

What's the Problem?

Sunita and Jo are painting a room. They have a tin of red paint and a similar sized tin of blue paint. Though they want to paint the room two colours, they want the two colours to be more similar to each other.

Jo says:

Sunita says:

Jo thinks it wouldn't make any difference. Who is right?

The Puzzler

One quarter of this rectangle has been shaded. Can you divide the remaining part into four identical pieces?

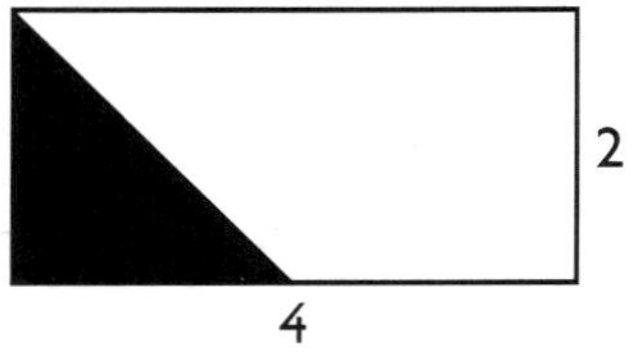

Looking for Patterns

Look at this method for adding all the numbers from 1 to 10.

Explain the method.

Using this method, what are the answers to each of the following calculations?

Show your working.

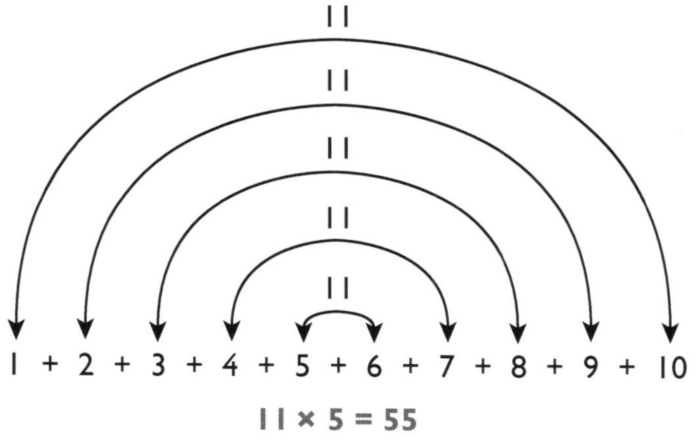

1 + 2 + 3 + 4 + … + 16 + 17 + 18 + 19 + 20

6 + 7 + 8 + 9 + 10 + 11 + 12 + 13

15 + 16 + 17 + 18 + 19 + 20

52 + 53 + 54 + 55 + 56 + 57 + 58 + 59 + 60 + 61

What about these calculations? Look carefully and don't be tricked!

Don't forget to show your working.

1 + 2 + 3 + 4 + 5 + 6 + 7

9 + 10 + 11 + 12 + 13 + 14 + 15 + 16 + 17

24 + 25 + 26 + 27 + 28

67 + 68 + 69 + 70 + 71 + 72 + 73

Name:

The Maths Herald

Volume 4

Date:

At Home

Use food advertisements to plan a dinner for four people.

You can spend up to £20.

Write about what you plan for dinner. List the price of each item of food.

How much money did you spend?

How much money do you have left over?

How could you have saved more money?

Focus on Science

What foods do you think are healthy?

What foods do you think are unhealthy?

Make two lists.

Look at a collection of supermarket till receipts.

Is it cheaper to eat more healthily?

Sports Update

Make a list of ten different exercise movements, such as touching your toes, star jumps, sit ups, knee bends.

Assign between 1 and 5 points for each movement, depending on how difficult you think the movement is. The more difficult the movement, the more points.

Make a poster showing the ten movements and the points you have assigned for each movement.

Create two exercise routines, each lasting for about 5 minutes, using a number of repetitions of your ten movements. Make one of the routines much more difficult than the other.

Now make another poster for each of your exercise routines showing the total value of each routine.

Let's Investigate

Write down your telephone number.

Separate the digits into one-digit or two-digit numbers and find the total.

Investigate separating the digits into other one-digit or two-digit numbers, and find the total each time.

What is the largest answer you can get by separating the digits into one-digit or two-digit numbers and finding the total?

What is the smallest answer you can get?

9828 7493

98 + 28 + 74 + 93 =

9 + 82 + 87 + 49 + 3 =

9 + 8 + 2 + 8 + 7 + 4 + 9 + 3 =

98 + 2 + 8 + 74 + 9 + 3 =

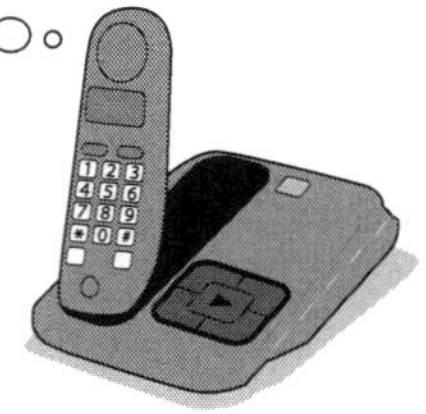

Looking for Patterns

In these addition calculations, different letters stand for different digits.

Each letter always stands for the same digit in the three calculations.

What digit does each letter stand for?

ME + ME + ME = BE

```
  XYZ
+  ZY
-----
  XXX
```

```
  TUB
+ NOT
-----
  XUN
```

The Puzzler

Using a set of normal double-six dominoes, choose dominoes so that the sum of each of the four sides in each domino square totals 12.

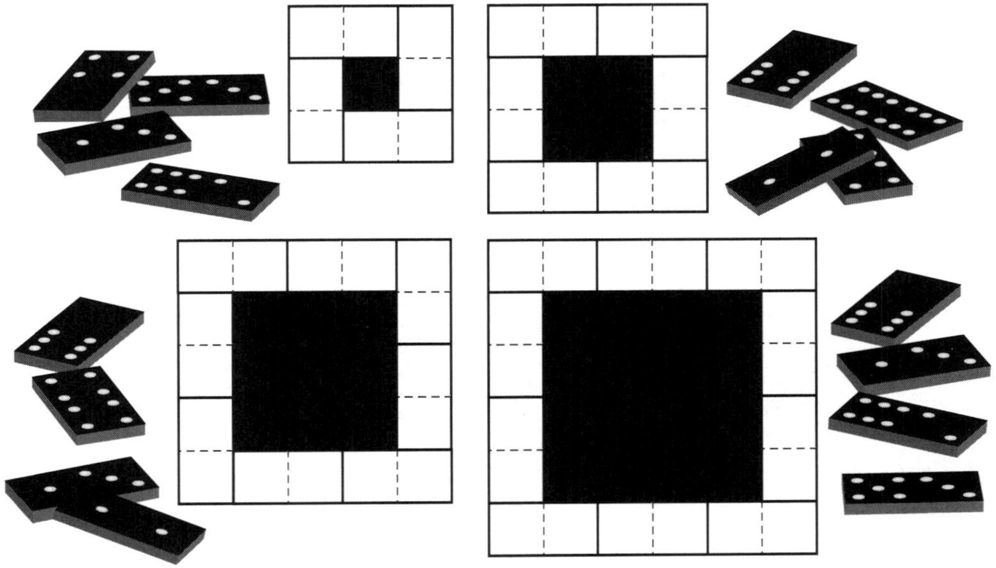

Let's Investigate

Look at this diagram.

What do you notice?

What would you expect the next stage of this diagram to look like?

Keep going. (You may need to rewrite and enlarge some of the smaller triangles as you go along.)

Investigate similar diagrams. Start by writing any three numbers at the three corners of the largest triangle.

Write about what you find out.

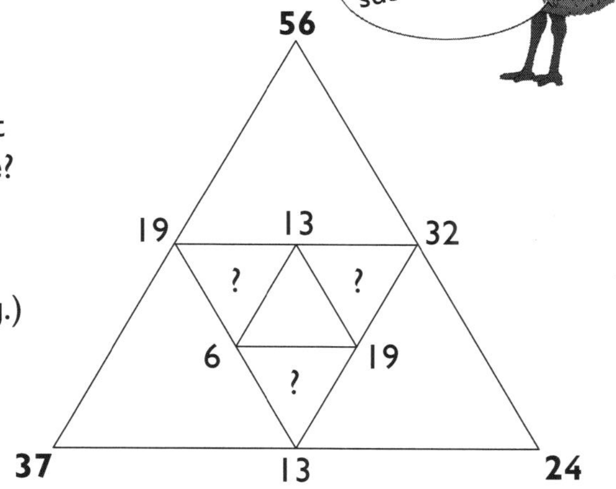

The Puzzler

What number am I?

I am a two-digit number one less than a square number and I am not divisible by 3 or 7.

What number am I?

I am a two-digit number. The difference between my two digits is 3 and I'm a square number.

Make up some problems similar to these. Try to include some subtraction.

Name:

The Maths Herald

Volume 4

Date:

The Puzzler

Here is a magic trick. It involves addition and multiplication, but the final stage of the trick relies on subtraction. Follow these steps to amaze your friends.

- Ask your friend to secretly choose a card from a pack of playing cards.
- Then tell them to:
  - add the number that is 1 more than the number of the card
  - multiply the answer by 5
  - add the value of the suit
  - add 637
  - subtract 642.
- To find the card they chose, the first digit (or two digits, if the final answer is a three-digit number) equals the card number. The last digit is the suit value.

Try this out several times yourself before trying it out on a friend.

Record the calculations of your trial.

For this trick:	Value of the suits:
Ace = 1	♥ Hearts = 1
Jack = 11	♦ Diamonds = 2
Queen = 12	♣ Clubs = 3
King = 13	♠ Spades = 4

Looking for Patterns

In these subtraction calculations, different letters stand for different digits.

Each letter always stands for the same digit in the three calculations.

What digit does each letter stand for?

EA – AM = HE

NGO	MNE
– AN	– TOM
AMN	ANT

Let's Investigate

Here is how a simple subtraction can make a very difficult addition calculation so easy.

Step 1: Write down a five-digit number.	67 893
Step 2: Look at each digit in the number, find the difference between each of these digits and 9, and write down each answer to form a new five-digit number.	32 106
Step 3: Repeat Step 1.	89 617
Step 4: Repeat Step 2.	10 382
Step 5: Repeat Step 1.	83 381
Step 6: Subtract 2 from the number in Step 5.	83 379
Step 7: Place a 2 in front of the answer to Step 6.	283 379
Step 8: Add together the five numbers in Steps 1 to 5.	?

What do you notice?

Why does this happen?

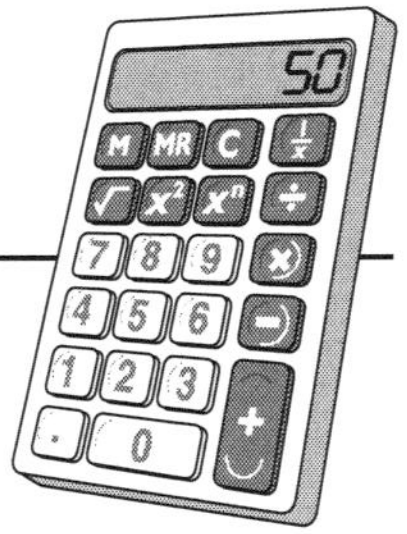

What's the Problem?

Using all the numbers from 1 to 99 with either an addition or subtraction sign between each number, make an answer of exactly 50.

1 ◇ 2 ◇ 3 ◇ 4 ◇ 5 ◇ 6 ◇ … ◇ 95 ◇ 96 ◇ 97 ◇ 98 ◇ 99 = 50

What's the Problem?

Using any of the four operations and only the 5 digit, reduce 61 to 0.

The Puzzler

Write only the digits 3 or 5 in each of the empty boxes to complete each of these subtraction calculations.

□□□ – □□ = 282

□1□ – 1□□ = 380

□□□ – □2□ = 228

6□□ – □□7 = 296

Write about how you worked out what the missing digits were.

Let's Investigate

Look at this subtraction calculation. What is the answer?

$$\begin{array}{r} 1243 \\ -\ 748 \\ \hline \\ \hline \end{array}$$

Write about your method for working it out.

Look at this method for working it out.

$$\begin{array}{r} 1243 \\ -\ 748 \\ \hline \\ \hline \end{array} \quad \text{is equivalent to} \quad \begin{array}{r} 1295 \\ -\ 800 \\ \hline 495 \\ \hline \end{array}$$

Can you explain what is happening?

Use this method to work out the answers to these subtraction calculations.

$$\begin{array}{r} 846 \\ -\ 358 \\ \hline \\ \hline \end{array} \quad \begin{array}{r} 495 \\ -\ 159 \\ \hline \\ \hline \end{array} \quad \begin{array}{r} 634 \\ -\ 347 \\ \hline \\ \hline \end{array} \quad \begin{array}{r} 663 \\ -\ 448 \\ \hline \\ \hline \end{array} \quad \begin{array}{r} 702 \\ -\ 514 \\ \hline \\ \hline \end{array}$$

Is this a method you might use?
If not, why not? If so, when?

Focus on Science

How long each day do you spend looking at a screen, either a computer screen or a television screen?

Does this change from day to day?

Is it different at weekends from weekdays?

Approximately how long do you spend each week looking at a screen?

Think about how long this is each year.
Is it different during holidays than during term time?

Show how you worked out each of these approximations.

Looking for Patterns

53 × 104   46 × 98

Work out the answers to the calculations above. Show all your working.

Here is one method you can use to work out the answer to each of the calculations.

53 × 104 = 53 × (100 + 4)
= (53 × 100) + (53 × 4)
= 5300 + 212
= 5512

46 × 98 = 46 × (100 – 2)
= (46 × 100) – (46 × 2)
= 4600 – 92
= 4508

= ○ × (□ + △)
= (○ × □) + (○ × △)

= ○ × (□ – △)
= (○ × □) – (○ × △)

The equations above use symbols to show how each of these methods work.

Use these methods to work out the answers to these calculations:

42 × 103   37 × 106   58 × 95   62 × 97

Name:

The Maths Herald

Volume 4

Date:

Looking for Patterns

In these multiplication calculations, different letters stand for different digits.

Each letter always stands for the same digit in the three calculations.

What digit does each letter stand for?

IS × F = HOS

AH × TO = AHO

Z × TOO = ZOO

Money Matters

Sunita went to the post office and bought an equal number of 5p and 40p stamps. She spent £9. How many of each type of stamp did she buy?

Focus on Science

Buttercups have 5 petals and clovers have 3 leaves.

One day Grace found a total of 28 buttercups and clovers.

Altogether she counted 110 petals and leaves.

How many buttercups did Grace find?

How many clovers did she find?

Looking for Patterns

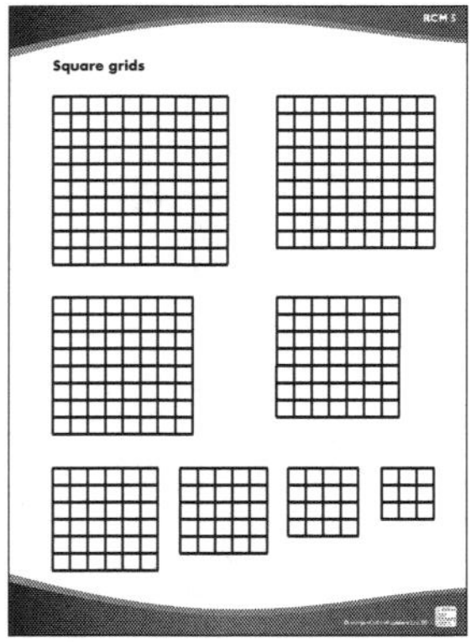

Look at the grids on the RCM.

Imagine each of these as number grids similar to a 1–100 number square, with number 1 starting in the top left hand square and numbers continuing in order.

Choose a number between 2 and 10.

Shade in all the multiples of your secret number on every grid.

Write about the patterns you notice.

What if you chose a different number?

1	2	3	4	5	6	7	8
9	10	11	12				

Let's Investigate

Step 1: Write down a known times-table fact. $3 \times 4 = 12$

Step 2: Double each of the two numbers you multiplied together to make a new calculation. $6 \times 8 = 48$

Step 3: Keep doing this for as long as you can. $12 \times 16 = ?$

What do you notice about the answers?
Does this always work?
What if you only double the first number?
What if you only double the second number?
What do you notice?

Famous Mathematicians

John Napier (1550–1617) was a Scottish mathematician. He developed a method for solving multiplication calculations using a set of 10 rods marked with numbers. By placing selected rods side by side you can multiply quickly and accurately. His method is known as 'Napier's Bones' (because they were originally made from bones!) or 'Napier's Rods' (see RCM).

This is how you would answer 58×36 using Napier's Rods.

3	6	×
0/3	0/6	1
0/6	1/2	2
0/9	1/8	3
1/2	2/4	4
1/5	3/0	5
1/8	3/6	6
2/1	4/2	7
2/4	4/8	8
2/7	5/4	9

Place rods 3 and 6 side by side.

- Put the 'Index' rod beside them.
- To multiply 36 by 8, look at the 8 row on the 'Index' rod.
- Add the numbers shown between the diagonal lines, reading the answer from left to right.

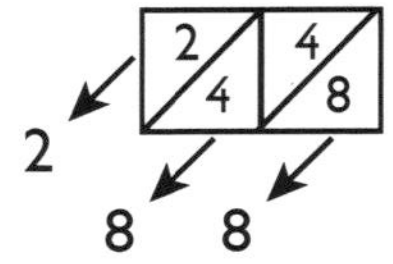

- Now to multiply 36 by 50, look at the 5 row and repeat, multiplying the result by 10.

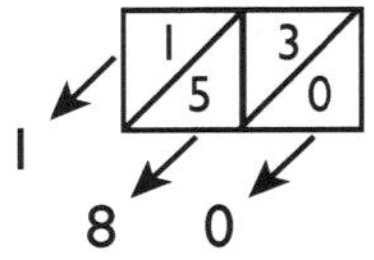

$180 \times 10 = 1800$

- Finally add the two products together, i.e. $288 + 1800 = 2088$

Write some multiplication calculations of your own and use Napier's Rods to work out the answers.

How would you use Napier's Rods to answer a calculation such as 58×327?

Is this a method of multiplication that you would regularly use? Why, why not?

Looking for Patterns

Work out the answer to each of the calculations below.

999 999 ÷ 7 =

1 999 998 ÷ 14 =

2 999 997 ÷ 21 =

What do you notice?

What are the next two calculations in the pattern?

Looking for Patterns

The first number in a division calculation is called the *dividend*.

So in the calculation below the number 63 is the dividend.

63 ÷ 9 = 7

Look at the dividends in the five calculations in the Looking for Patterns activity above.

All the digits in each of these five dividends share a special relationship.

Can you work out what it is?

Name:

The Maths Herald

Volume 4

Date:

Around the World

How much does it cost to post a letter to someone in the UK?

What about Europe, Australia or the USA?

Consider the distance that each letter has to travel.

Which letter is the cheapest per mile / per kilometre?

Looking for Patterns

In these division calculations, different letters stand for different digits.

Each letter always stands for the same digit in the three calculations.

What digit does each letter stand for?

PA ÷ A = I

HM ÷ O = MY·A

BYE ÷ ME = BY

What's the Problem?

A group of children went out looking for conkers. They found enough for each child to have four with none left over.

Along came two more friends which made it impossible to divide the conkers evenly. However, after finding one more conker and adding it to the others, there were enough for each child to have three with none left over.

How many conkers were divided between how many children?

The Arts Roundup

The money that television stations make by televising advertisements is used to pay for the cost of making (producing) television programmes.

What are your favourite television programmes? Choose programmes that are produced in the UK.

Find out how much it costs to produce one episode.

Assume that a half hour programme will have seven minutes of adverts and an hour programme 14 minutes of adverts. Calculate the cost of airing an advert during each of the programmes.

Let's Investigate

A *palindrome* is a word or number that reads the same backwards as forwards.

For example, 'MADAM', 'NURSES RUN', 5775, 2002.

True or False?

What generalisations can you make?

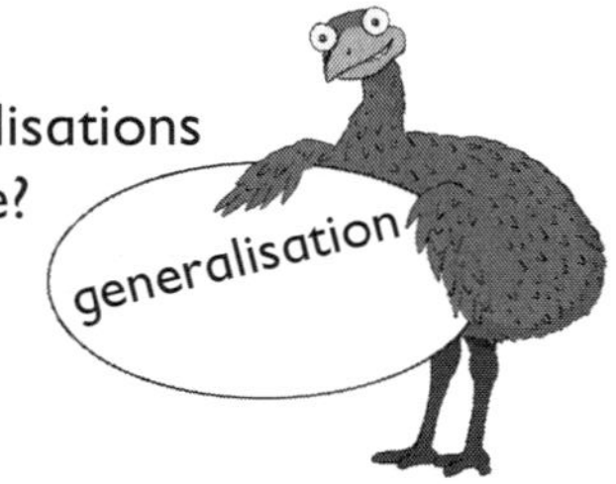

Let's Investigate

Step 1: Write down a three-digit number in which all the digits are different. 758

Step 2: Add together all the digits in the three-digit number. 7 + 5 + 8 = 20

Step 3: Write down all the possible two-digit numbers you can make using each of the digits in the three-digit number (there should be six different two-digit numbers). 75, 78, 57, 58, 87, 85

Step 4: Add together the six two-digit numbers. 87 + 85 + 78 + 75 + 58 + 57 = 440

Step 5: Divide the answer to Step 4 by the answer to Step 2. 440 ÷ 20 = ?

Repeat the above several times starting with a different three-digit number each time (making sure that all the digits are different).

What do you notice?

Looking for Patterns

111 222 333 444 555 666 777 888 999

Without working out any calculations, predict what will happen when you:

- divide each of the three-digit numbers above by the only digit in that number
- divide the answer by 3.

Write about what you think will happen.

Now test your predictions.

Why does this happen?

$(555 \div 5) \div 3 =$

Looking for Patterns

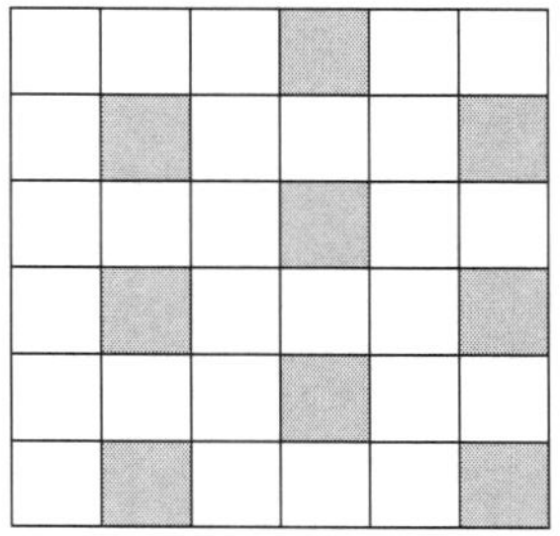

Look at the grid on the right.

Imagine that this is a number grid similar to a 1–100 number square but smaller, with number 1 starting in the top left hand square and numbers continuing in order.

What multiples have been shaded on this grid?

Below are sections from four different grids.

Can you work out what multiples have been shaded on each grid?

How wide might the grids be?

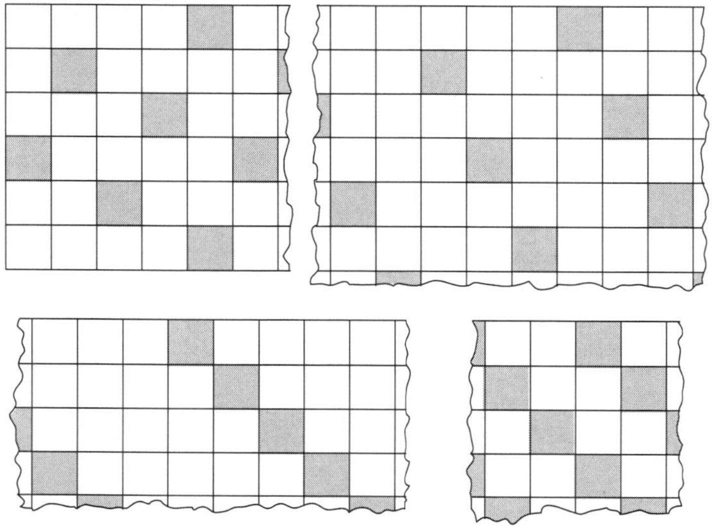

Let's Investigate

1 4 9

Using only the digits 1, 4 and 9 and any of the four operations, can you make all the even numbers from 2 to 30?

Notes:
- You can use each digit no more than twice.
- Don't forget to use brackets.

Here are two to get you started. $2 = (9 - 1) \div 4$ $4 = 4 \times 1$

Name:

The Maths Herald

Volume 4

Date:

Money Matters

Imagine you are 18 years old – you are an adult! You have £2000 to spend on a holiday anywhere in the world.

With this money you need to pay for your travel ticket, travel insurance, accommodation and any other expenses, including food.

Write an expenses sheet for your holiday.

Things that will affect the cost of your holiday
- How long you plan to go for
- When you plan to go
- If you are going to travel alone or with someone else

Around the World

London to New York is one of the busiest plane routes in the world.

Every day different airlines make numerous flights between the two cities.

Investigate the differences in prices of travelling from London to New York.

Present your results in a table.

Write statements comparing the differences in prices.

Looking for Patterns

Algebra is where letters and other symbols represent numbers in a formula or calculation. Mathematicians and scientists use algebra to explain complex concepts.

Look at this 'think of a number' puzzle.

- Think of a number.
- Add 3.
- Double it.
- Subtract 6.
- Divide your answer by 2.

The puzzle can be explained using algebra.

Look at the following:

Draw a cloud to stand for the number you are thinking of.

• Think of a number.	☁
• Add 3.	☁ + 3
• Double it.	2 × (☁ + 3) or ☁ + ☁ + 3 + 3
• Subtract 6.	☁ + ☁
• Divide your answer by 2.	☁

Use algebra to explain this 'think of a number' puzzle.

- Think of a number.
- Multiply it by 2.
- Add 4.
- Halve it.
- Subtract 2.

Try making up some 'think of a number' puzzles of your own.

Make sure you can explain how they work using algebra.

The Puzzler

For each of these function machines, the output number is the same as the input number.

What are the numbers?

Using the RCM, make some function machines of your own where the output number is the same as the input number.

Give your function machines to a friend. Can they solve your puzzles?

Technology Today

Use a calculator to work out the answer to each of these calculations.

However, although the calculator display will show the number '4', the '4' key on the calculator is broken.

436 + 569	46 × 9	96·6 − 48·3	762 ÷ 4
604 − 265	411 ÷ 6	3·4 × 5	46·7 + 55·4

Write down the keys you pressed in order to work out each of the answers.

Remember: You can't use the '4' key!

Money Matters

What is the total cost of a wedding?

Think about:

- invitations
- clothing
- wedding rings
- wedding cake
- flowers
- transport
- hiring of the reception venue
- music
- food and drink
- photographs
- honeymoon
- other expenses.

Write a detailed list, itemising each expense.

What assumptions have you made when working out the total cost?

The Puzzler

3, 5, 8, 12, 16

Use any three of the numbers above to complete each of the following calculations.

◇ + ◇ – ◇ = 0

◇ – ◇ × ◇ = 1

◇ ÷ (◇ – ◇) = 4

◇ ÷ ◇ + ◇ = 5

◇ × ◇ ÷ ◇ = 6

(◇ + ◇) ÷ ◇ = 4

What's the Problem?

Pascal the baker starts work at 4:00 a.m.

By 5:00 a.m. he has baked his first batch of bread.

At 7:00 a.m. he bakes a dozen more than double the amount he baked at 5:00 a.m.

At 9:00 a.m. Pascal bakes twice the amount of bread he has baked already this morning.

So far Pascal has baked 198 loaves of bread.

How many loaves of bread has Pascal baked by 5:00 am?

Name:

The Maths Herald

Volume 4

Date:

What's the Problem?

$$a + b = 23 \qquad a \times b = 112$$

What are the values of *a* and *b*?

How did you work out the two values?

Let's Investigate

When a number is multiplied by itself, the answer, or product, is called a *square number*.

We can write such calculations using the abbreviation: ^{2}

Look at this short cut for finding the square of a number ending in 5.

	Example 1	Example 2
	85^2 =	135^2 =
• Look at the digit (or digits) to the left of the 5. Multiply the number(s) by the number(s) itself + 10 more.	80 × 90 = 7200	130 × 140 = 18 200
• Add 25 to the result.	7200 + 25 = 7225	18 200 + 25 = 18 225

Can you use this method for any number ending in 5? Investigate.

Technology Today

Lakshmi is playing a game of Space Invaders.

She scores 10 points each time she hits a flying saucer.

She loses 2 points each time she misses one.

After 12 flying saucers have passed she has scored 60 points.

How many flying saucers has Lakshmi hit?

The Puzzler

In a *magic square* the sum of each column, row and diagonal add up to the same number – this is the magic number.

Using a set of normal double-six dominoes, choose dominoes to complete this 4 × 4 magic square.

Hint! You can arrange the dominoes anyway you like.

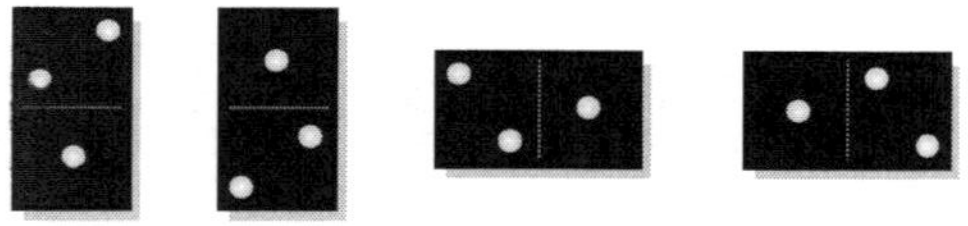

Can you make more than one magic square?

Money Matters

In recent years it has become very popular for people to grow their own fruit and vegetables, and even raise their own chickens.

Consider the cost of 'growing your own'.

Think about the cost of:

- seeds and plants
- soil / compost
- fertilisers and weed killers
- tools
- any other expenses.

Write a detailed list of all the expenses involved in 'growing your own'.

Is 'growing your own' cheaper than buying fruit and vegetables from a supermarket?

Justify your conclusions with examples.

Focus on Science

Approximately how many hours are the classroom lights on in a whole school year?

Write an explanation as to how you arrived at this number.

Also show the calculations you did to work out your approximation.

How many kilowatt hours of energy is this?

Approximately how much does this electricity cost the school?

How could this bill be reduced?

Looking for Patterns

Consecutive numbers are numbers that follow in order. For example, 1, 2, 3 or 46, 47, 48, 49.

- Which two consecutive numbers have a sum of 29?
- Which two consecutive numbers have a product of 156?
- Which three consecutive numbers have a sum of 66?
- Which three consecutive numbers have a sum of 54?
- Which two consecutive even numbers have a sum of 74?
- Which two consecutive even numbers have a product of 224?
- Which three consecutive even numbers have a sum of 60?
- Which two consecutive odd numbers have a product of 323?

How did you work out what the numbers were?

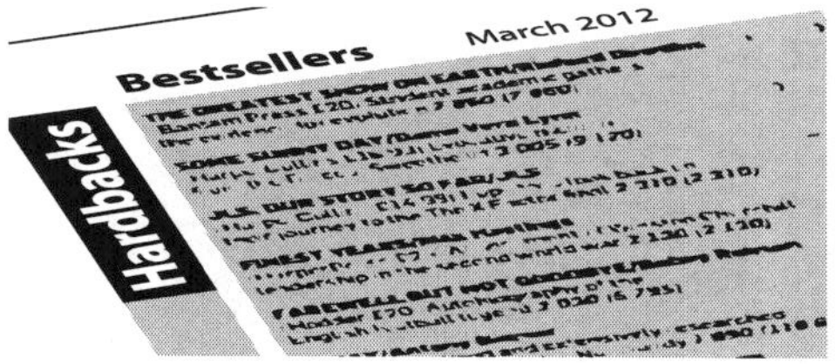

The Arts Roundup

Look through the culture / arts section in a Sunday newspaper for the listing of the bestselling books for the past week.

These listings usually show the top five or ten books in order, starting with the book that has sold most copies in the past seven days.

For each book the listings usually give:

- the books recommended retail price (RRP)
- an estimate of how many copies of the book were sold during the past week
- an estimate of the total number of sales for the book since it was published.

Write several statements comparing the sales, price and order of the books in the listing.

You might want to think about:

- the difference in the number of copies sold
- how much money a book costs or has made altogether
- how a book's 'popularity' has changed.

Name:

The Maths Herald

Volume 4

Date:

In the Past

A healthy adult at rest takes 12 breaths per minute.

Approximately how many breaths did each of these people take during their lifetime?

Focus on Science

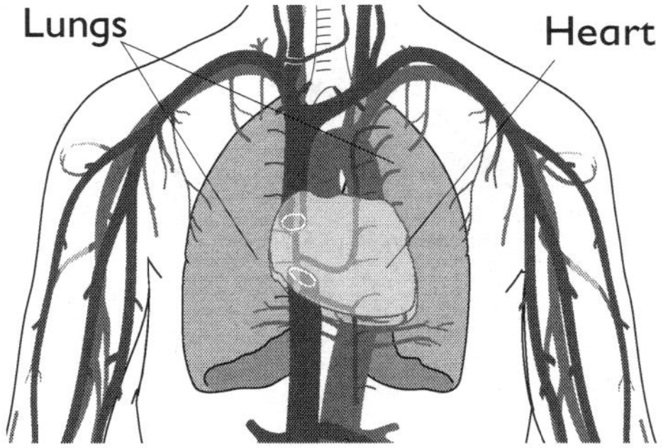

Breathing is the process of taking air into the lungs and pushing it out again.

Find out the number of breaths you take in one minute.

At this rate, calculate the number of breaths that you take in a year.

Approximately how many breaths have you taken during your life so far?

Looking for Patterns

A 2 × 2 box is placed on a number grid, covering four numbers.

The numbers in the opposite corners are multiplied together and the difference between their products is found. For example:

6 × 11 = 66   7 × 10 = 70   70 – 66 = 4

1	2	3	4
5	6	7	8
9	10	11	12
13	14	15	16

What happens when the box moves around the number grid?

Multiply the opposite corners together and find the difference between their products.

What do you notice?

This number grid uses four columns.

Using the RCM, investigate grids with different numbers of columns.

What do you notice?

What patterns or rules do you notice?

Money Matters

A *budget* is a plan of how money is spent. A total sum of money is divided into smaller amounts that are used for specific purposes.

Families, cities, schools and governments all use budgets to plan spending.

Look at the diagram on the right. It is called a *pie chart*. It is divided into sectors that each represent a proportion of a whole.

These proportions are shown as *percentages*.

Percentages are fractions out of 100.

So 20% means $\frac{20}{100}$ or $\frac{1}{5}$.

This pie chart shows the different areas that a family might spend their *income* on.

If a family's income is £22 000 a year, how much money do they spend in each of these areas?

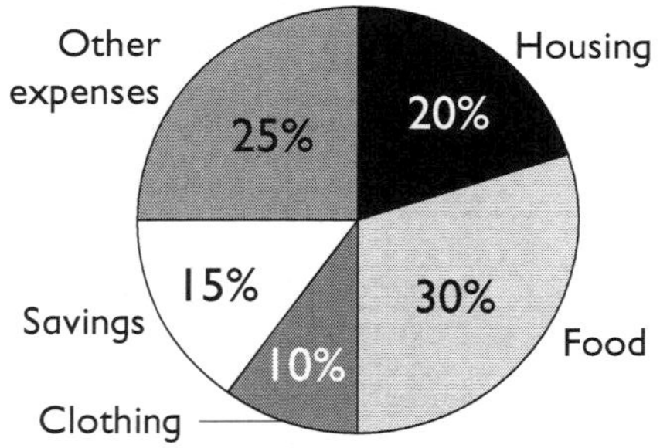

Money Matters

When you eat a meal in a restaurant it is usual to add a little extra money to the bill. This additional amount of money, called a *tip* or *service charge*, is given for good service.

A tip is usually somewhere between 10% and 20% of the cost of the meal.

Remember, percentages (%) are fractions out of 100. 20% means $\frac{20}{100}$ or $\frac{1}{5}$.

So, to work out 20% of £26.00:

$\frac{1}{5}$ × £26.00 = £5.20

Work out what the service charge will be for each of these bills.

Then calculate the total cost of each meal.

FOOD BASKET

TINKER LANE
MIDSOMMER TWIGGY
GLOUCESTERSHIRE
GL23 4GG

VAT No. 34058767675

21st June 2012 12:35pm

1 Cheeseburger	£6.00
1 Chicken salad	£8.00
1 Ice cream	£3.00
1 Lemon Pie	£4.00
2 Soft drinks @ £2.50	£5.00
Sub-Total	£26.00
Service charge (20%)	£5.20
Total	£31.20

THANK YOU FOR YOUR SERVICE

Sub-total	£28
Service charge (10%)	£
Total	£

THANK YOU FOR YOUR SERVICE

Sub-total	£45
Service charge (10%)	£
Total	£

THANK YOU FOR YOUR SERVICE

Sub-total	£48
Service charge (15%)	£
Total	£

THANK YOU FOR YOUR SERVICE

Sub-total	£37
Service charge (20%)	£
Total	£

THANK YOU FOR YOUR SERVICE

Money Matters

The average wedding costs £18 500.
This is how the money is spent.

Wedding reception	$\frac{7}{20}$
Flowers & decoration	$\frac{1}{20}$
Clothing for bride, groom and attendants	$\frac{3}{20}$
Wedding cake	$\frac{1}{50}$
Photography	$\frac{1}{10}$
Honeymoon	$\frac{1}{5}$
Transport, stationary, gifts etc.	$\frac{13}{100}$

Work out how much money is spent on each of these categories.

Let's Investigate

Use the digits 2, 3, 4, 5, 6, 7, 8 or 9 only once in each number sentence.

How many different solutions can you find for each number sentence?

$\frac{\square}{\square} + \frac{\square}{\square} = 2$ $\qquad$ $\frac{\square}{\square} + \frac{\square}{\square} = 3$

$\frac{\square}{\square} - \frac{\square}{\square} = 1$ $\qquad$ $\frac{\square}{\square} - \frac{\square}{\square} = 2$

Name:

The Maths Herald

Volume 4

Date:

What's the Problem?

The viewing platform at an Adventure Park can hold a maximum of 60 adults or 96 children. If there are 45 adults on the platform, how many children can get on as well?

What's the Problem?

Marcus and his friends were playing a game with their football cards.

In the first game, Marcus lost one-quarter of all his cards.

In the second game, he won six cards.

In the third game, he won the same number of cards as he had at the end of the second game.

In the fourth game, he lost one-fifth of his cards.

In the fifth game, he won two cards.

By the end of the game Marcus had a total of 50 cards.

How many cards did Marcus have to start with?

What's the Problem?

Sammi went shopping.

She spent one-quarter of her money on a skirt and another quarter on a top. One-fifth of her remaining money was spent on a drink and a cake.

She counted how much she had left, and spent a third of this on a CD.

When she got home, her brother asked her if she could lend him some money, so she gave him a half of what she had left.

After all this, Sammi had only £8 remaining.

How much money did Sammi go shopping with?

Focus on Science

The purity of gold in jewellery is traditionally measured in *carats*.

24 carat gold is pure gold.

18 carat gold is $\frac{3}{4}$ gold and $\frac{1}{4}$ other metals.

12 carat gold is $\frac{1}{2}$ gold and $\frac{1}{2}$ other metals.

Calculate how many grams of pure gold there are in each of the following pieces of jewellery:

- An 18 carat gold ring weighing 24 g
- A 12 carat gold brooch weighing 270 g
- An 18 carat gold chain weighing 428 g
- A 24 carat gold necklace weighing 137 g
- A 12 carat gold bracelet weighing 294 g

What's the Problem?

Farmer Dobbs had a farm of 430 hectares. When he retired, he decided to keep a quarter of his farmland for himself and divide the rest up between his four children.

He gave $\frac{3}{10}$ to his eldest child, $\frac{1}{4}$ to the second eldest, $\frac{1}{5}$ to the third child and the rest to the youngest.

How many hectares did each person get?

What's the Problem?

Half the children around a dinner table are drinking water, a quarter are drinking milk, a third are drinking neither, and two are drinking both milk and water.

How many children are sitting around the dinner table?

The Language of Maths

A *formula* is a mathematical rule or principle represented in symbols, numbers or letters.

The term *laws of mathematics* refers to the general mathematical rules or principles that are thought to be true.

The following formulae show some of the different laws of mathematics.

Commutative law of addition	Commutative law of multiplication	Associative law of multiplication	Distributive law
A + B = B + A	AB = BA	A(BC) = (AB)C	A(B +C) = AB + AC

Explain what each of these laws mean.

Write two different calculations that illustrate each of the above formulae.

Formula rule:

A multiplication calculation such as A × B can be written without the multiplication sign, that is AB.

But you can't do this if you use numbers:

A × B = AB

6 × 4 ≠ 64

Focus on Science

Approximately how many hairs do you have on your forearms?

Write about how you arrived at your approximation.

Name:

The Maths Herald

Volume 4

Date:

Let's Investigate

Look at the calculations on the right.

When a number is multiplied by itself, the answer, or product, is called a *square number*.

We can write such calculations using the abbreviation: ^{2}

2 × 2 = 4	$2^2 = 4$
3 × 3 = 9	$3^2 = 9$
4 × 4 = 16	$4^2 = 16$
5 × 5 = 25	$5^2 = 25$
6 × 6 = 36	$6^2 = 36$

Look at this short cut for finding the square of decimals such as $6{\cdot}5^2$ or $18{\cdot}5^2$.

	Example 1	Example 2
	$6{\cdot}5^2$	$18{\cdot}5^2$
• Multiply the whole number by the number itself + 1 more.	6 × 7 = 42	18 × 19 = 342
• Add 0·25 to the result.	42 + 0·25 = 42·25	342 + 0·25 = 342·25

Can you use this method for any number ending in 0·5? Investigate.

How could you use this method for working out the answer to calculations such as: $(4\frac{1}{2})^2$ or $(12\frac{1}{2})^2$?

Let's Investigate

Using no more than four 9s, write calculations to make each of the following answers.

81	90	0	1
2	11	20	162

The Puzzler

Martin went out shopping for some new clothes.

He spent one-fifth of the cash that was in his wallet on a pair of trousers.

He then spent another fifth of his remaining cash on a shirt.

Altogether Martin spent a total of £72.

- How much money did Martin originally have in his wallet?
- What was the price of the trousers?
- What was the price of the shirt?

Money Matters

What is a bank account?

What are debit cards?

How do they work?

Money Matters

What is credit?

What are credit cards? How do they work?

What are the similarities and differences between credit cards and debit cards?

How do credit card companies make money?

Provide some examples.

In what situations might it be useful to use a credit card?

When might it not be so good?

Do you think credit cards are a good thing or not? Justify your reasoning.

At Home

Supermarkets stock many different *brands* of the same, or very similar, groceries.

For example:

- flour
- orange juice
- ground coffee
- butter
- baked beans
- crisps

Visit a local supermarket.

Choose three or four different groceries that each offers a wide range of choice.

Look carefully at the printed price label on the supermarket shelf. It will not only show the cost of the grocery, but also the price per kilogram or per litre.

Make a note of the brands and price per kilogram or per litre.

Which is the cheapest brand of each of your chosen groceries?

Let's Investigate

- Write down a three-digit number in which all the digits are the same. 444
- Find the sum of the digits. 4 + 4 + 4 = 12
- Divide the original three-digit number by the sum. 444 ÷ 12 = ?

Repeat for other three-digit numbers in which all the digits are the same.

What do you notice?

Money Matters

Instead of keeping all their money at home, or in their pockets or bag, most people keep the majority of their money in a bank.

They have an account at the bank that keeps a record of all the money they have put in to the bank (*deposits*) and all the money that they have taken out (*withdrawals*).

Every month or two, the bank sends them a *bank statement* that lists all the deposits and withdrawals they have made, and the amount of money that they have left in the account (*balance*).

Below is part of a bank statement.

Complete the balance column of the statement to find out how much money is in this bank account after depositing the 'Cheque from Mrs Grant'.

Date	Transaction	Deposit	Withdrawal	Balance
1/7/2011	Salary	1562.00		1562.00
3/7/2011	Go! Supermarket		15.60	1546.40
6/7/2011	Electricity bill		69.70	
11/7/2011	Better Electrics		399.00	
14/7/2011	Go! Supermarket		27.38	
18/7/2011	Cheque from Mrs Grant	50.00		

Name:

The Maths Herald

Volume 4

Date:

Focus on Science

Blinking is an automatic process that helps keep the eyes moist.

Every time you blink, the eyelid closes and a tiny amount of moisture is spread over the sclera – the outermost layer of the eye.

Find out how many times you blink in one minute.

At this rate, calculate the number of times you blink in one hour.

What about in a day?

What about in a year?

Approximately what is the number of blinks you have made during your life so far?

In the Past

Look at the answers you got for the Focus on Science activity above.

Assuming that the total number of blinks you make in a year is similar for other people, approximately how many blinks did each of these people make during their lifetime?

Queen Elizabeth I — Albert Einstein — William Shakespeare — Sir Isaac Newton

The Arts Roundup

Bomaderry Primary School has an orchestra.

Use the following clues to work out how many musicians are in the orchestra.

- If the number is not a multiple of 8, it is a number between 31 and 40.
- If the number is not a multiple of 7, it is a number between 21 and 30.
- If the number is a multiple of 4, it is a number between 1 and 20.

What's the Problem?

Dennis was collecting football player cards which the newspaper was giving away free.

There were 11 player cards in each team, and the newspaper was giving away one each day of the week, for one team after another.

His Mum asked him how many he had collected.

He said:

The offer was running for eleven weeks.

How many cards had Dennis collected already?

Issue 19 Calculating – General

The Arts Roundup

The director of the Shellharbour Symphony Orchestra has only enough money to pay his 50 musicians for 40 days. This is not enough to last until the next amount of money arrives in 90 days time.

After 10 days he lays off 30 musicians.

Will he have enough money to pay the remaining 20 musicians until the next amount of money arrives?

Looking for Patterns

$\square \times \bigcirc + \square \times \triangle = \square \times (\bigcirc + \triangle)$

$\square \times \bigcirc - \square \times \triangle = \square \times (\bigcirc - \triangle)$

The equations above have been written using symbols. For each equation the expression to the right of the equals sign provides a quicker and easier way of working out the answer. Look at these examples.

$$6 \times 4 + 6 \times 7 = 6 \times (4 + 7) = 6 \times 11 = 66$$

$$9 \times 8 - 9 \times 3 = 9 \times (8 - 3) = 9 \times 5 = 45$$

Use the quicker and easier method to work out the answers to these calculations:

$7 \times 8 + 7 \times 5$ $\quad$ $9 \times 12 + 9 \times 7$ $\quad$ $6 \times 8 - 6 \times 2$

$10 \times 9 - 10 \times 5$ $\quad$ $14 \times 6 + 14 \times 7$ $\quad$ $16 \times 7 - 16 \times 3$

Construct

It is possible to fold a sheet of A4 paper into each of these different shapes (one A4 sheet per shape). Can you do this?

square
- 4 equal sides
- 4 equal angles
- 4 lines of symmetry

equilateral triangle
- 3 equal sides
- 3 equal angles

kite
- 2 pairs of adjacent sides equal
- 1 pair of opposite angles equal
- 1 line of symmetry

rhombus
- 4 equal sides
- opposite angles equal
- 2 lines of symmetry

regular hexagon
- 6 equal sides
- 6 equal angles

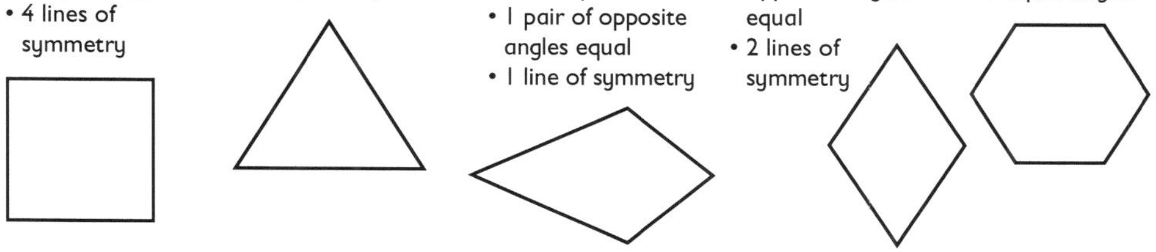

Only once you've attempted to make each of the shapes, look at the RCM. Follow the instructions to make each of the shapes a second time.

What is similar and different about each of the first set of shapes you made when compared with the second set of shapes?

Construct

Look at the Let's Investigate activity at the bottom of page 3.

Investigate bridges, buildings and other structures and comment on how they are made rigid.

What shapes are commonly used to ensure something is rigid?

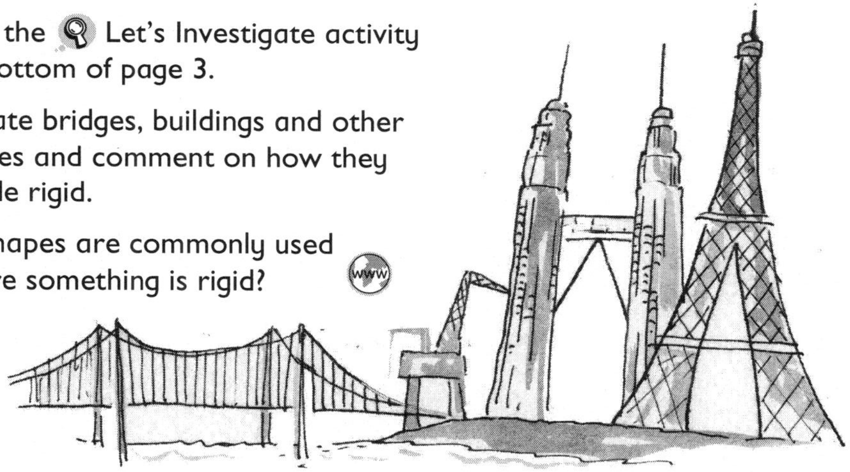

Name:

The Maths Herald

Volume 4

Date:

The Arts Roundup

Abstract artists often use lines, shapes and geometric patterns in their work.

Investigate the work of some of the following artists.

Georges Braque (1882–1963)
M.C. Escher (1898–1972)
Auguste Herbin (1882–1960)
Wassily Kandinsky (1866–1944)
Paul Klee (1879–1940)
Fernand Léger (1881–1955)
Henri Matisse (1869–1954)
Piet Mondrian (1872–1944)

Comment on how shape and lines have influenced each of the artists, using specific examples of the artist's work to justify your comments.

Construct

By making two straight cuts, the paper square on the right has been cut into three other shapes – two right-angled triangles and a hexagon.

Using a selection of paper squares, which of these shapes can you make with two cuts?

- equilateral triangle
- right-angled triangle
- isosceles triangle
- irregular quadrilateral
- oblong
- parallelogram
- trapezium
- kite
- pentagon
- hexagon
- heptagon
- octagon

Looking for Patterns

How many triangles are there in each of these diagrams?

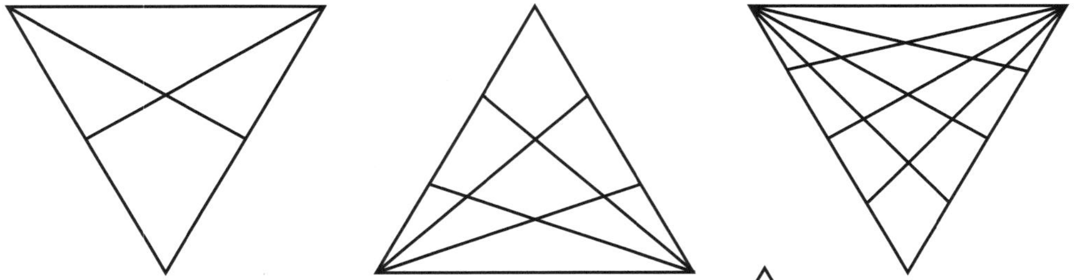

What patterns do you notice?

Can you predict how many triangles there are in this shape?

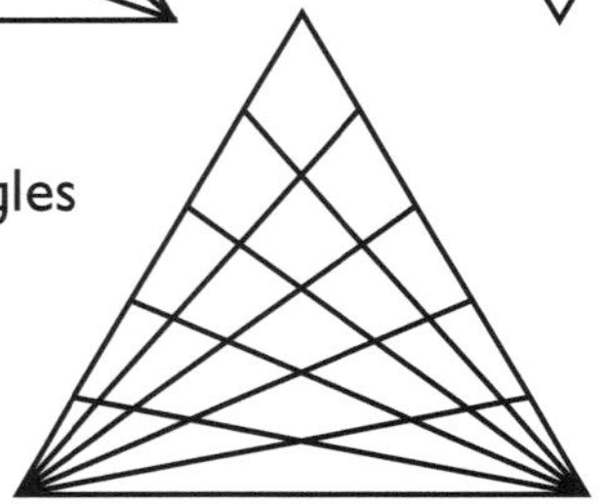

Let's Investigate

This large square has been divided into four smaller squares.

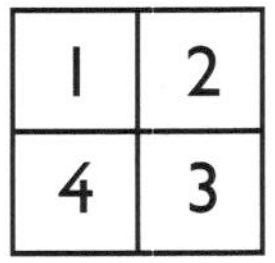

This large square has been divided into six smaller squares.

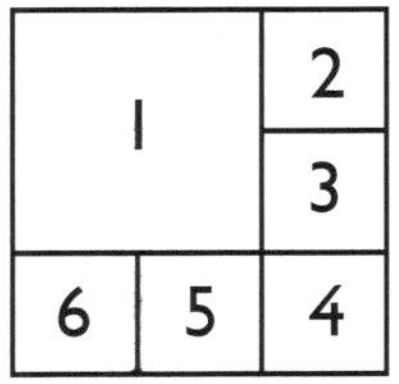

This large square has been divided into seven smaller squares.

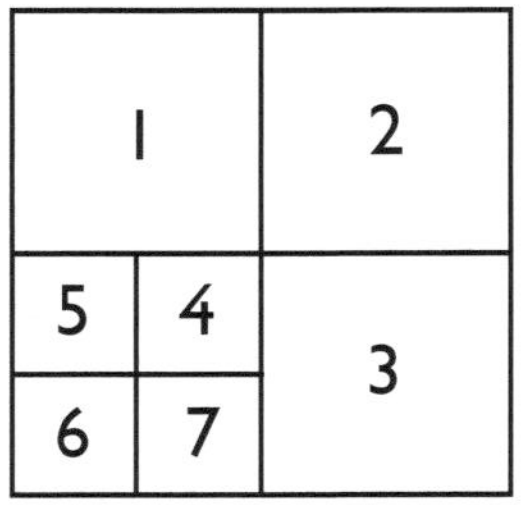

Divide larger squares into 8, 9, 10, 11 and 12 smaller squares.

Use squared paper to record your results.

Looking for Patterns

The triangle on the right can make a fascinating pattern known as the *Sierpinski Triangle*.

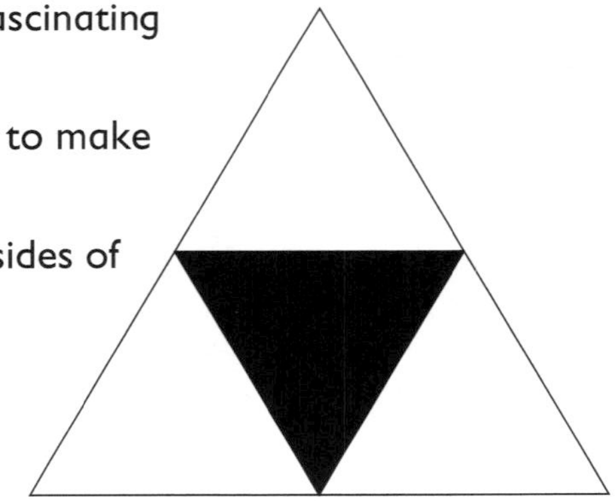

Using the RCM, follow the steps below to make the pattern.

Step 1: Connect the midpoints of the sides of each of the three white triangles.

Step 2: Shade the centre triangles.

Step 3: Repeat Steps 1 and 2.

Step 4: Repeat Steps 1 and 2.

Let's Investigate

Using geostrips, make an equilateral triangle and a rectangle. Make sure to fasten the corners tightly.

Gently push the triangle in the direction of the arrow.

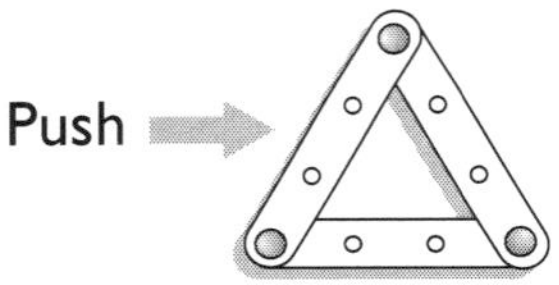

The triangle should not move because it is a *rigid* shape.

Now gently push the rectangle in the direction of the arrow.

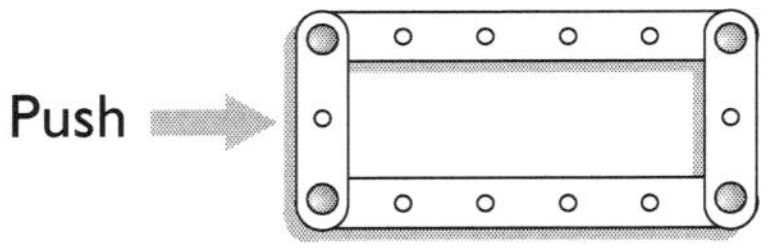

Is the rectangle rigid?

Now put another geostrip diagonally through the rectangle. This geostrip acts as a support *strut*.

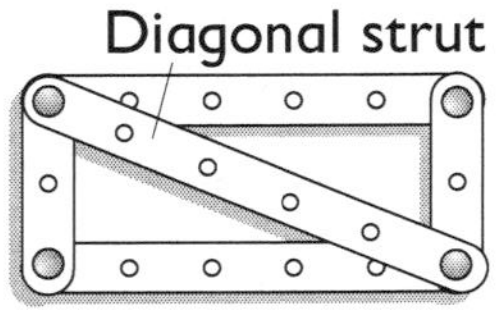

Is the rectangle rigid now? Why?

How many struts do each of the following shapes need to make them rigid? Why?

- pentagon
- hexagon
- heptagon
- octagon

The Puzzler

These three shapes can be fitted together to make a cube in two different ways.

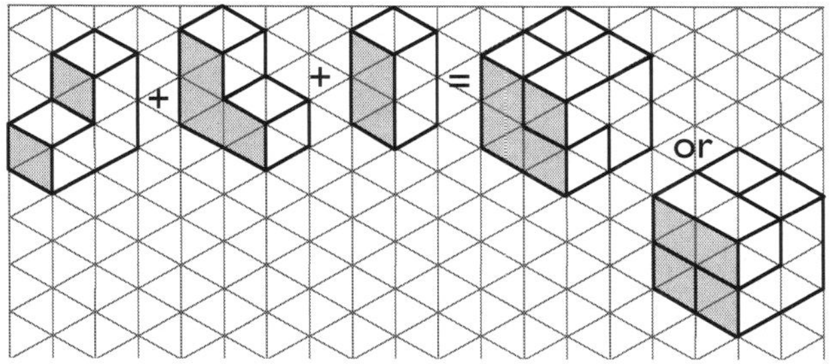

Fit these four pieces together to make a 2 × 2 × 2 cube.

How many different ways can you do it?

Draw your answers on isometric paper.

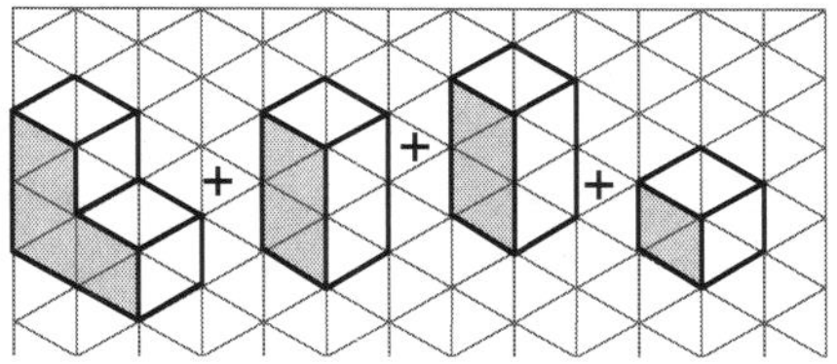

Now fit these four pieces together to make a 3 × 3 × 3 cube.

How many different ways can you do it?

Draw your answers on isometric paper.

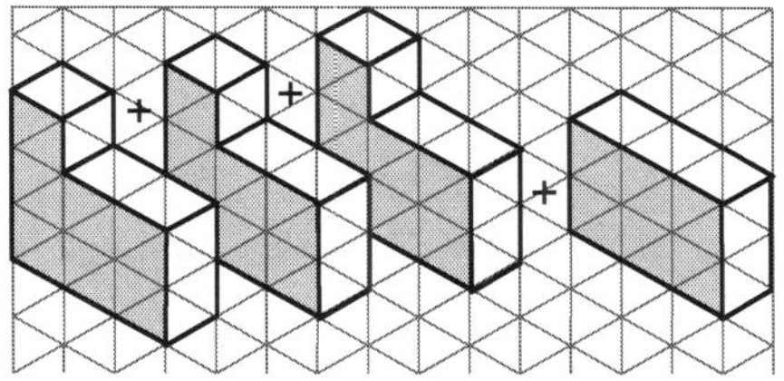

Now fit these seven pieces together to make a 3 × 3 × 3 cube.

How many different ways can you do it?

Draw your answers on isometric paper.

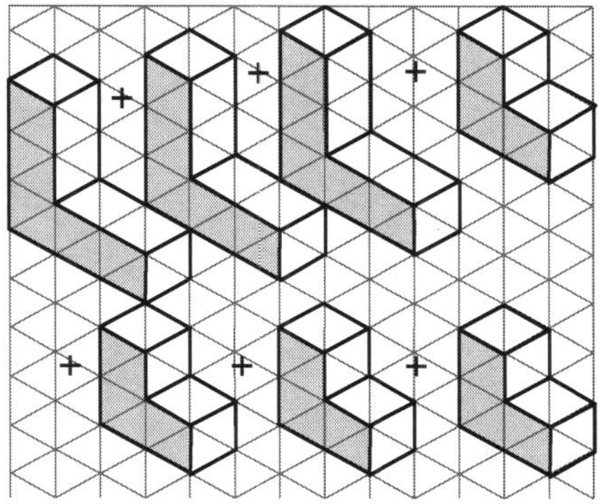

Construct

Here is the net of a cube.

Change this into the net of a cuboid.

Draw the net on squared paper.

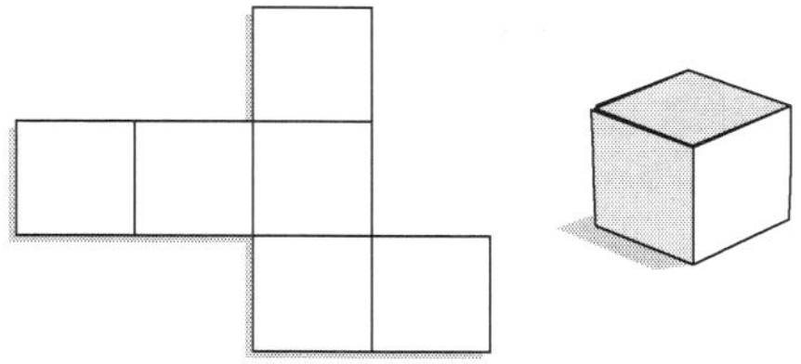

Name:

The Maths Herald

CN PM

Volume 4

Date:

Construct

Origami is the Japanese art of paper folding. Follow these instructions to make a rectangular box. You will need a large square sheet of coloured paper.

Step 1

Fold the paper in half, then open.

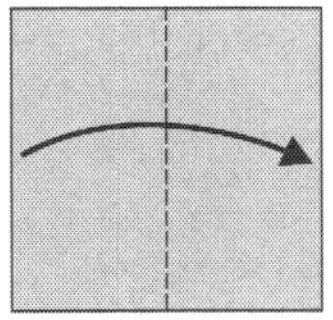

Step 2

Fold the side edges to the centre fold.

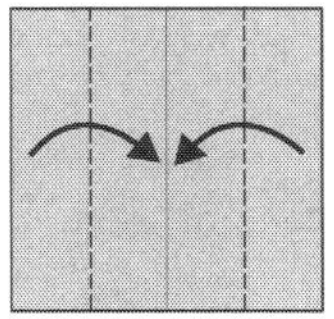

Step 3

Fold the paper outwards along the creases as shown.

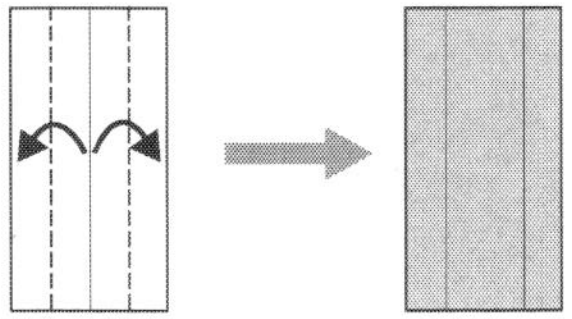

Step 4

Turn the paper over and fold the side edges into the centre fold. Crease then unfold.

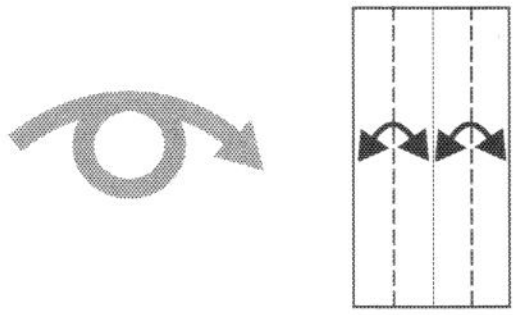

Step 5

Take the bottom corner and fold it up to the third crease.

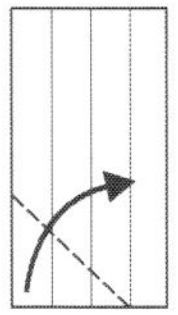

Step 6

Fold the small corner as shown.

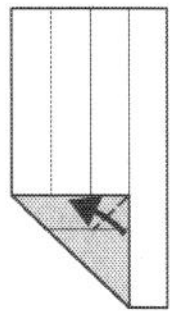

Step 7

Fold up the other corner and tuck under.

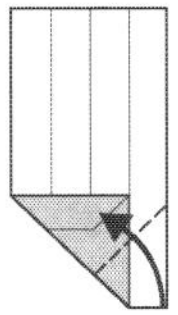

Step 8

Fold up the bottom corner and tuck under.

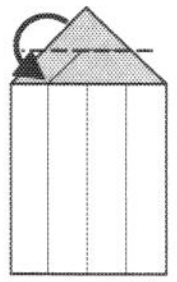

Step 9

Turn round the paper and repeat Steps 5 to 8 on the other end of the paper.

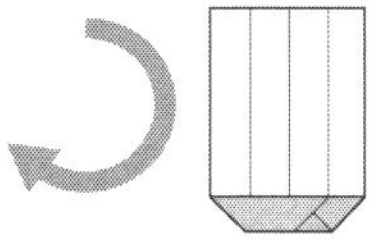

Step 10

Pull the sides out.

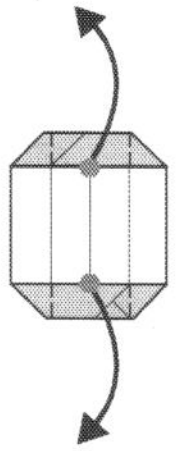

Your finished box should look like this:

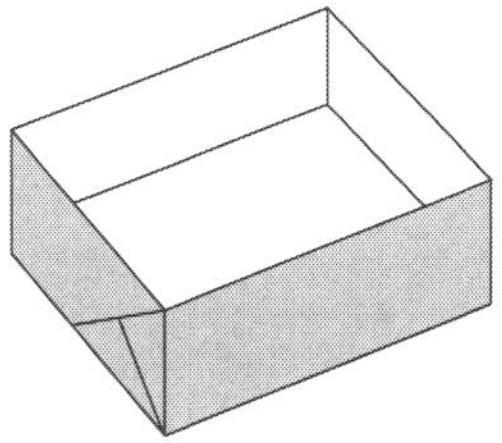

Construct

Origami is just one way of making a paper box.

Using another sheet of A4 paper, design and make a different rectangular box about the same size as your Origami box.

Try and use as few other resources as you can.

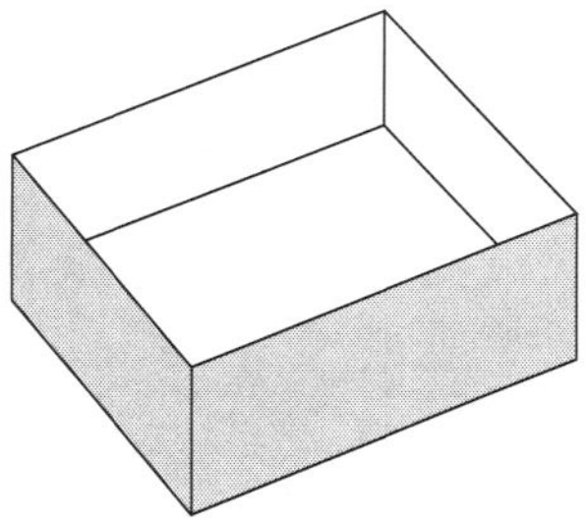

Construct

Look at this shape.
It has been drawn using isometric paper.

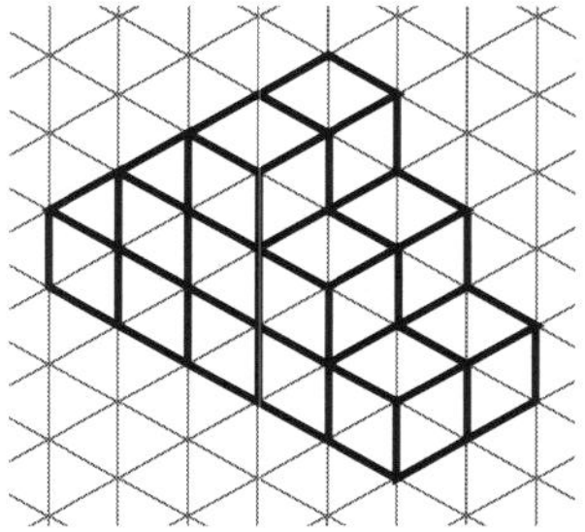

Here are its front view, top view and side view.

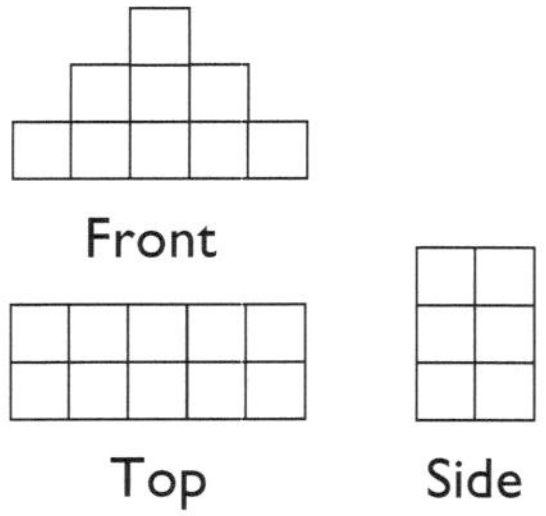

Below you can see the front view, top view and side view of four other shapes.

Draw each of these shapes using isometric paper.

1

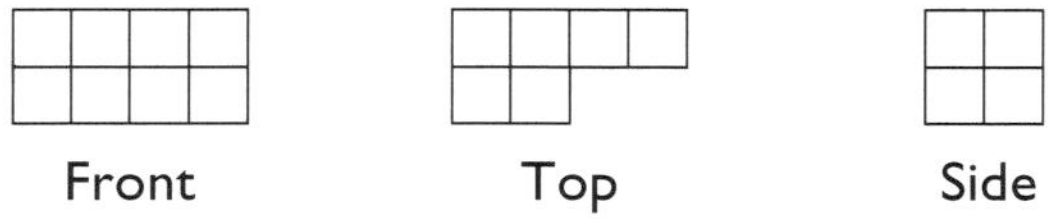

2

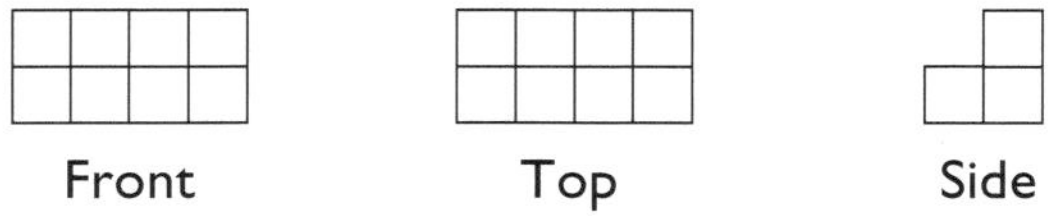

3

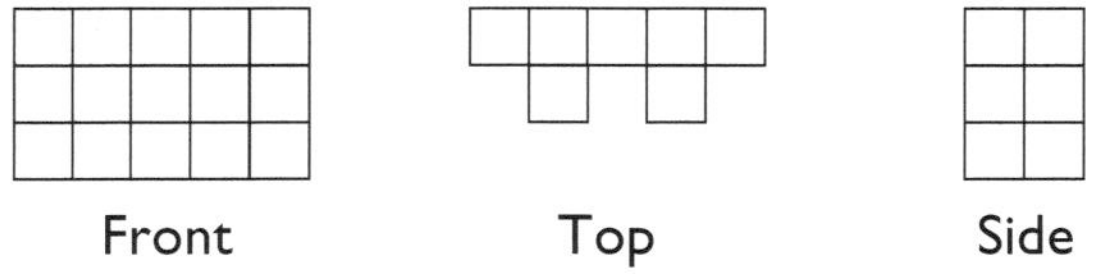

4

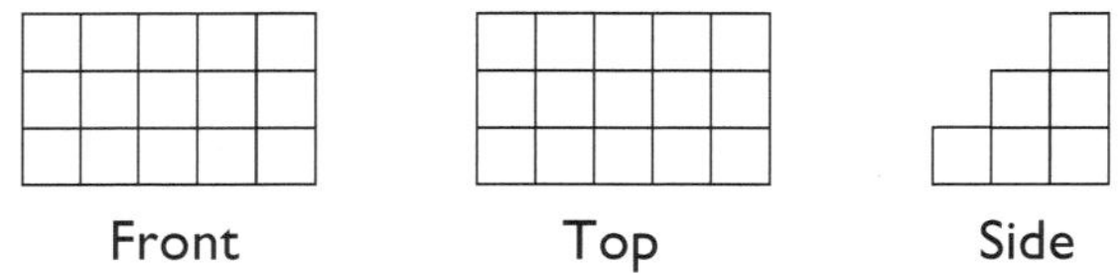

Construct

The circumference of a circle is always $\frac{22}{7}$, or 3·14, times its diameter.

So, if the diameter of a circle is 2 cm, its circumference is 3·14 × 2 cm = 6·28 cm.

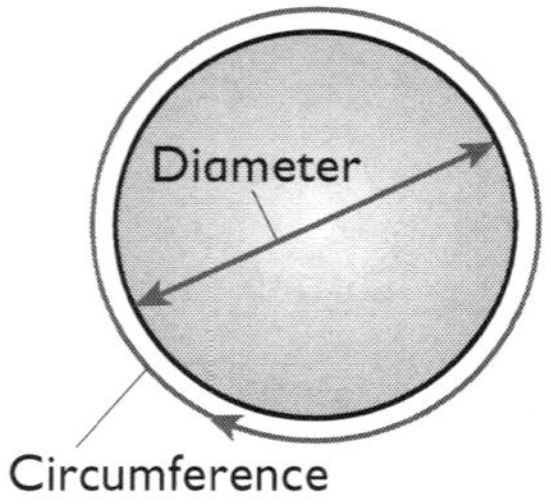

Draw the net of this cylinder.

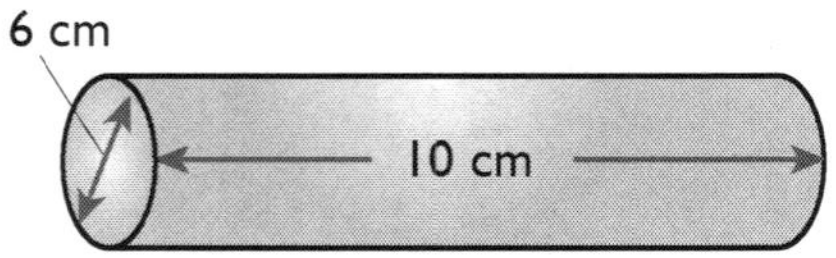

Cut it out, leaving the circles attached to the rectangle by a small amount of paper. Then assemble it.

Now draw the net of this cone.

Cut it out and then assemble it.

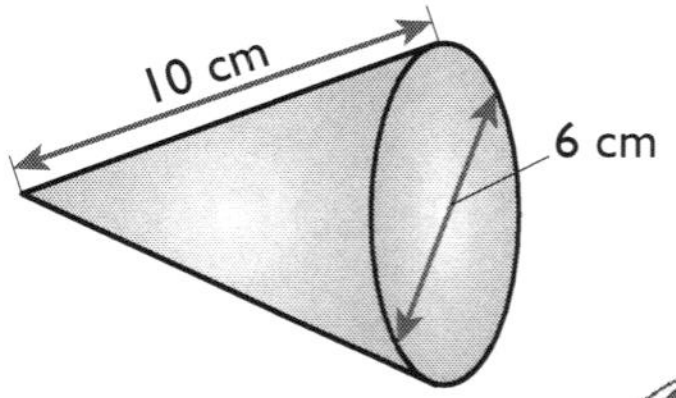

Looking for Patterns

Which of these is the net of a triangular prism?

1

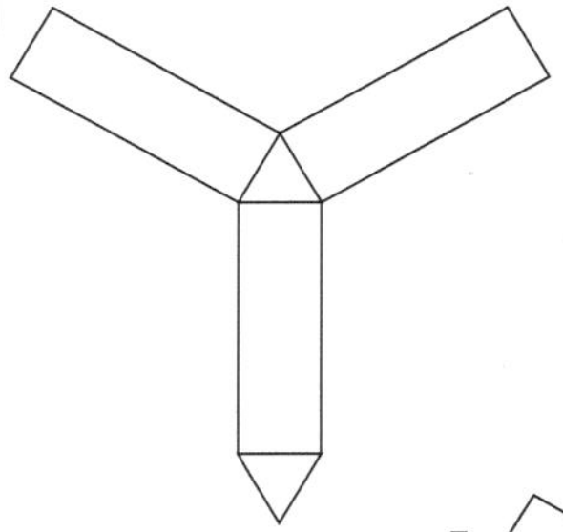

2

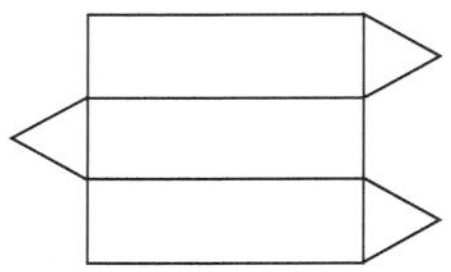

3

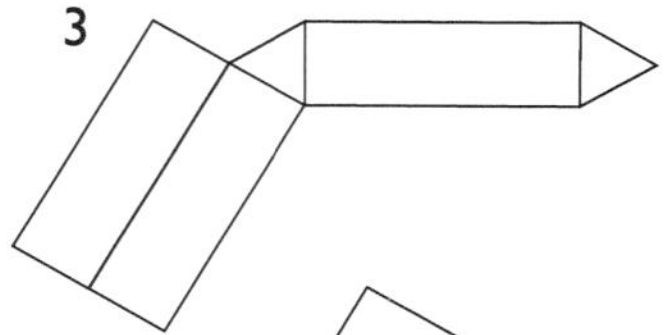

4

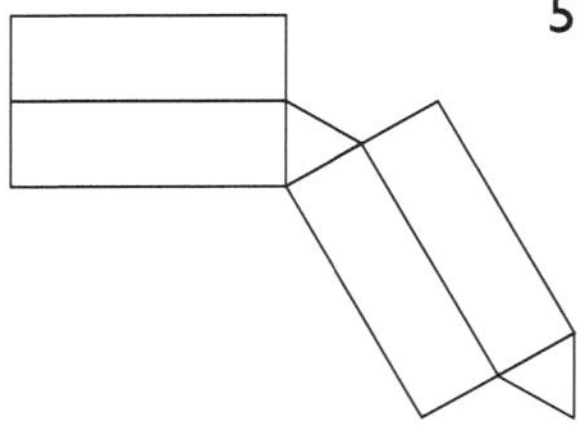

5

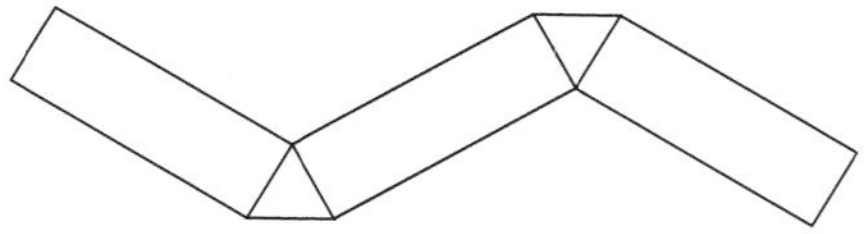

6

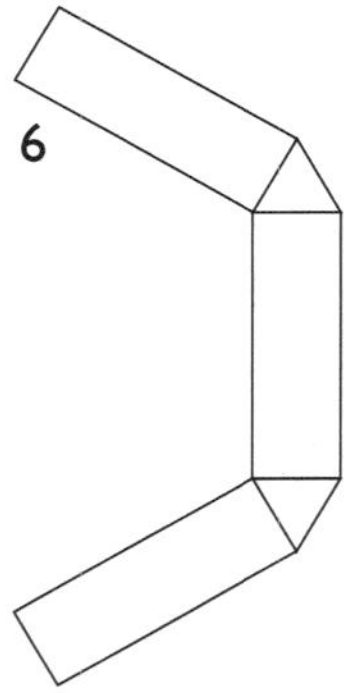

Focus on Science

Draw simple pictures of different animals (including fish and birds) showing them from an angle where they have a line of symmetry.

What do you notice about the lines of symmetry that you have drawn on all your animals?

Why do you think this is?

Let's Investigate

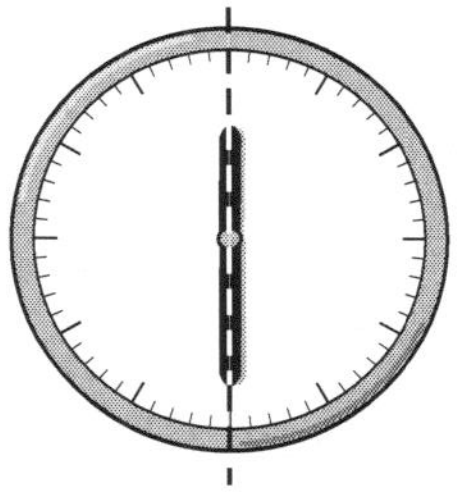

When an analogue clock shows 6 o'clock the hands form a line of reflective symmetry through the middle of the clock.

Use the RCM to show six different times where there is a line of reflective symmetry through the middle of the clock. Be as accurate as possible with the clock hands.

Draw on the lines of symmetry.

Around the World

Here are the floor plans of three famous buildings that show reflective symmetry.

Draw all the lines of symmetry on each building.

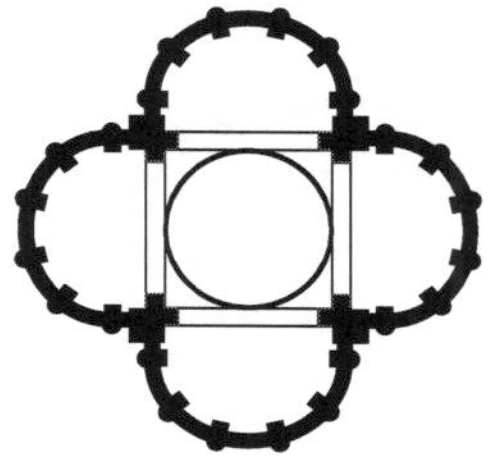

Santa Maria della Consolazione
Todi, Italy

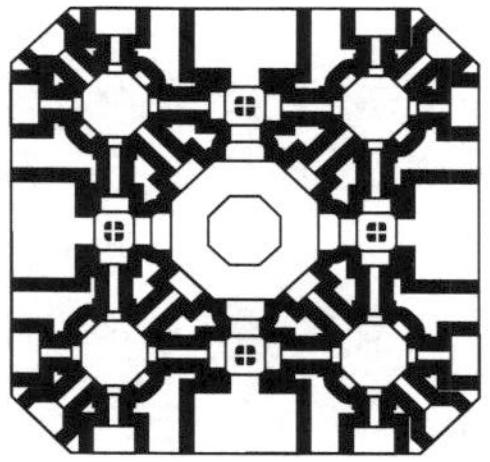

The Taj Mahal
Agra, India

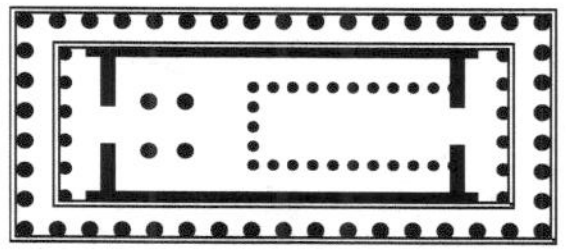

The Parthenon
Athens, Greece

Find floor plans of other famous buildings that show reflective symmetry.

Draw all the lines of symmetry on each building.

Name:

The Maths Herald

Volume 4

Date:

Focus on Science

Which fruits have symmetry?

Have they got rotational or reflective symmetry?

Can you show where their lines or axes of symmetry are?

Which fruits have no symmetry?

Looking for Patterns

On a 10 × 10 square, draw a vertical line of symmetry down the middle of the square.

Using four different colours, colour in the squares to make a pattern that shows reflective symmetry about this line.

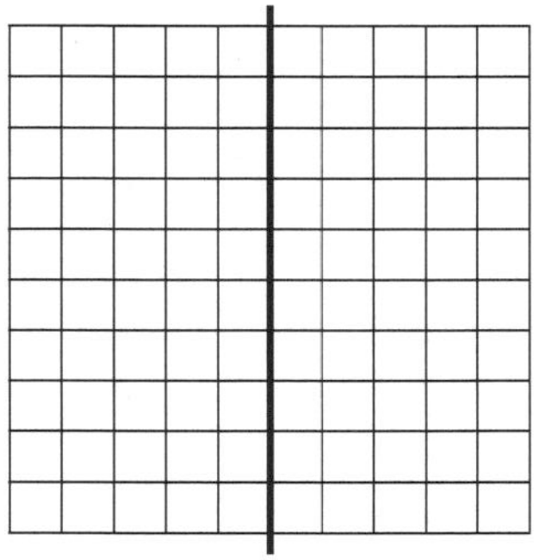

On a new 10 × 10 square, draw a vertical line of symmetry down the middle and a horizontal line of symmetry across the middle of the square.

Using four different colours, colour in the squares to make a pattern that shows reflective symmetry about both lines.

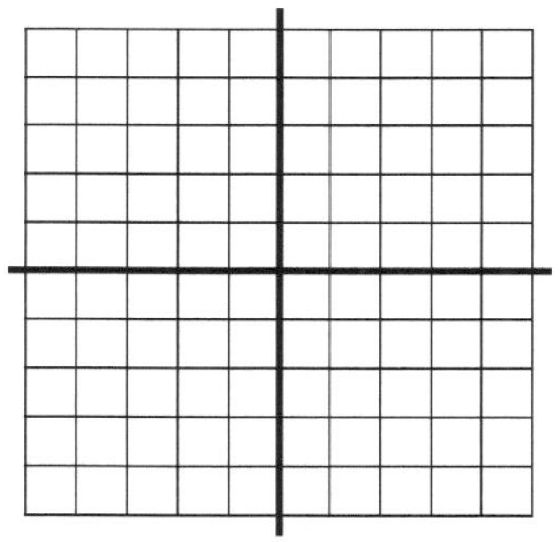

Construct

Fold a sheet of A4 paper in half.

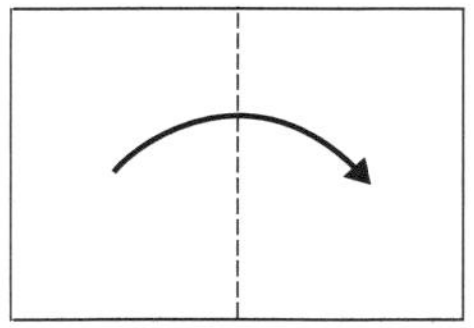

Open it up and fold the two edges of the paper in to the centre crease.

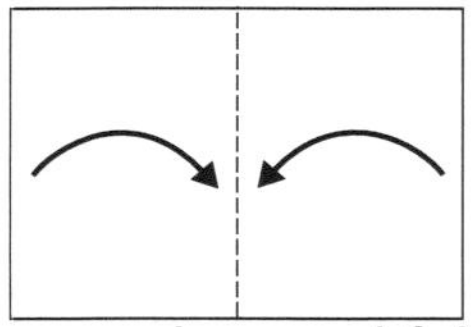

Take the two edges and fold them back to the two creases you have just made.

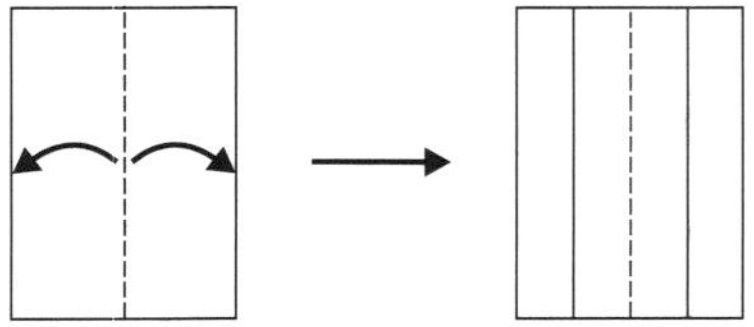

Fold the paper back together along the first centre crease.

Now take one of the edges and fold it back to the centre crease and flatten.

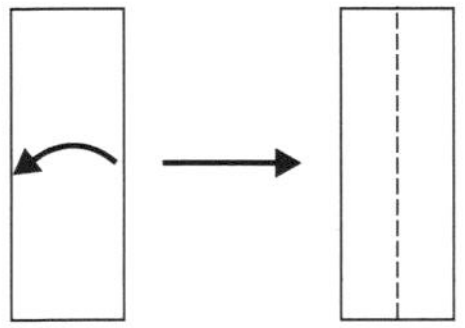

Turn the paper over and repeat the step above.

Your sheet of paper should now look like this:

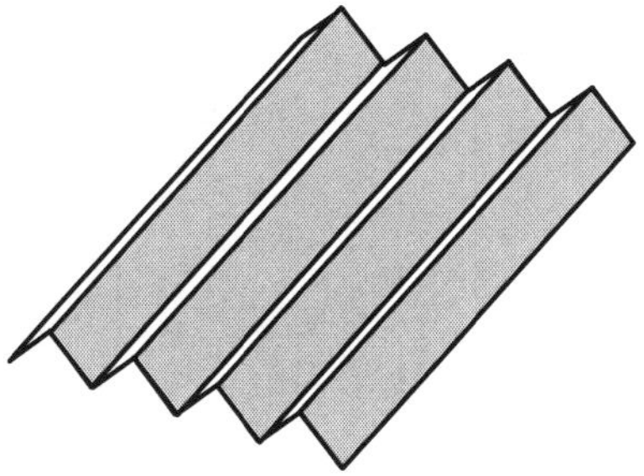

Use two paper clips to keep your concertina flat with all the faces together.

Use scissors to cut some shapes out of the two long edges. Don't cut too far across the concertina or it will break apart.

Keeping your concertina together, take another sheet of paper and draw what you think the pattern will look like when you open it out. Remember that there will be seven creases, making seven parallel lines, equally spaced across the page. You may want to draw these in.

Now open out your concertina and compare it to the drawing you made.

Were your predictions correct?

Looking for Patterns

Take a square piece of paper.

Fold it in half to make a rectangle, and then in half again so you have a small square.

Use scissors to cut patterns into the four sides of the square. Don't make the cuts too big, or your paper will fall apart.

Now open out your paper.

Write about what you notice about the pattern.

Can you now find a way of folding and cutting your paper to make the pattern symmetrical about the two diagonal axes as well?

Focus on Science

Think of all the different types of transportation there are.

Can you draw a line of symmetry if you viewed an aeroplane from this angle?

What if you viewed an aeroplane from this angle?

What about from this angle?

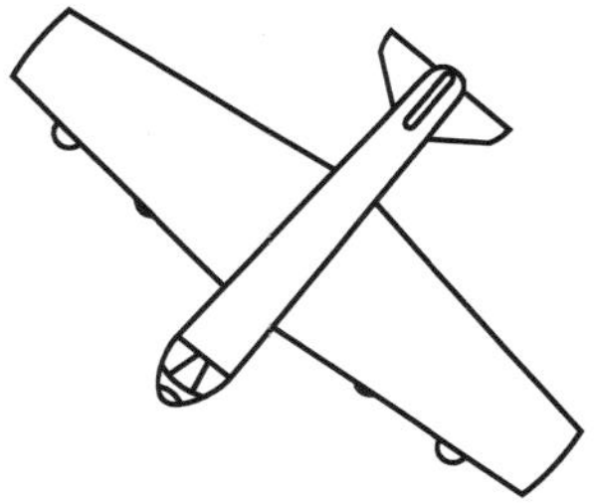

Do simple drawings of all the forms of transport you can think of, showing them from an angle where you can draw a line of symmetry on each one.

What do you notice about the lines of symmetry that you have drawn on all your forms of transport?

Why do you think this is?

Around the World

What is a *compass*?

How does it work?

When might you use a compass?

Use a compass to describe directions from your classroom.

Around the World

For this activity you need to know about 24-hour time. If you're not sure how this works, ask your teacher or have a look at The Maths Herald Issue 30.

You can use an analogue watch, that is a watch with hands, just like a compass.

Here's what you do:	Example:
• Read the time on the watch using 24-hour time.	13:20
• Round the time to the nearest hour.	13:00
• Divide this number by 2.	06:30
• If the answer is a half past time, ignore the 30 min.	06:00

- Move around so that the hour answer is pointing towards the sun.
- Without moving, look at the direction of 12:00 on the watch. This is north.

If you know where north is, you should be able to work out the directions of south, east and west.

Go into the playground and experiment with your watch compass.

Check using an actual compass.

How accurate is your watch compass?

Name:

The Maths Herald

Volume 4

Date:

Construct

The Morris family have just moved home. The removal company have dumped all the furniture for the sitting room in the middle of the room as shown on the grid below.

Using 1 cm squared paper, draw a grid and label 14 horizontal squares A to N and 12 vertical squares 1 to 12 as in the diagram below. This is the sitting room.

Move each piece of furniture into a new position that you think would be suitable.

Then write the grid reference of the new position of each piece of furniture.

For example, the current position of the coffee table is G3, H3 and I3.

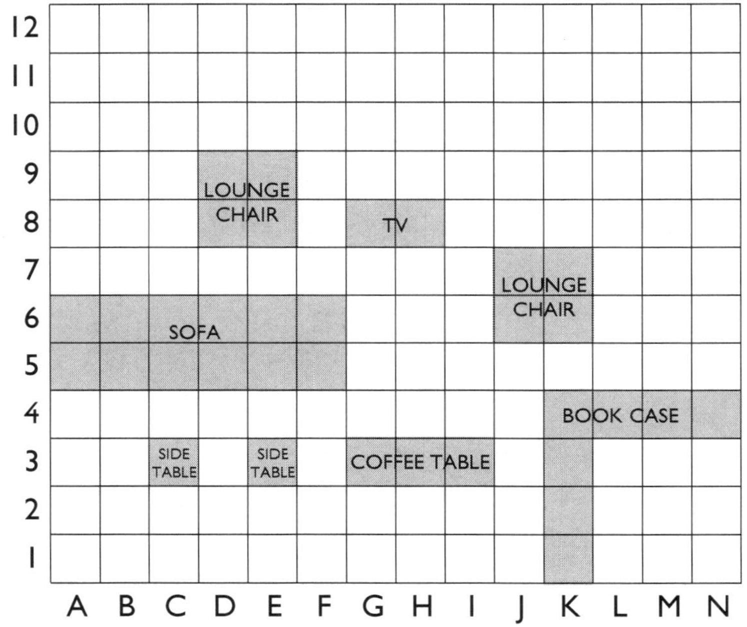

Around the World

Satellite navigation systems (Sat Navs) are devices used for finding specific locations and giving directions between places. Many cars and mobile phones now have this system built in as standard features.

Most Sat Navs show a map of the route and also provide a set of verbal instructions.

Choose two different locations in your school.

Draw a map of the route and write the instructions for a Sat Nav.

Construct

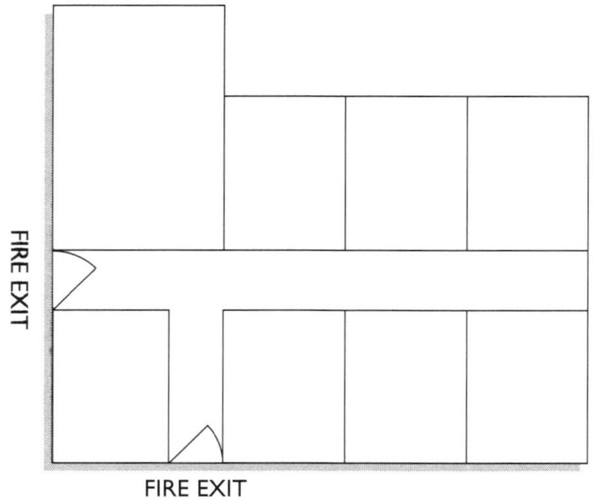

Draw a plan of your school building marking in all the exits. Remember to include fire exits.

Where in the school is furthest from an exit?

If there were a fire at the school, how would each class escape?

What are the existing escape routes? Can you improve them?

Draw a plan for each class showing the best escape route in case of fire.

Also show an alternate route in case there is a fire near any of the exits.

How would a disabled child or teacher leave the building from their classroom?

What can be improved to make this safer for them?

Construct

Hugh drives up to a T-junction and sees this sign.

How far is it from Luxton to Longridge?

How far is it from Luxton to Elfton?

How far is it from Elfton to Longridge?

Draw a map, showing the positions of the towns, the distance between them, and the position of Hugh and the sign.

Around the World

Road maps and street directories help us navigate our way between different places.

Many road maps show the distance (in kilometres or miles) between various points of roadway. These distances are often shown between pairs of arrow points.

Referring to a road map or street directory, use the distance markers to calculate the distance between various places. For example:

- The distance between Timbury and Trombone is 3 miles.
- The distance between Combing and Thursty via Rushton is 9 miles.

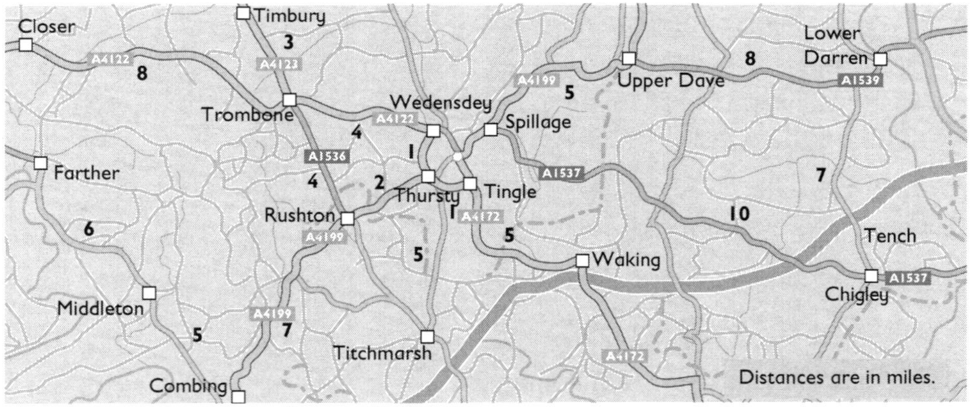

In the Past

The Pyramids at Giza, in Egypt were built approximately 4500 years ago.

They are regular, square-based pyramids.

The largest one was about 150 m high when it was built.

- If you wanted to climb directly from the ground to the top, which would be the steepest route?
- Which would be the least steep route?
- Which is the shortest route?
- Which is the longest?

The Pyramids are built from millions of blocks of stone. Each block is several metres long and weighs thousands of kilos – as much as an elephant. It is thought that the ancient Egyptians built the pyramids by pushing and pulling these blocks up a zig-zag path built against the side of the pyramid.

- Why do you think the ancient Egyptians used a zig-zag path to raise the stones up the pyramids as they were building them?

Name:

The Maths Herald

Volume 4

Date:

At Home

How many *right angles* can you find in your home?

What about *acute* angles?

What about *obtuse* angles?

Make a list for each type of angle.

Which type of angle are there more examples of? Why do you think this is?

Focus on Science

Every 24 hours the Earth spins around its axis by 360°.

So, between midday on one day and midday the next day, the Earth turns through 360°.

- By how many degrees does the Earth spin between midday and midnight?
- By how many degrees does the Earth spin between midday and 6 p.m.?
- How many degrees does the Earth turn through between 10 a.m. and 10 p.m.?
- How many degrees does the Earth turn through between 11 a.m. and 5 p.m.?
- How many degrees does the Earth turn through between 4 a.m. and 10 a.m.?
- Give two times between which the Earth turns through 60°.
- Give two times between which the Earth turns through 30°.

Looking for Patterns

A *linear spiral* is a pattern made from a series of straight lines that constantly increase or decrease in size and change direction.

This is a 1, 2, 3 linear spiral.

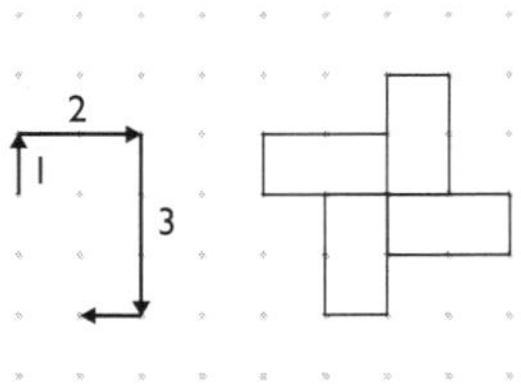

To draw the spiral, you start at a point facing up and:

- move 1 unit forward, then turn clockwise 90°
- move 2 units forward, then turn clockwise 90°
- move 3 units forward, then turn clockwise 90°.

Continue the 1, 2, 3 pattern.

A 1, 2, 3 pattern makes a *closed linear spiral.*

This is a 1, 2, 3, 4 linear spiral.

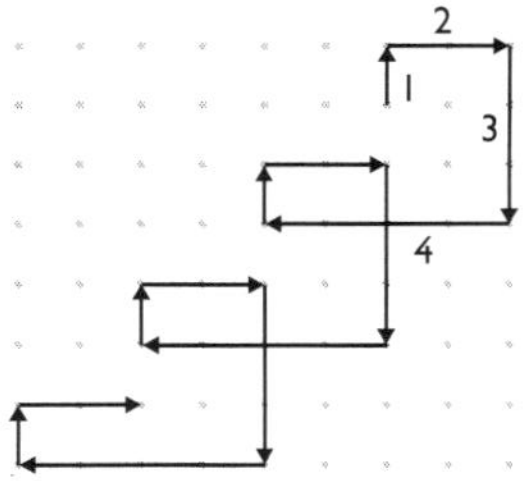

To draw the spiral, you start at a point facing up and:

- move 1 unit forward, then turn clockwise 90°
- move 2 units forward, then turn clockwise 90°
- move 3 units forward, then turn clockwise 90°
- move 4 units forward, then turn clockwise 90°.

Continue the 1, 2, 3, 4 pattern.

A 1, 2, 3, 4 pattern makes an *open linear spiral.*

Draw the following linear spirals using squared dot paper. Write whether each one is an example of a closed or an open linear spiral.

1, 2, 4	1, 2, 3, 3	3, 1, 1, 1	3, 1, 1
1, 2, 3, 4, 5	3, 3, 1, 5	2, 3, 3, 1, 1	1, 4, 2, 1

What conclusions can you draw about what makes a closed linear spiral and what makes an open linear spiral?

Write two patterns that will each make a closed linear spiral.

Write two patterns that will each make an open linear spiral.

Now test your patterns by drawing the four linear spirals.

Around the World

You are the captain of the yacht 'Albatross'.

Each day you must tell the crew which direction to sail so that, using their compass, they know where to head for. Your instructions should be in the form:

> Day 1: We sail on a route 20° clockwise from north.

The route you need to follow is shown on the chart below. Measure the angles and write down your instructions for each day. If you are not accurate, you will end up on the rocks.

Bon voyage.

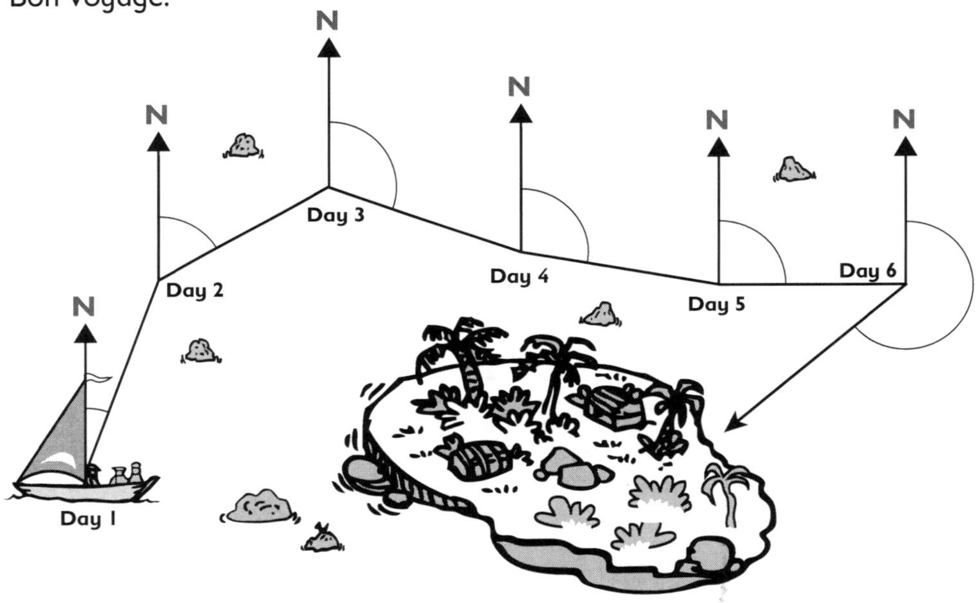

Let's Investigate

Two or more shapes are *congruent* if they are exactly the same shape and size.

The two 4 × 4 squares on the right have each been divided into two congruent parts.

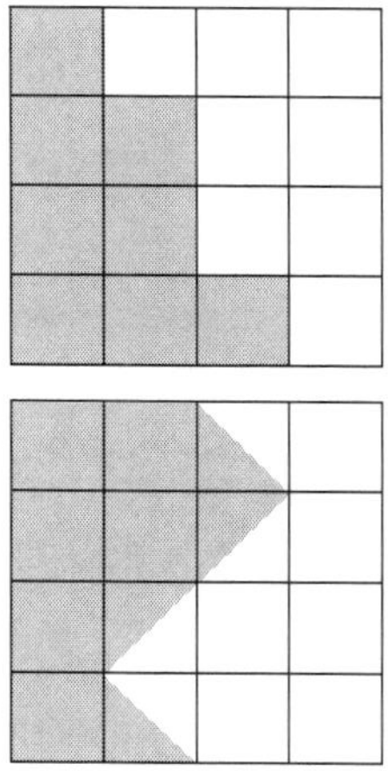

How many different ways can you find to divide a 4 × 4 square into two congruent parts?

Try to be as imaginative as possible.

Looking for Patterns

Imagine you are at a funfair. You go on the Ferris wheel. You get into basket 1. The wheel starts turning clockwise.

- How many degrees will the wheel have turned through by the time your basket is in the position of basket 3?
- How many degrees will the wheel turn through as your basket moves from position 3 to position 7?
- How many degrees will the wheel turn through as your basket moves from position 7 to position 8?
- How many degrees will the wheel turn through as your basket moves from position 8 to position 3?
- Your basket is in position 3. The wheel turns through another 135°. What position are you in now?
- If your basket is in position 2 and the wheel turns through another 225°, what position will you be in?

Name:

The Maths Herald

Volume 4

Date:

Construct

Design the ideal classroom.

Remember:

- It has to accommodate the same number of children that are in your class now.
- It has to allow for all the things that you regularly do in your classroom.

What special features might you add? Why?

Draw a plan of your classroom. Label your plan including dimensions.

The Puzzler

Draw the 16 shapes on the grid so that no shape or pattern appears more than once in the same row, column or diagonal.

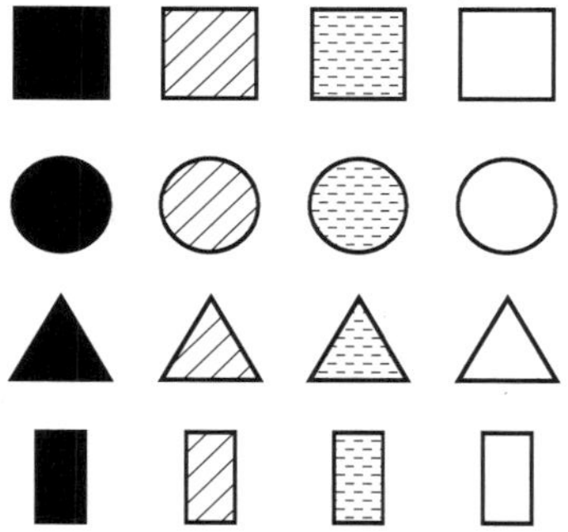

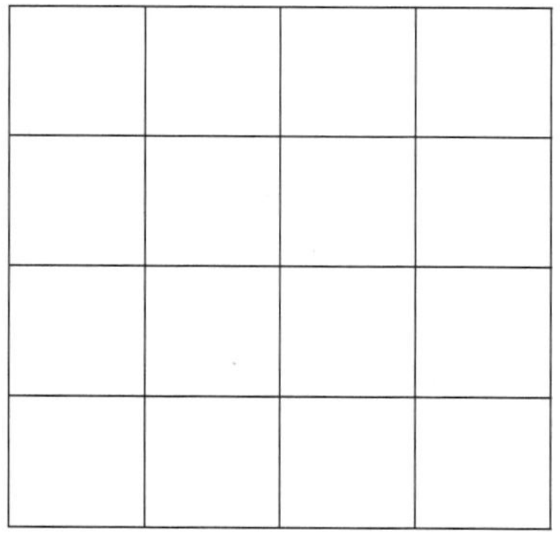

The Puzzler

Dean and Alice went for a picnic with their parents. They came to a river that was too deep to cross on foot. There was a small rowing boat tied up by the bank, but it was only big enough for one adult or two children – one adult and one child would sink it.

Dean and Alice figured out a way of getting everyone across the river.

What did they do?

Construct

Using five interlocking cubes, join them together to make a shape that is one cube deep.

There are 12 different five-cube shapes that you can make.

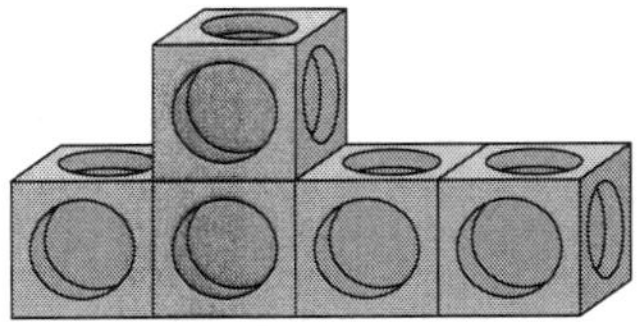

Can you find them all?

Record your different shapes on isometric paper.

Note: These two shapes are considered identical. One is simply the reflection of the other.

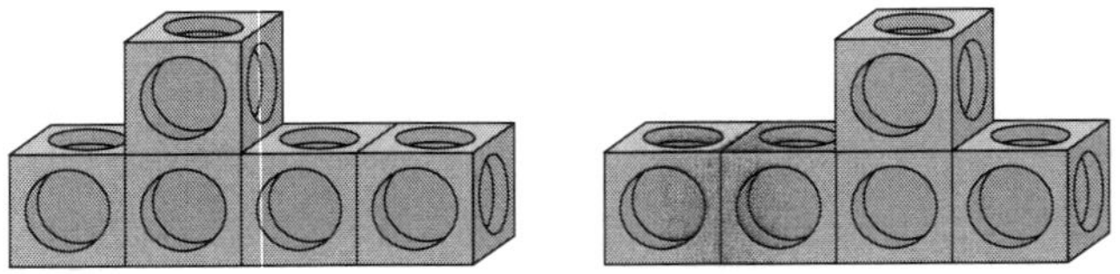

Looking for Patterns

Look at the 12 different five-cubed shapes you made in the Construct activity on the left.

Which shapes, when replicated five times, will fit together to make a 5 × 5 square?

Record your results on isometric paper.

The Language of Maths

Find out which direction north is in relation to your classroom.

Write a description of how you can get from the door of your classroom to your desk without bumping into anything. Include phrases like "*Walk northwest five steps. Turn 45 degrees to the left and walk seven steps west ....*"

Give your directions to a friend and see if they can walk to your desk without hitting anything.

With the help of a friend, write a description of how you get from the school gate to your classroom, using compass directions. Bear in mind all the time which direction is north.

The Language of Maths

Eight 2-D shapes and 3-D solids were all chatting together on a social networking site.

They didn't want to give their identities away and say what shape or solid they were, so instead they described themselves to each other.

This is how they each described themselves.

1 There are two sides to me, one of which is curvy.

2 I have only one side and that's smooth.

3 I'm circular and solid too, but also a bit flat. I'm never sharp.

4 I'm circular and solid, but I'm two faced and can be sharp.

5 I'm solid but totally square.

6 I'm solid and smooth and have no edges.

7 I'm not a cube but I am square. I'm triangular and have five good points.

8 I'm rectangular and pentagonal.

Let's Investigate

A shape made from five identical squares is called a *pentomino*.

There are 12 different pentominoes.

Here is one:

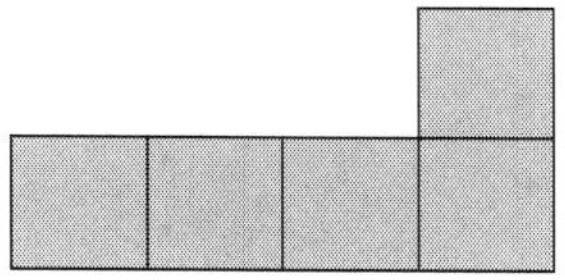

Note: These two pentominoes are the same.

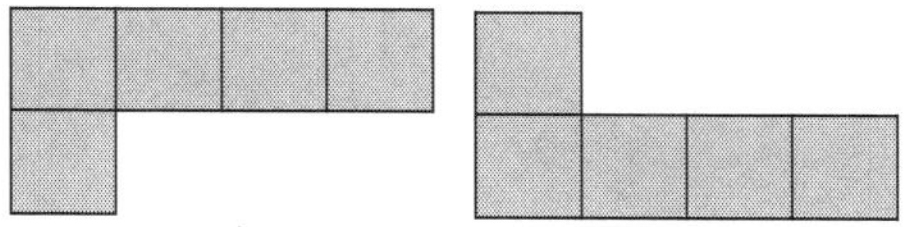

Using 2 cm squared paper, draw and cut out the 12 pentominoes.

Now try to arrange them into a rectangle.
You can rotate and turn over your pentominoes to fit.

Looking for Patterns

Look at the 12 different pentominoes you made in the Let's Investigate activity above.

Draw all the lines of symmetry on each of the pentominoes.

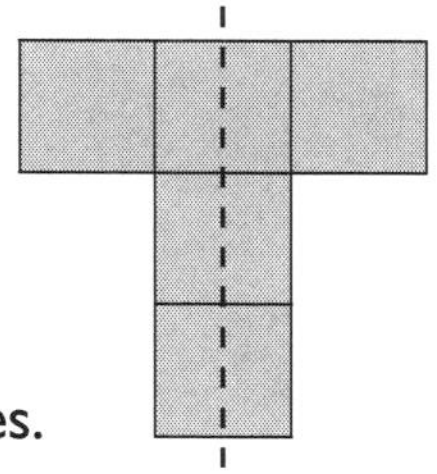

The Language of Maths

Look at the 12 different pentominoes you made in the Let's Investigate activity above.

Each of these pentominoes can be labelled using a different letter of the alphabet.

Can you work out which letter each pentomino represents?

Note: Some pentominoes can be labelled using more than one letter.

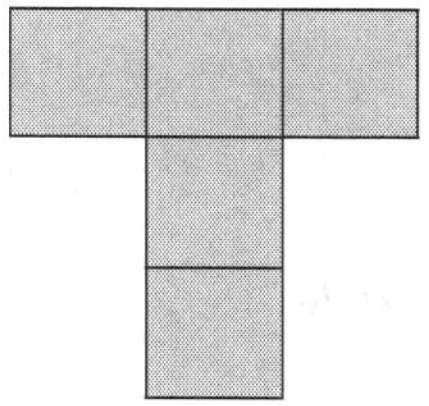
T

Name:

The Maths Herald

Volume 4

Date:

Let's Investigate

A shape made from two identical squares is called a *domino*.

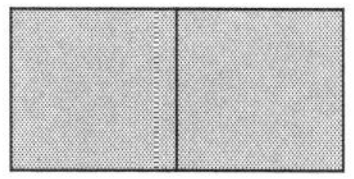

A shape made from three identical squares is called a *tromino*.

A shape made from four identical squares is called a *tetromino*.

There are five different tetrominoes.

Here is one:

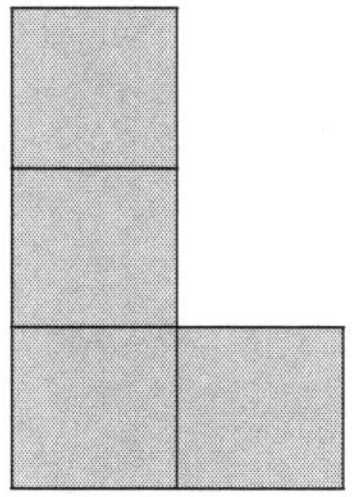

Note: These two tetrominoes are the same.

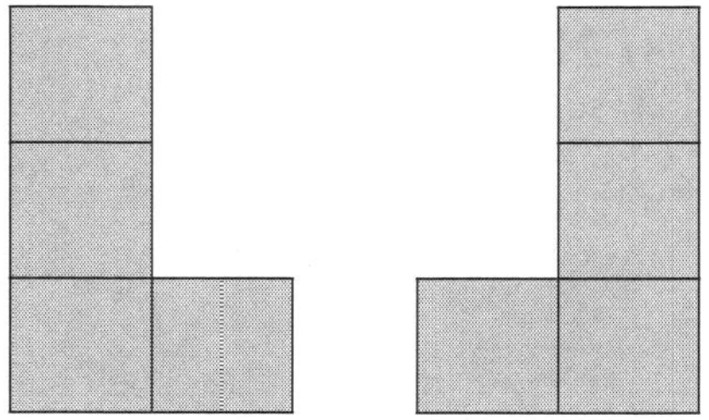

Using 2 cm squared paper, draw and cut out the five tetrominoes.

Now find a friend. Each of you put your set of five tetrominoes on the table so there are 10 tetrominoes altogether.

Arrange your tetrominoes into a rectangle.

You can rotate and turn over your tetrominoes to fit.

Famous Mathematicians

August Ferdinand Möbius (pronounced Mer–bius) was a famous German mathematician and astronomer. Amongst other things, he discovered the very strange properties that a strip of paper has when it's twisted and the two ends are stuck together.

This is how you make a *Möbius strip*.

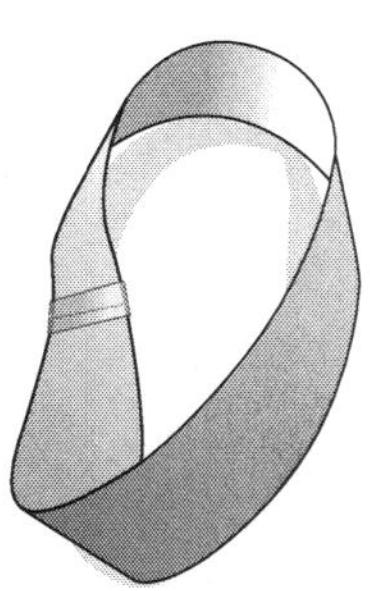

Cut a strip of paper, about 5 cm wide, from the length of an A4 sheet of paper.

Hold the two ends together and turn one end over.

Now stick the two ends together as shown.

You have just made a Möbius strip.

Strange property no. 1

Put your pen or pencil in the middle of the width of your Möbius strip and, without raising your pen off the paper, draw a line down the middle of the strip.

Move the strip of paper so you can carry on drawing the line, without taking your pen off the paper. Keep going until you get back to the place where you started the line.

Now look at your strip of paper. You will see both sides of the strip have a line down the middle, although you never took your pen off the paper. Unlike a normal piece of paper that has two sides, your Möbius strip has only one side.

Strange property no. 2

Put your pen or pencil near one edge of your Möbius strip and, without raising your pen off the paper, draw a line along the edge of the strip.

Move the strip of paper so you can carry on drawing the line, without taking your pen off the paper. Keep going until you get back to the place where you started the line.

Now look at your strip of paper. You will see that there is a line along both edges. Your Möbius strip has only one edge.

Strange property no. 3

Using a pair of scissors, cut along the line down the middle of your Möbius strip until you get back to where you started. You have cut your Möbius strip in two. Or have you?

Open out your strip. What do you find?

Is this magic? Some things are stranger than they seem!

Construct

The sum of the three angles inside a triangle is always 180°.

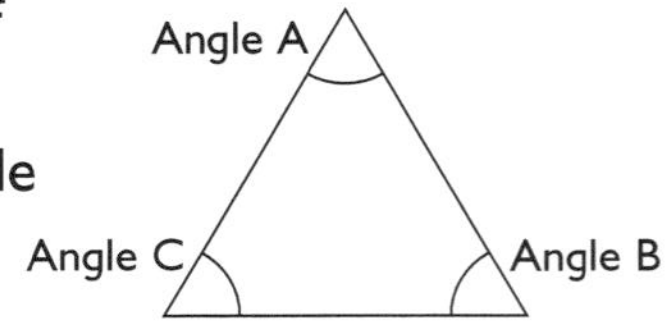

$$A^\circ + B^\circ + C^\circ = 180^\circ$$

The sum of the four angles inside a quadrilateral is always 360°.

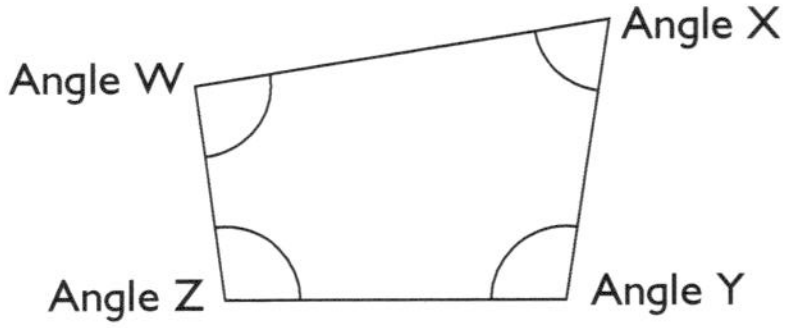

$$W^\circ + X^\circ + Y^\circ + Z^\circ = 360^\circ$$

Draw a small triangle with straight sides on a piece of cardboard.

Cut it out.

Now trace around the triangle to make a total of 12 congruent triangles.

Label all the same angles A, all the same angles B and all the same angles C.

Cut them out.

Try to fit the 12 triangles together, corner-to-corner, so that there are no gaps between them.

Do you notice a pattern in the way they fit together? If so, why do you think this is?

Now draw an irregular quadrilateral with straight sides on a piece of cardboard.

Cut it out.

Trace around it to make a total of 12 congruent irregular quadrilaterals.

Label all the same angles W, all the same angles X, all the same angles Y and all the same angles Z.

Cut them out.

Try to fit the 12 quadrilaterals together, corner-to-corner, so that there are no gaps between them.

Do you notice a pattern in the way they fit together? Why do you think this is?

Around the World

The *equator* is an imaginary ring around the Earth. It is located half way between the North and South Poles. The equator divides the Earth in half: the Northern Hemisphere and the Southern Hemisphere. The length of the equator is 40 075 km.

The distance between any city and the equator can be calculated using the number of degrees the city is from the equator. *Lines of latitude* give the distance of a place north or south of the equator. The equator is at zero degrees, which is written as 0°.

Fact: 1 degree of latitude equals 111 kilometres.

Using the fact above, calculate the distance of each of the following cities from the equator.

London, UK 51°	Sydney, Australia 34°	Bangkok, Thailand 14°
Edinburgh, UK 56°	Hong Kong, China 22°	Washington DC, USA 39°

Around the World

Find out the latitude of the town or city in which you live. If you can't find the exact latitude, find the nearest latitude you can.

Using the fact given in the previous Around the World activity, calculate the distance your town or city is from the equator.

Find out the latitudes of other cities near you and in other parts of the world. Calculate their distances from the equator.

Name:

The Maths Herald

Volume 4

Date:

Around the World

Look at the labels from a collection of supermarket fruit and vegetables.

How many 'food miles' did each piece of fruit or vegetable travel?

What 'hidden extras' are you paying for when you buy this fruit or vegetable?

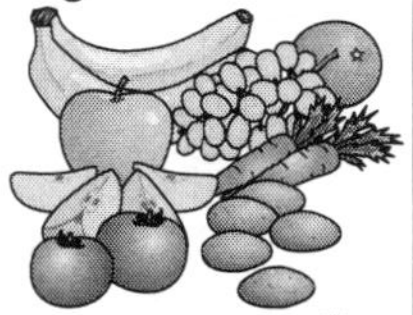

How does the price of *imported* fruit and vegetables compare with those produced locally?

Around the World

The Great Wall of China is over 4000 miles long.

Using the scale in an atlas, find different places that are about the same distance apart as the length of the Great Wall of China.

Around the World

The diagram on the right shows the approximate heights of two of the world tallest buildings.

Mark the approximate heights of the following buildings:

- 381 m Empire State Building (USA)
- 235 m One Canada Square (UK)

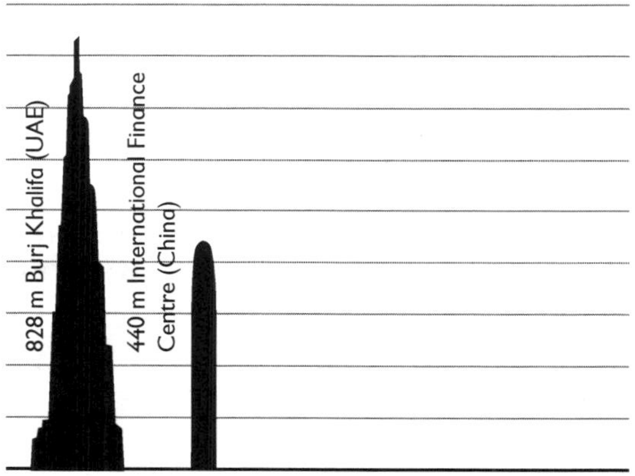

In the Past

When cars were first invented in the late 19th century, the speed that most cars could travel was about 10 miles per hour.

In the early 1900's, approximately how long would it have taken to drive from London to Brighton?

How does that compare with how long it would take today? Explain the difference.

Apart from the speed at which a car can travel, what else could affect the time it takes to drive from London to Brighton?

What similarities and differences are there between a journey in 1900 compared with today?

Around the World

This table shows the lengths of the five longest rivers in the world.

River	Length (km)	Location
Nile	6695	Africa
Amazon	6486	South America
Yangtze	6300	China
Mississippi	5993	USA
Huang He	5464	China

Round the length of each river to the nearest 100 km and draw a scale drawing showing the relative sizes of the five longest rivers in the world.

The table below shows the lengths of the five longest mountain ranges in the world.

Round the length of each mountain range to the nearest 100 km and draw a scale drawing showing the relative sizes of the five longest mountain ranges in the world.

Mountain range	Length (km)	Location
Andes	7242	South America
Rocky Mountains	6035	North America
Himalayas	3862	Asia
Great Dividing Range	3621	Australia
Transantarctic Mountains	3541	Antarctica

Money Matters

Which is worth more: 60 centimetres of 5-pence coins placed side by side or 40 centimetres of 10-pence coins placed side by side? About how much more?

Around the World

Using a road map of the local area, with a scale, investigate which towns and cities are less than 100 km from your town.

Which towns or cities are about 50 km from the town in which you live?

Around the World

Mount Everest, a mountain in the Himalayas, is 8848 metres above sea level. It is the highest point on Earth.

At 828 metres, the world's tallest building is the Burj Khalifa in Dubai.

The Eiffel Tower in Paris is 324 metres high. *

The London Eye is 135 metres high. *

Write statements comparing the height of these three structures to that of Mount Everest.

Find the heights of other tall buildings throughout the world and compare their heights with Mount Everest.

* Mark these two structures on the chart on the last Around the World activity on page 1.

Focus on Science

A flea is the most amazing little creature. It can pull a weight 100 000 times its own weight.

The weight of an average 10-year-old is 32 kilograms.

If the average 10-year-old could pull a weight that is 100 000 times their own weight, what sorts of things might they be able to pull?

What's the Problem?

A dragon weighs one and a fifth times as much as a giant.

A giant weighs 1200 kg less than a dragon.

How much does a dragon weigh?

The Puzzler

You have 60 coins. One of them is slightly lighter than all the others.

Using a scale balance, can you find which one it is with a maximum of four weighings?

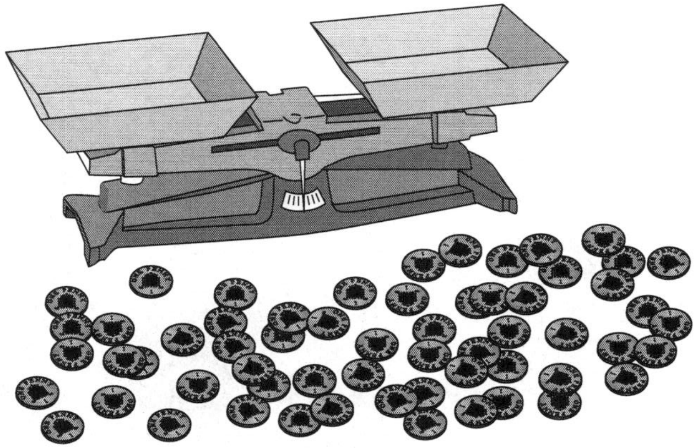

Name:

The Maths Herald

Volume 4

Date:

Focus on Science

What material is best for a shopping carrier bag?

Test different materials for strength.

Design and make a shopping bag to carry a minimum of 5 kg of food, using the material you think is best.

Test your design.

In the Past

The units of measurement we use most commonly for weighing objects are *grams* (g) and *kilograms* (kg). This measuring system is called the *metric system*.

However before 1995, most people in the UK used the *imperial system* that measures weight in *pounds* (lb) and *ounces* (oz).

Using only the weights below, can you make each of the weights from 1 oz to 32 oz?

What's the Problem?

The total weight of a cereal box full of Wheat Puffs is 500 grams.

The total weight of a cereal box exactly the same, but full of Muesli weighs 900 grams.

If Muesli weighs three times as much as Wheat Puffs, what is the weight of the empty boxes?

At Home

What is the difference in weight between cooked and uncooked:

- pasta?
- rice?
- lentils?
- potatoes?

The next time you have a meal at home that requires the cooking of a food item such as those mentioned above, weigh the item before and after it is cooked.

What conclusions can you draw?

Is the difference between the weight of cooked and uncooked food the same for all foods?

Which foods have the greatest difference between cooked and uncooked?

Which have the least difference?

What's the Problem?

Mrs Andes takes three parcels to the post office. Each parcel is a different weight.

Together parcels A and B weigh 13 kg.

Parcels B and C together weigh 16 kg.

Parcels A and C together weigh 21 kg.

What is the weight of each parcel?

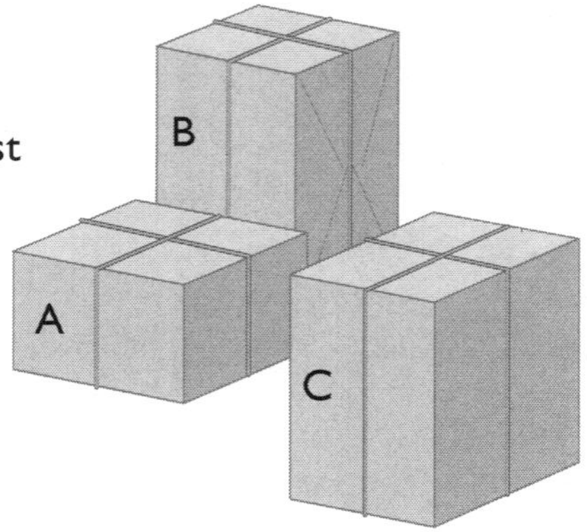

The Puzzler

In each of these problems, the first two sets of scales balance.

Work out how many hearts are needed to balance the third set.

Write a statement about how you worked out how many hearts were needed to balance the third sets of scales.

What's the Problem?

Mrs Mittal was organising the drinks for a picnic.

She packed enough fruit juice to give each person exactly 400 ml.

Two more children than she had expected came along, so there was only enough juice for everyone to have 350 ml.

How many people came on the picnic?

What's the Problem?

Tamar asked Sandeep how much petrol he had left in his petrol can.

Sandeep replied:

How much petrol does Sandeep have?

Name:

The Maths Herald

Volume 4

Date:

Focus on Science

How much water are you meant to drink each day to keep you healthy?

How much water do you drink each day?

What about other children in your class?

Write a record describing how much water most children in your class drink each day, whether this is enough, and what you could do to encourage everyone to drink the daily recommended amount of water.

Focus on Science

Cars, trucks, planes and boats run on petrol, diesel or other similar types of fuel.

It is important to know how much the fuel tank of a vehicle holds and how far it will travel on a tank full of fuel.

In the UK, petrol used to be sold in gallons, and advertisers still quote 'miles per gallon' when talking about a car's *fuel economy*. This means the number of miles a car will travel using one gallon of fuel. The higher the figure, the less fuel the car uses.

Nowadays however, petrol is sold in litres and car petrol tanks are measured in litres.

For a car that does 55 miles per gallon, work out:

- how far it will travel on 1 litre of fuel
- how far it will travel on a full tank of fuel if the tank holds 47 litres.

Round your answers to two decimal places.

Around the World

In many countries in Europe, the fuel economy of cars is quoted as 'litres per 100 km'. This means the number of litres of fuel a car uses to travel 100 km. The lower the figure, the less fuel a car uses.

Work out how many 'litres per 100 km' the car mentioned in the second Focus on Science activity on page 1 uses. Round your answer to two decimal places.

Investigate whether this car is economical or not, compared to other cars.

Money Matters

Shores Café uses 15 litres of milk a day.

Milk is sold in 2-litre cartons at £2.90 each, or 5-litre cartons at £7.30 each.

How many cartons of each size must the café buy to get the best value for money? How much will this cost them?

What's the Problem?

What does 1 million litres look like?

Think of different objects that hold vast amounts of water.

How many of each of these would you need to make 1 million litres?

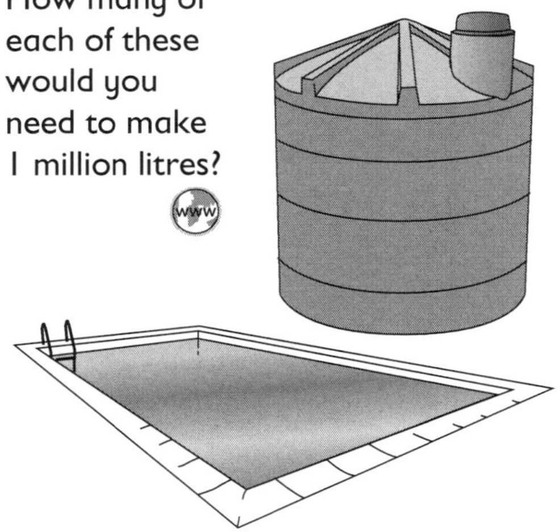

What's the Problem?

The Moneypenny's house gets all its water from a well.

Every 24 hours the well fills up with 1200 *l* of water.

The Moneypennys usually use 750 *l* of water a day, but in summer they water the garden three times a week and use 1250 *l* each time.

The well can hold a total of 4000 *l*.

Will the well run dry? If so, when?

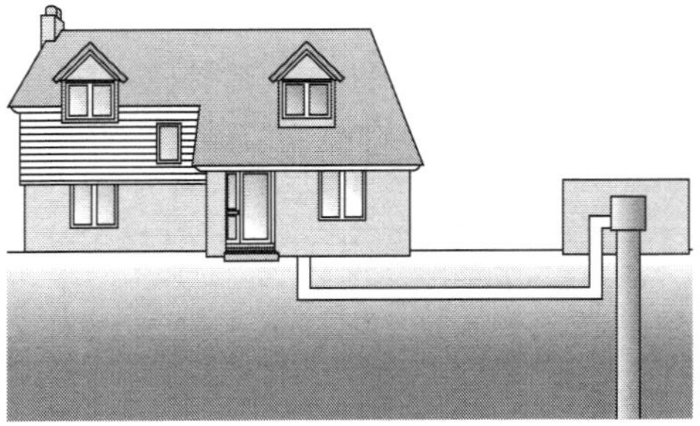

What's the Problem?

Sonia needs to buy a water pump to supply water to her garden irrigation system.

There are nine sprinklers in her garden. Four of them use 2.5 *l* of water each minute, four of them use 4.5 *l* of water each minute and one uses 8.5 *l* of water each minute.

There are four sizes of water pump in the shop. They can pump 1000, 2000, 3000 or 4000 litres of water each hour.

Which size of water pump should Sonia buy?

The Language of Maths

Order these quantities from smallest to largest.

3 pints | 1 quart | 0·75 *l* | 350 ml | 6.5 cl

$\frac{1}{2}$ pint | 4·5 *l* | 1 gallon | 1·75 *l* | 1 pint

The Language of Maths

There are two different ways of telling the time. One is called *12-hour time*, the other *24-hour time*.

In most cases we use 12-hour time, for example:

"Half past nine in the morning."

"Two-fifteen p.m."

When we use 12-hour time, we often have to use words such as *morning*, *afternoon*, *evening* or *night*, or terms such as *a.m.* and *p.m.*, to clarify what part of the 24-hour day we are referring to.

However, when we use 24-hour time, we don't need to use such words.

"09:30"

"14:15"

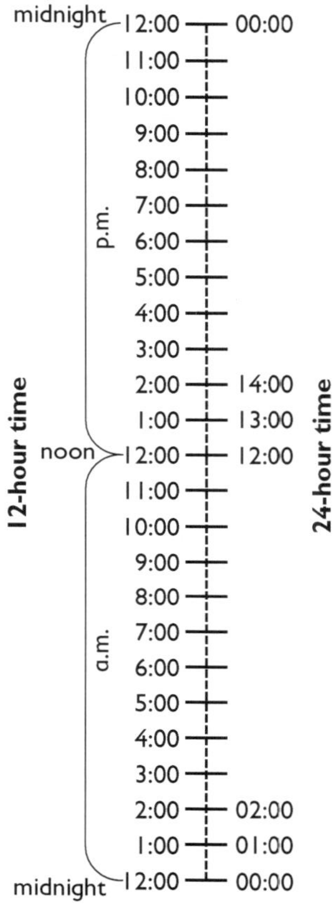

The time-line on the left shows the relationship between 12-hour and 24-hour time.

Complete the time-line.

Write down the following times using both 12-hour and 24-hour notation.

- You wake up
- Leave home for school
- School starts
- Break starts
- Lunch starts
- Lunch ends
- School ends
- You go to bed

The Arts Roundup

It takes Simon 30 hours to write a song by himself. Together with Paul he can write a song in 10 hours.

How long would it take Paul to write a song alone?

Name:

The Maths Herald

Volume 4

Date:

Construct

Make a sundial as follows:

- Place a stick, about a metre long, in the ground somewhere in the school playground that gets sunlight all day.
- Use a piece of string about half a metre long, and make a small loop at each end. Loop one end of the string around the base of the stick and loop something like a small stick in the loop at the other end of the string. Now draw a circle around the taller stick.
- Throughout the day, mark and label the places on the circle that the shadow points towards at 9:00 a.m., 10:00 a.m., 11:00 a.m., 12:00 noon, 1:00 p.m., 2:00 p.m. and 3:00 p.m.
- For the next few days check your sundial to make any adjustments until it is as accurate as you can make it.

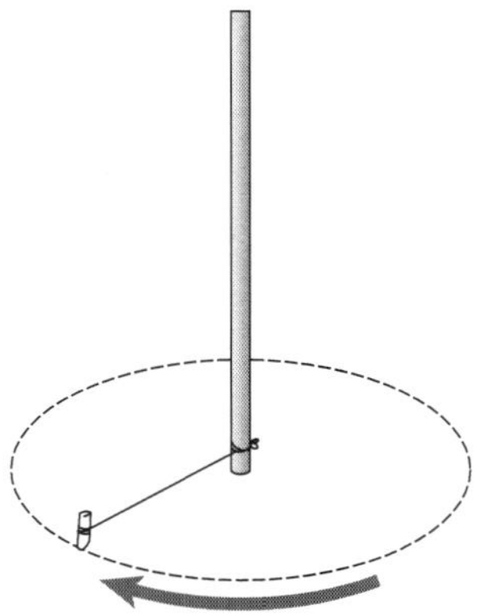

Write about what you notice about the experiment. In particular, mention what happens to the length of the shadow throughout the day.

In the Past

Draw a time-line showing the major developments in transportation since 1900.

What's the Problem?

Mrs Beavers has two chiming clocks that are meant to strike every hour on the hour. Although they both keep the correct time, one of the clocks always chimes every 55 minutes and the other clock every 50 minutes.

Today at 12:00 noon, they both chime at the same time.

When will be the next time that both clocks will chime together?

The Puzzler

James was born in 2001.

In the year 2015 his mother will be 3 times his age.

In what year was James's mother born?

How old was James's mother when she gave birth to James?

In the Past

Could your great-great-grandfather have taken tea with Queen Victoria? Be prepared to justify your answer.

Issue 30 Time

What's the Problem?

Exactly how many days a year do you spend at school?

That's assuming that you are never absent!

Once again, assuming that you have never been absent from school, so far during your lifetime, how many days have you been in school?

How many different year groups are there in your school? Imagine there is a boy at your school called Christopher Clever-Clogs. If Christopher spends a full year in each year group at your school, how many days will Christopher have spent in school altogether? (Christopher is never absent from school – that's why he's so clever!)

What's the Problem?

Caen and Able are building a tree house.

Caen can build the tree house alone in 40 days and Able can build it alone in 60 days.

Caen starts building it alone for 10 days, then Able joins him and they finish it together.

Working together, how many more days will it take Caen and Able to finish building the tree house?

Construct

Using squared dot paper, enclose a 4 × 4 square.

Using different colours, draw as many different sized squares within the 4 × 4 square as you can.

Here are two.

Draw more 4 × 4 squares if your square becomes too cluttered.

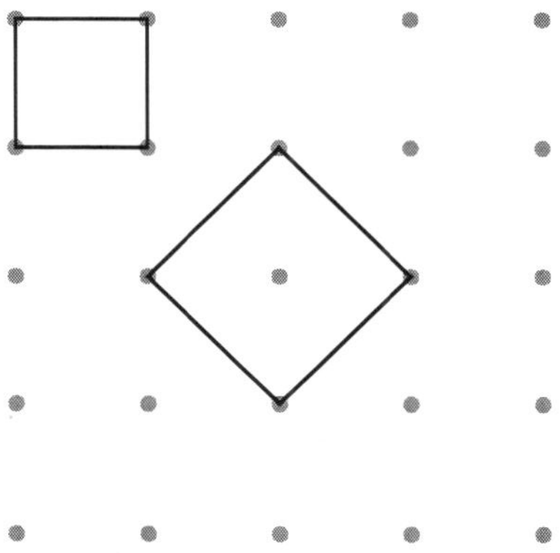

Construct

Imagine that you have been allocated an allotment of 9 m by 30 m.

Design a planting plan for your allotment.

Think about the different fruit and vegetables you are going to grow.

How much of the total area of the allotment are you going to devote to each type of fruit or vegetable?

What else are you going to have on your allotment? How much space is this going to take up?

Use the information you discovered in the Around the World activity on page 1 to help you design your planting plan.

Your plan should include all the dimensions that show the area you intend to allocate to each fruit and vegetable, and any other land usage.

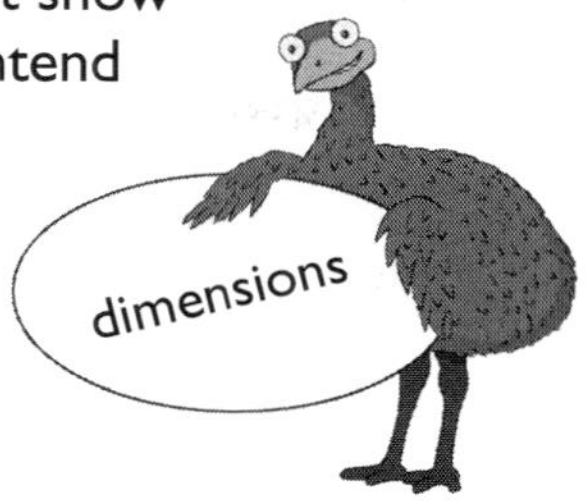

Name:

The Maths Herald

Volume 4

Date:

Around the World

An *allotment* is an area of land set aside by the local council that people can rent so that they can grow their own fruit and vegetables.

Find out all you can about allotments.

What size are most allotments?

What type of fruit and vegetables are commonly grown on allotments?

What else do people use the land for apart from growing fruit and vegetables?

Construct

Using a tin or another cylindrical object, make a label that completely covers the curved surface.

Think about:

- how you are going to measure the height of the tin or cylinder
- how you are going to measure the distance around the tin or cylinder.

Draw your label on a piece of paper and write on it how you measured your tin or cylinder.

Work out the label's area.

Now cut it out and see if it fits.

Does it fit well? Is it too big or too small? If so, why do you think this is?

Looking for Patterns

What is the area of each of these triangles?

Write about how you worked out the answers.

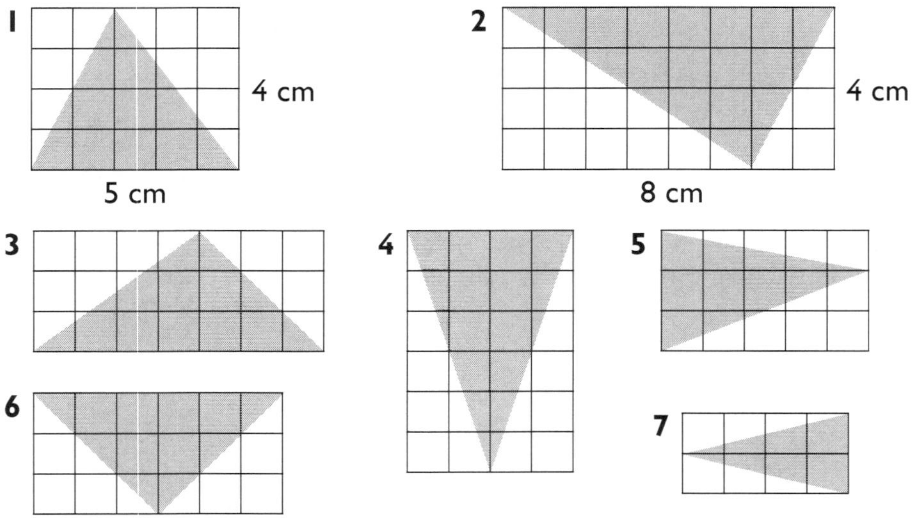

Let's Investigate

Find the area of each of these rectangles.

Investigate what happens to the area if the length of each side is doubled.

Justify your conclusions by providing appropriate diagrams.

What happens to the area if the length of each side is multiplied by 3?

What if the sides are multiplied by 4 or 5?

Once again justify your conclusions with diagrams.

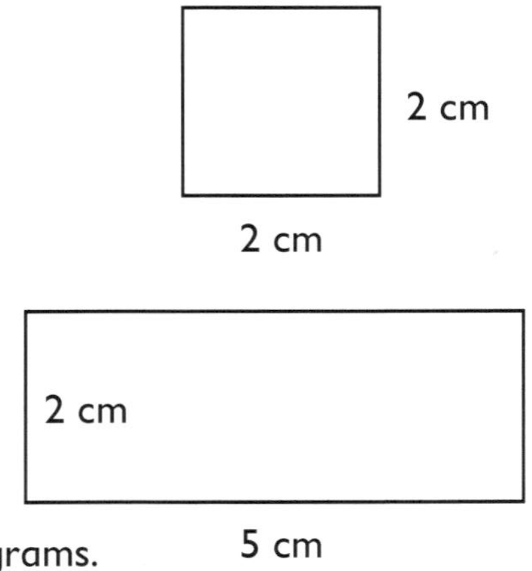

What's the Problem?

A nursery school has a large square play area with a tree at each corner.

How could the nursery school double the area of the play area without moving the trees and still keep it square?

Sports Update

Most team games, like football, rugby, volleyball or hockey, are played on pitches or courts.

They are all of different dimensions and areas.

Find out the dimensions and areas of the pitches of as many different team sports as you can.

Why are they the sizes that they are?

Is there a relationship between the area and the number of players? Or the way the ball is passed about, i.e. thrown, kicked, hit with a racket?

Write about any relationships you find.

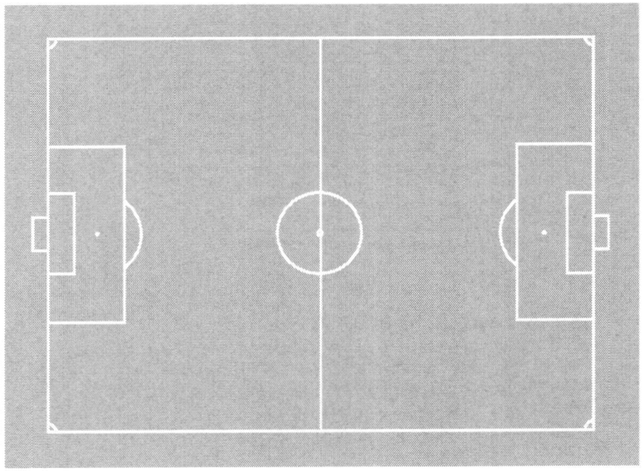

What's the Problem?

Jonny has bought some plants for his garden.

He has enough to fill 16 m^2.

He could put them all into one square flower bed like this:

4 m

4 m

But he would prefer to spread them out so they can be seen better.

He wants the bed, or beds, to have the maximum perimeter possible, but no bed can have a side less than 1 m, and if there is more than one bed they must all be touching.

How should he arrange his plants?

What is the maximum perimeter possible?

Let's Investigate

Put a sheet of paper flat on your desk and use 12 matchsticks to make a 2-D shape on it.

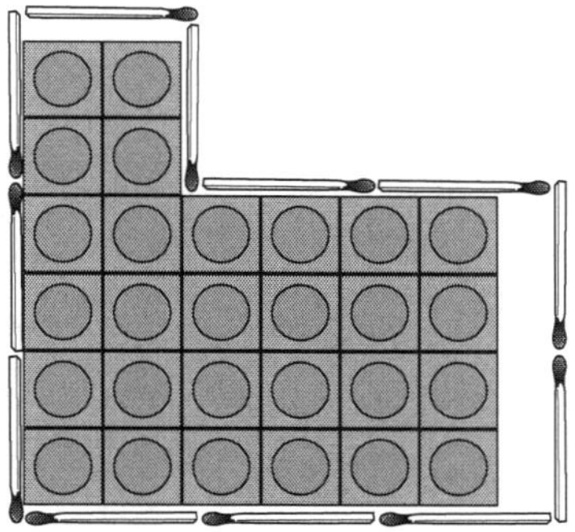

How many interlocking cubes can you fit inside the shape in one layer?

Now make another shape with the 12 matchsticks and see how many cubes you can fit inside it.

When you have found the shape that fits the most cubes inside it, draw its outline on the sheet of paper.

Compare your shape with a friend's.

Do they look similar or not?

Why do you think this is?

Name:

The Maths Herald

Volume 4

Date:

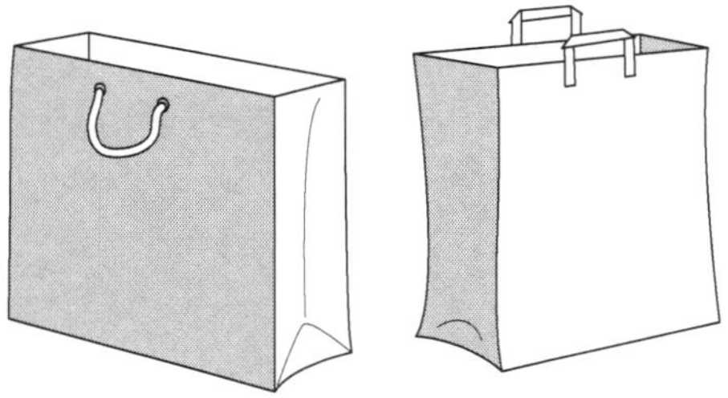

Construct

Design and construct two different paper bags, each with a perimeter of exactly 1 metre.

Let's Investigate

The words *diameter* and *circumference* are used when describing measurements of a circle.

The *diameter* refers to a straight line that connects two points on the perimeter of a circle and passes through the centre.

The *circumference* refers to the perimeter of the circle – the distance around the edge of the circle.

Measure the diameters and circumferences of the tyres on different types of cars in the school's car park.

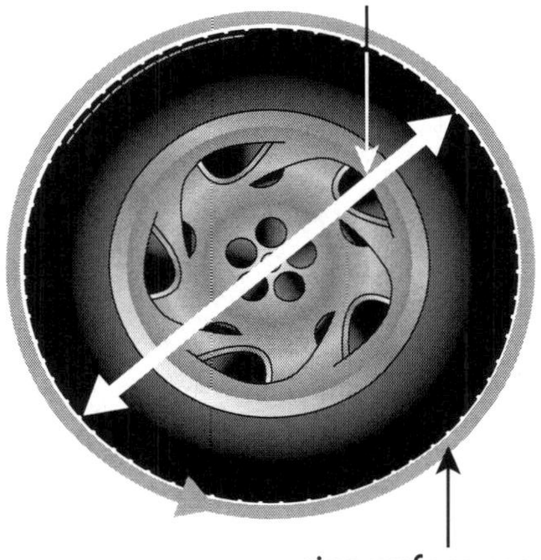

Are they all the same?

Is there a *correlation* between tyre size and vehicle size?

The Puzzler

Look at this chessboard.

What is the perimeter of the whole chessboard in 'square' units?

Which line of squares has the same perimeter as the whole chessboard?

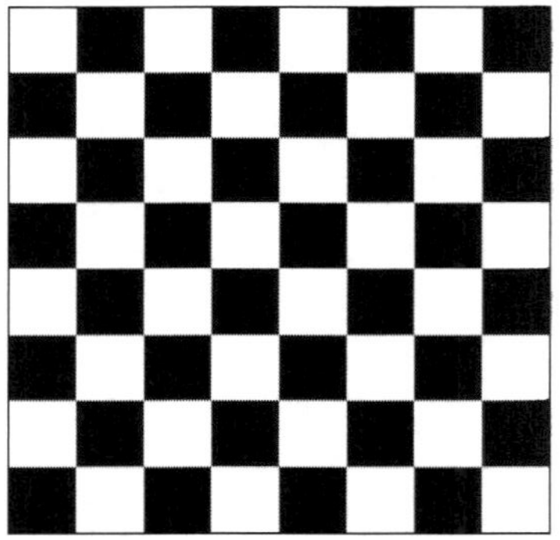

What's the Problem?

Sam and Toni live next door to each other.

Both their gardens are rectangular and the side of each garden that forms the common border is the same length. However, the sides of Toni's garden are 20 m and 40 m longer than the sides of Sam's.

If the perimeter of Toni's garden is twice that of Sam's, what are the measurements of Sam's and Toni's gardens?

The Puzzler

A *tetromino* is a four square polyomino and a *pentomino* is a five square polyomino.

A *hexomino* is a six square polyomino.

This is the simplest hexomino. It has a perimeter of 14 units.

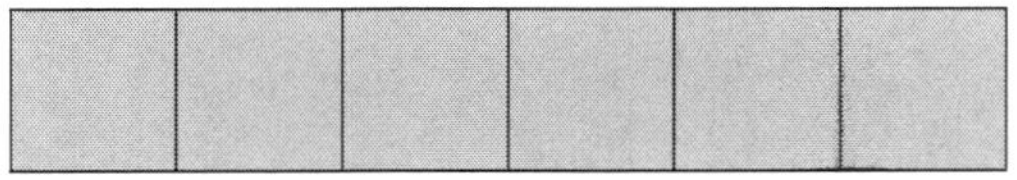

Using squared dot paper, draw as many different hexominoes with 14 unit perimeters as you can.

Remember, mirror images and rotations do not count as different hexominoes.

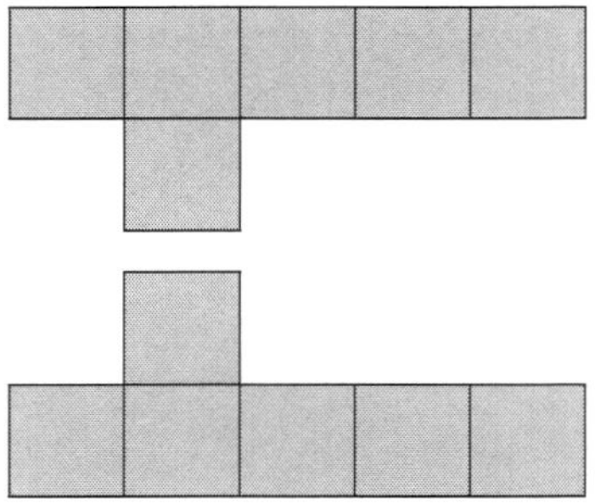

Let's Investigate

On 1 cm squared dot paper, draw an isosceles triangle as shown:

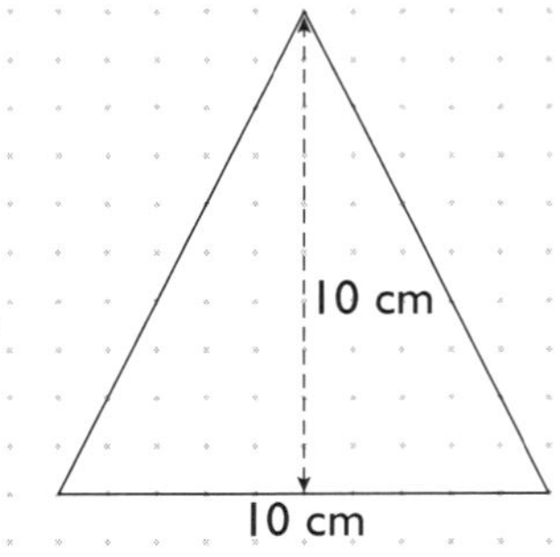

Draw a line from the top corner to the midpoint of the opposite side.

Imagine you were to cut out the triangle and cut it in half down the line you have drawn.

Now rotate one half through 180° and put the diagonal sides together to form a rectangle.

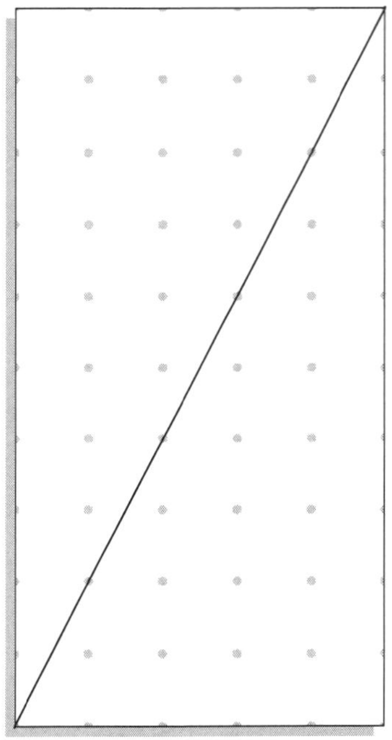

Would this rectangle have the same area and perimeter as the triangle?

Measure it and see.

The Puzzler

Two 10p coins are put flat on a table.

One coin is held motionless while the other coin is rolled around the perimeter of the first coin, edge to edge, without slipping.

How many revolutions does the moving coin make before it gets back to its starting point?

Now try it.

Would the answer be different if you used two £2 coins?

Focus on Science

Too much exposure to the sun's rays can be very harmful to your skin. Skin that is exposed to the sun such as the face, arms and legs can be protected if you use a sunscreen.

The length of time it takes to burn in the sun depends on your skin tone and colour. The fairer your skin, the quicker you are likely to burn.

The majority of health experts agree that after 15 minutes exposure to the sun most people begin to burn.

Sunscreen manufacturers have a rating system to guide people when buying sun protection products. This system is called the *Sun Protection Factor* (SPF).

The SPF number indicates how much time you are able to spend in the sun before your skin starts to burn.

You can use the SPF to calculate how long different sunscreens will protect you from the sun.

For example:

Using SPF 5 means that it will take 5 times longer for your skin to start burning.

Given that most people's skin starts to burn after 15 minutes, using SPF 5 means that it will be 15 min × 5 (SPF) = 75 minutes = 1 h 15 min, before you start to burn with the SPF 5 sunscreen on.

Investigate the range of SPF sunscreens. Calculate how many hours and minutes of protection they each provide.

Sports Update

A messenger runs at 18 km per hour for one hour, and then at 12 km per hour for the next two hours. How far does he run?

What is his average speed?

Name:

The Maths Herald

Volume 4

Date:

Focus on Science

Galileo was born in 1564 in Pisa, in Italy.

He made many amazing discoveries in science and mathematics.

How high can you throw a ball?

One of Galileo's experiments discovered the relationship between how long a ball stays in the air, and the maximum height it reaches when it is thrown vertically in the air.

Total time in the air (seconds)	Maximum height (m)
1	1·2
2	4·8
3	10·8
4	19·2
5	30·0

Use the table to discover the formula for Galileo's discovery.

Work with a friend to find out how high you can throw a ball. Be sure to use your formula.

Around the World

Draw a map of what you think your school would look like from a hot air balloon.

Try and make the scale of your map as accurate as possible.

Construct

Work with a friend to design and create a paper plane that will travel the fastest over the longest distance.

You are allowed to design, create and trial up to six different planes.

You need to be able to find ways of measuring both the distance travelled and the time it took to travel that distance.

Record the results for all your planes in a table, showing both the distance and the time.

Which of your paper planes travelled the fastest over the longest distance?

Be prepared to justify your decision.

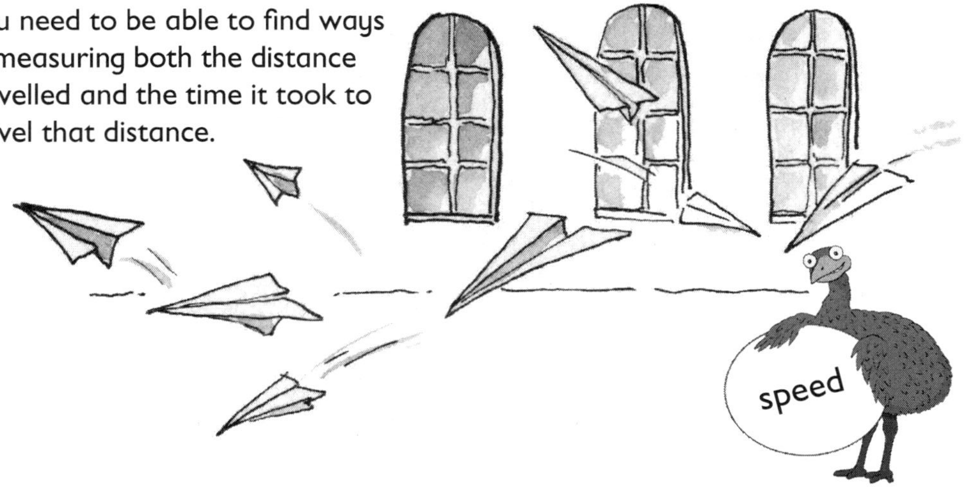

Sports Update

What is the perimeter of this doubles tennis court?

What is the area of this doubles tennis court?

What is the perimeter of a singles tennis court?

What is the area of a singles tennis court?

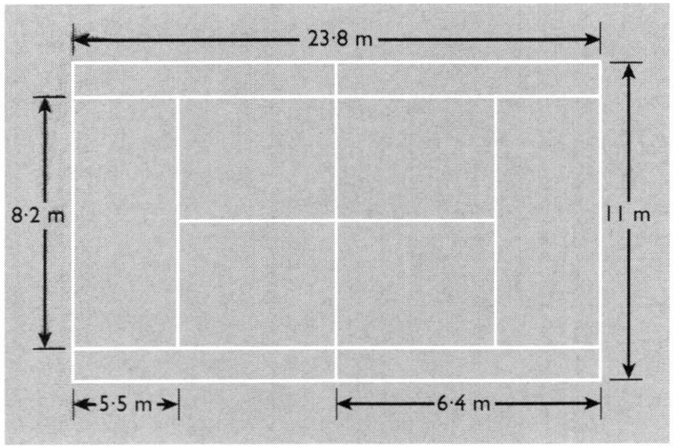

At Home

Supermarkets stock many different brands of the same, or very similar, product.

For example:

- still mineral water
- strawberry jam
- cola
- white bread
- soap

Visit a local supermarket.

Choose three or four different products that each offers a wide range of choice.

Make a note of the brands and prices.

Be careful that you are comparing products that are very similar. Make sure that the amount, size, weight, volume … of each product you are comparing is the same.

For each product, write a report comparing the differences in prices between the different brands.

What conclusions can you make?

Focus on Science

The number of times your heart beats in one minute is called your *pulse rate*.

Your pulse rate changes in different situations.

Take your pulse rate for one minute during each of these situations.

- Sitting
- Standing
- Lying down
- Walking
- After running on the spot for 2 minutes
- After eating a meal
- During PE
- After you've had a hot bath or shower
- As soon as you wake up in the morning
- Just before you go to sleep

Write statements describing how your pulse rate changes in each of these situations.

Let's Investigate

With the help of a friend, measure how long your own pace is.

How long would your *mille* or *mile* be?

How much longer or shorter than a *Roman mile* is it?

Let's Investigate

Look through a selection of different newspapers for the same day to find the weather section.

Cut them out and use them to make a display.

Comment on the similarities and differences between how each of the different newspapers displays the temperature.

Do all the newspapers forecast the same temperature?

What's the Problem?

You have a scale balance and a 40 g weight.

How do you measure 440 g of sugar from a 1 kg bag using the scale balance only twice?

Name:

The Maths Herald

Volume 4

Date:

Construct

Work with a friend to design and create a parachute that will stay airborne for as long as possible.

You are allowed to design, create and trial up to six different parachutes.

You need to be able to find ways of measuring accurately how long the parachutes stay airborne.

Record the results for all your parachutes in a table, showing how long each of the parachutes stayed airborne.

Which of your parachutes stayed airborne the longest?

Be prepared to justify your decision.

What's the Problem?

A family of snakes was going for a walk in single file, one behind the other. From the nose of the front snake to the tip of the tail of the back snake, they took up 3·5 m of the path. They left 10 cm between each other.

Two of the snakes were the same length as each other, and the other three snakes were the same length as each other.

There was 30 cm difference in length between the longer and the shorter snakes.

The lengths of both types of snake were multiples of 10 cm.

How long were the snakes?

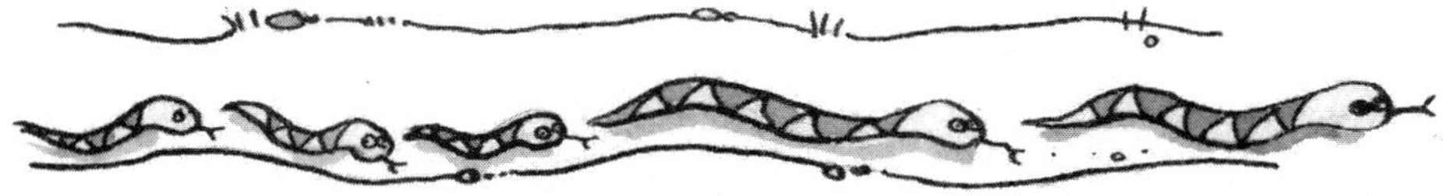

Focus on Science

A *knot* is a unit of measurement for speed.

1 knot = 1·85 kilometres per hour

= 1·15 miles per hour

A cyclone is a storm with winds of 64 knots or more.

What is the wind speed of a cyclone of 64 knots in kilometres per hour?

What about in miles per hour?

Around the World

Investigate the world's most powerful cyclones.

For each cyclone write about:

- where it occurred
- when it occurred
- what the wind speed was in knots
- what the wind speed was in kilometres per hour
- what the wind speed was in miles per hour

The Puzzler

A train takes 6 seconds to enter a tunnel that is 2 km long.

If the train is travelling at 120 km per hour, how long will it take to pass completely through the tunnel?

Sports Update

Sam and Alex are having a running competition.

They each have a home base, 500 m apart. Starting from their home bases, the first person to reach the other's base and then race back to their own home base wins.

They first pass each other 200 m from Sam's base.

Assuming that both Sam and Alex run at constant speeds, who wins? Where do they pass each other a second time?

In the Past

The Romans were the first people to measure distances in miles.

The word *mile* comes from the Roman word *mille* meaning 1000, because a *Roman mile* was the distance a soldier could walk in 1000 paces. (A pace is two steps – start from the left foot, then the right foot, then the left foot.)

A pace was divided into 5 feet.

A Roman mile was 1480 m.

How long was a Roman pace?

How long was a Roman foot?

Let's Investigate

Make a note of the registration numbers of all the cars in the school car park.

Sort the number plates in as many different ways as you can.

Try and record your results in tables, Venn diagrams and / or Carroll diagrams.

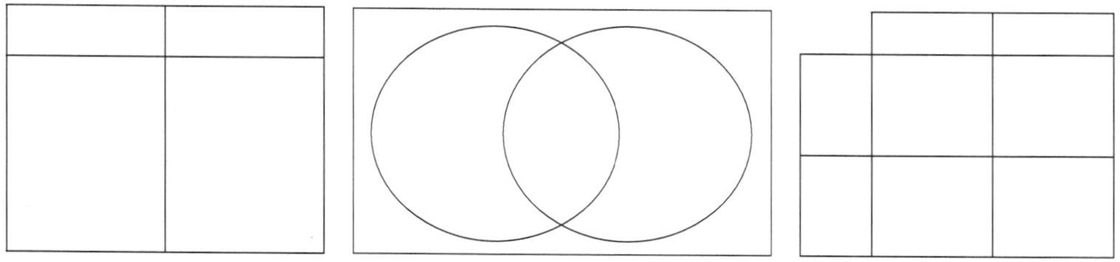

In the Past

The first Model T Ford was built by Henry Ford in Detroit, USA in 1908. It was the first mass produced automobile which could be afforded by everyone. Between 1909 and 1927, the Ford Motor Company built more than 15 million Model T cars.

What is the most common make of vehicle in your community?

The Language of Maths

certain very likely not very likely impossible

Using the terms above, describe some things you might see through a window in your classroom.

Name:

The Maths Herald

Volume 4

Date:

Let's Investigate

What is the average age of all the children in your class?

Follow these steps:
Step 1: Plan
Step 2: Collect data
Step 3: Process the data
Step 4: Represent the data
Step 5: Interpret and discuss the data

Give your answer in years and months.

At Home

Draw a Venn diagram.

Label one section 'Me', and the other section with the name of someone in your family.

In the section labelled 'Me', list different characteristics that describe you, but not your family member.

In the other section, list the different characteristics that describe your family member but not you.

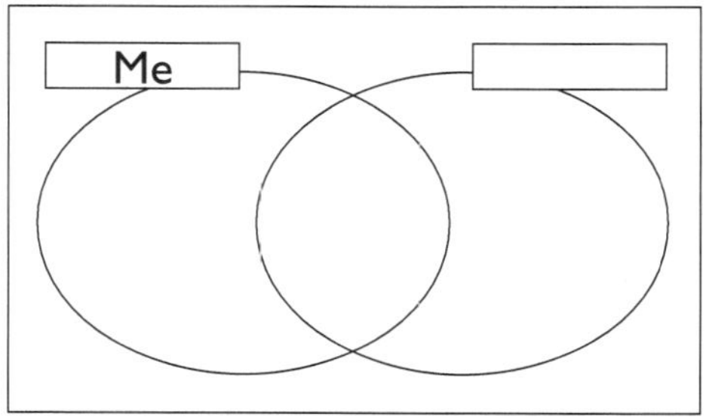

In the intersecting section, list all the characteristics that you both share.

Try drawing different Venn diagrams for other members of your family.

Sports Update

The World Cup is the world's most prestigious football competition.

Here are the results from the 2010 World Cup.

Write as many different statements as you can to describe the results.

Group A	Pts	Group B	Pts	Group C	Pts	Group D	Pts
Uruguay	7	Argentina	9	United States	5	Germany	6
Mexico	4	South Korea	4	England	5	Ghana	4
South Africa	4	Greece	3	Slovenia	4	Australia	4
France	1	Nigeria	1	Algeria	1	Serbia	3

Group E	Pts	Group F	Pts	Group G	Pts	Group H	Pts
Netherlands	9	Paraguay	5	Brazil	7	Spain	6
Japan	6	Slovakia	4	Portugal	5	Chile	6
Denmark	3	New Zealand	3	Ivory Coast	4	Switzerland	4
Cameroon	0	Italy	2	North Korea	0	Honduras	1

Knock-out Results

Let's Investigate

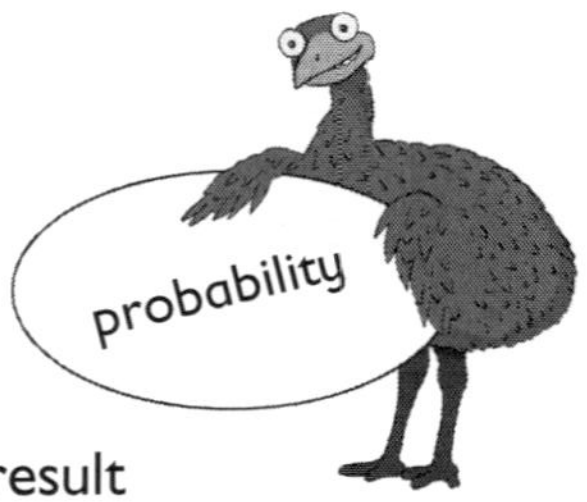

A *sample* is a selection, or a small part, of a group that is used to show what the whole group is like.

For example, if you asked 10 children in your class what was their favourite television programme, the result could be considered a sample of the opinions of all the children in your class.

When taking a sample, you must make sure that you ask enough people, and that you ask a range of different people.

Based on a sample only, what is the most common surname in your school?

Follow these steps:

Step 1: Plan
Step 2: Collect data
Step 3: Process the data
Step 4: Represent the data
Step 5: Interpret and discuss the data

Write a statement about your sample and how it is representative of all the children in your school.

Around the World

Compare the prices of organic and non-organic fruit and vegetables.

Is organic produce always more expensive?

What exactly does 'organic' mean? Do some research to find out.

Sports Update

Apart from the basic skipping rope method, there are at least four other different, more difficult, styles of skipping.

Jogging skip

Scissors skip

Ski skip

Cross-over skip

Design an experiment to find out which of the four skips listed is the easiest and hardest to master.

Follow these steps:

Step 1: Plan
Step 2: Collect data
Step 3: Process the data
Step 4: Represent the data
Step 5: Interpret and discuss the data

Things to think about:

- How many children are you going to ask?
- What previous experience do the children you ask have with skipping? How may this affect your experiment?
- Over how long a period are you going to allow the children to practise?
- How are you going to measure progress?
- How are you going to keep a record of the progress made?

Be prepared to justify your conclusions with the results from your experiment.

Name: ____________

The Maths Herald

Volume 4

Date: ____________

Famous Mathematicians

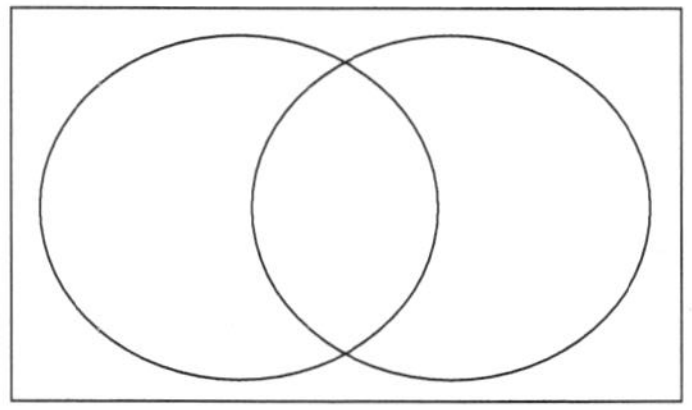

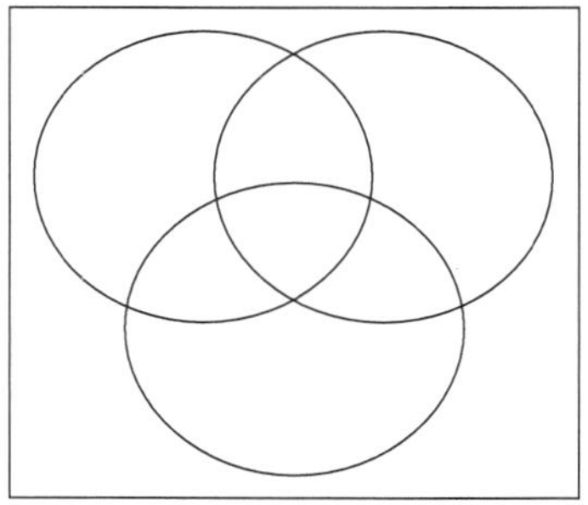

John Venn was a British mathematician who lived from 1834 to 1923. Venn was extremely interested in logic and probability. He created the sorting diagram that bears his name.

Draw a Venn diagram to show the following information. Then answer the question.

These are the results of a class survey.

18 children are boys.

15 children are 7 years or older.

16 children enjoy reading.

8 children are boys who are 7 years or older.

8 children are 7 years or older who enjoy reading.

7 children enjoy reading and are boys.

5 children are boys who are 7 years or older and who enjoy reading.

All the girls less than 7 years old like reading.

Altogether how many children are there in the class?

Money Matters

Many companies raise money by issuing *shares* in their company.

These shares can be bought by anyone who then becomes part owner in the company. People who buy shares in a company are called *investors* or *shareholders*.

Individual investors buy and sell shares on the *stock market*.

Daily newspapers list stock market information in the business section.

Look through the business section of a newspaper for the listing of companies that are on the stock market. Choose a company that you have heard of, or a company you think sounds interesting. Beside the company name there will be a price. This price shows how much it costs to buy one share in the company.

Keep a record of the price for the share over a period of 10 days.

After the tenth day, draw a graph of the rise and fall of the share price for your company.

What do your results tell you about the company over this period?

Let's Investigate

What is the average height of all the children in your year group?

What is the average height for all the children in each of the other year groups in your school?

Draw a bar chart showing the average height in each of the year groups in your school.

The Language of Maths

Many people say 'Err …' and 'Umm …' a lot when talking. Have you noticed this?

It often seems that the less someone knows about the subject they are talking about, the more times they say 'Err …' and 'Umm …'.

With a friend, devise a way of testing whether this is true or not.

These are some things to consider:

- How will you know whether a person knows what they are talking about?
- Will you grade their knowledge on a scale, e.g. from 1 – knows almost nothing, to 5 – very knowledgeable?
- How will you count the number of times they say these two words without them knowing what you are doing?
- Will you count the number of times they say it each minute, or in total?
- Do you test the same people twice, once when they are talking about something they know a lot about, and a second time when they are talking about something they know very little about?
- How will you present your results?

It is probably best to make your test anonymous, and not write down anyone's name!

Focus on Science

Your handspan is the distance between the tip of your little finger and thumb at widest stretch.

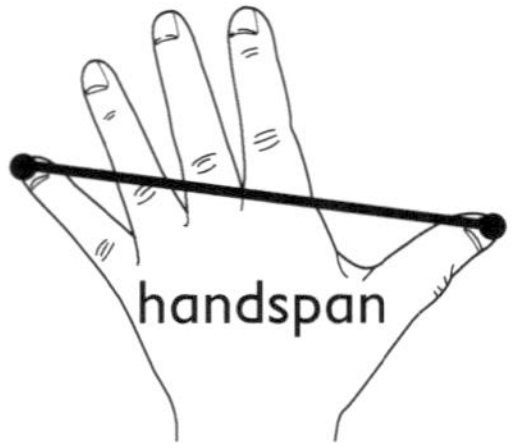

Investigate each of the following questions:

- Is a person's right handspan the same as their left handspan?
- Do taller people have larger handspans, and shorter people smaller handspans?
- Do people with large handspans also have large feet, and people with smaller handspans, smaller feet?

Represent the data you collect using graphs.

Write a report explaining your conclusions.

Refer to your graphs to justify your conclusions.

Teacher's notes

Issue 1 Whole numbers

Prerequisites for learning

- Identify and use patterns, relationships and properties of numbers
- Investigate a statement involving numbers and test it with examples
- Propose a general statement involving numbers
- Recognise and continue number sequences formed by counting on or back in steps of constant size
- Make estimations and approximations

Resources pencil and paper; RCM 2: My notes (optional); RCM 3: Pupil self assessment booklet (optional); calculator (optional); computer with internet access

Teaching support

Page 1
Famous Mathematicians

- Most children should know square numbers up to and including 10^2, but not all may be familiar with triangular numbers and oblong numbers.
- The important aspect of this activity is not being able to write the 5th to 10th square, triangular and oblong numbers, but rather working out a rule or formula for finding any square, triangular or oblong number.
- If children are not confident with writing a mathematical rule or formula, discuss with them possible ways of writing this, including the use of symbols such as *a* or *n*.
- If appropriate, discuss with the children the algebraic convention for omitting the multiplication sign when writing an algebraic expression, i.e. $n(n + 1)$ rather than $n \times (n + 1)$.

Page 2
The Puzzler

- Allow the children to use a calculator for reference.
- Children explore how many three-digit numbers they can make with, for example, ten light bars only. What about four-digit numbers with only ten light bars?
- Children include a decimal point or the minus sign to show a negative number. What is the smallest number possible they can display from a given number of light bars?

Page 2 continued

Famous Mathematicians

- Ensure children have completed the Famous Mathematicians activity on page 1 before attempting this activity.
- Work with the children, drawing a dot array for the first statement, e.g.

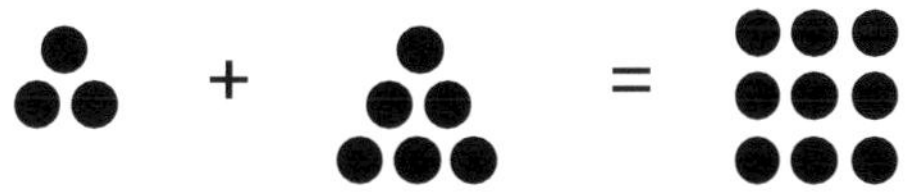

Page 3

Famous Mathematicians

- Ensure children fully understand the table and the problem before setting them off to work independently on the activity.
- Once the children have completed the activity, discuss with them their methods of working. Were they able to identify the pattern and apply the rule to working out how many pairs of rabbits there would be at the end of the year?

Page 4

Looking for Patterns

- Ensure children have completed the Famous Mathematicians activity on page 3 before starting on this activity.
- Children investigate further the life and work of Fibonacci.

Let's Investigate

- Ensure children complete this activity before starting on the Focus on Science activity which follows.
- Children discuss how they could use less paper. For example, working as a pair or group with only one taking notes.

Focus on Science

- Ensure children have completed the Let's Investigate activity above before starting on this activity.
- Estimates vary hugely from 8000 to 100 000 sheets, as to how much paper is produced from one tree. The most important aspect of this activity is the children justifying their comparisons.

AfL

- What is happening in this sequence?
- What pattern do you notice? What is the rule?
- How would you express this rule in words? What about using symbols?
- How else can you express this rule?
- How does this diagram show this relationship?
- How did you work out what the shape was?
- What are all the different possibilities? How can you be sure that you have accounted for them all?
- How did you arrive at your approximation / estimation?

Answers

Page 1

Famous Mathematicians

	Square number	Triangular number	Oblong number
5th	25	15	30
6th	36	21	42
7th	49	28	56
8th	64	36	72
9th	81	45	90
10th	100	55	110
50th	2500	1275	2550
Rule for any number	n^2	$\frac{n(n+1)}{2}$	$n(n+1)$

Page 2

The Puzzler The smallest number you can make from 12 light bars is 28. The largest number you can make from 12 light bars is 111 111.

Famous Mathematicians Diagrams will vary.

Page 3

Famous Mathematicians There would be 144 pairs of rabbits at the end of the year.

Page 4

Looking for Patterns The Fibonacci sequence is the sum of the previous two numbers in the sequence.

The first 20 Fibonacci numbers are: (0), 1, 1, 2, 3, 5, 8, 13, 21, 34, 55, 89, 144, 233, 377, 610, 987, 1597, 2584, 4181, 6765

Let's Investigate Results of the investigation will vary.

Focus on Science Results of the investigation will vary.

EMU

number sequence
An ordered series of numerical quantities.

Issue 2 Whole numbers

Prerequisites for learning

- Identify and use patterns, relationships and properties of numbers
- Investigate a statement involving numbers and test it with examples
- Propose a general statement involving numbers
- Recognise and continue number sequences formed by counting on or back in steps of constant size
- Partition, round and order four-digit whole numbers
- Add or subtract mentally combinations of one-digit and two-digit numbers
- Use written methods to record, support and explain multiplication and division of two-digit numbers by a one-digit number
- Multiply and divide numbers to 1000 by 10 and 100

Resources pencil and paper; RCM 2: My notes (optional); RCM 3: Pupil self assessment booklet (optional); lemon, banana, pear, pepper, cucumber, tomato; knife and plate; calculator (optional); 1, 1, 2, 2, 3, 3 digit cards (optional); computer with internet access

Teaching support

Page 1
Famous Mathematicians

- Most children should be able to successfully complete the table. However, some difficulty may arise when writing a rule or formula.
- If children are not confident with writing a mathematical rule or formula, discuss with them possible ways of writing this, including the use of symbols such as *a* or *n*.
- If appropriate, discuss with the children the algebraic convention for omitting the multiplication sign when writing an algebraic expression, i.e. $\frac{n(n + 1)}{2}$ rather than $\frac{n \times (n + 1)}{2}$.
- Children investigate further the life and work of Carl Gauss.

Page 1 continued

In the Past

- Discuss either of the following methods with the children:

  Method 1:

  (12 × 12 – 12) ÷ 2

  (12 × 12 – 12): Because the knights don't shake hands with themselves.

  ÷ 2: Because Knight A shaking hands with Knight B is the same as Knight B shaking hands with Knight A and counts as only one hand shake, not two.

  Method 2:

  1st knight shakes hands with 11 new people, the 2nd knight shakes hands with only 10 new people (because he's already shaken hands with the 1st knight), the 3rd knight shakes hands with only 9 new people (because he's already shaken hands with the 1st and 2nd knights) etc.

  Therefore 11 + 10 + 9 + 8 + 7 + 6 + 5 + 4 + 3 + 2 + 1 + 0 (because the last knight has already shaken hands with everyone.)

Page 2

Looking for Patterns

- As this activity revisits the Fibonacci sequence, it is advised that children have completed Volume 4, Issue 1 – Whole numbers, before attempting this activity.

Focus on Science

- Before attempting this activity, it is advised that children have completed the Famous Mathematicians activity on page 3, and the Looking for Patterns activity on page 4 of Volume 4, Issue 1 – Whole numbers, as well as the previous Looking for Patterns activity in this issue.
- Although this activity requires specific resources and some preparation, the effort required for this activity is well worth it, as it will provide the children with an opportunity to identify Fibonacci numbers in nature in a practical, hands-on way.
- Prior to the activity, cut each fruit and vegetable crosswise, i.e. to produce a slice of each.
- Children investigate Fibonacci numbers in different fruit and vegetables.

Teaching support continued

Page 3

The Puzzler

- Tell the children the correct position of some of the digits (see Answers).

The Puzzler

- Provide the children with digit cards to arrange and rearrange to find the solution.
- Tell the children that it is possible to make two different six-digit numbers. Can they find them both?
- Ask the children to arrange the digits 1, 1, 2, 2, 3, 3, 4, 4 to make an eight-digit number where:
  - each of the 1 digits is separated by one digit
  - each of the 2 digits is separated by two digits
  - each of the 3 digits is separated by three digits
  - each of the 4 digits is separated by four digits.

  (23 421 314 or 41 312 432)

Page 4

Looking for Patterns

- Ensure children realise that each sequence is made from two different repeating operations, e.g. × 3 and – 4 or ÷ 2 and × 5.

Let's Investigate

- The smallest number would have six beads on the Th column and nine beads on each of the others, making 6999. The next smallest number would have seven beads on the Th column, eight on the H column and nine on the other two, making 7899.
- The largest number would have six beads on the U column and nine on each of the others, making 9996.

AfL

- What is happening in this sequence?
- What pattern do you notice? What is the rule?
- How would you express this rule in words? What about using symbols?
- How else can you express this formula?
- What is the next number in this sequence?
- What are all the different possibilities? How can you be sure that you have accounted for them all?
- How did you work out the answer to this problem / solution to this puzzle?

Answers

Page 1

Famous Mathematicians

Formula is:

$$\frac{n(n + 1)}{2}$$

Counting numbers	Number in set (n)	Total
1	1	1
1 + 2	2	3
1 + 2 + 3	3	6
1 + 2 + 3 + 4	4	10
1 + 2 + 3 + 4 + 5	5	15
1 + 2 + 3 + 4 + 5 + 6	6	21
1 + 2 + 3 + 4 + 5 + 6 + 7	7	28
1 + 2 + 3 + 4 + 5 + 6 + 7 + 8	8	36
1 + 2 + 3 + 4 + 5 + 6 + 7 + 8 + 9	9	45
1 + 2 + 3 + 4 + 5 + 6 + 7 + 8 + 9 + 10	10	55

The numbers are all triangular numbers.
The total of the first 100 numbers is 5050.

In the Past The knights shook hands a total of 66 times.

Page 2

Looking for Patterns

The Fibonacci sequence.
The Fibonacci sequence is the sum of the previous two numbers in the sequence.
The next 10 numbers in the Fibonacci sequence are .... 13, 21, 34, 55, 89, 144, 233, 377, 610, 987.
Results of the investigation will vary.

Focus on Science Results of the investigation will vary. However, all of the fruit and vegetables show Fibonacci numbers.

Answers continued

Page 3

The Puzzler

			73 ▼	516 ▼	5204 ▼			54 ▼	026 ▼	118 ▼	
	5632 ► ▼	2	3	6	5	1466 ► ▼	6	4	6	1	5497 ▼
	6	1407 ► ▼	7	1	0	4	5098 ► ▼	5	0	8	9
42 ►	2	4	9512 ► ▼	5	2	1	9	172 ► ▼	2	1	7
103 ►	3	0	1	6204 ►	4	6	0	2	5413 ▼	5 ►	5
759 ►	5	7	9	45 102 ▼	1536 ►	6	5	1	3	45 132 ▼	4
	3512 ► ▼	1	5	2	3	1784 ►	8	7	4	1	9325 ▼
	5	620 ► ▼	2	0	6	367 ▼	208 ▼	552 ►	5	2	5
32 ►	3	2	1748 ►	4	1	7	8	321 ►	1	3	2
01 ►	1	0	75 160 ►	1	5	6	0	7	95 ►	5	9
62 ►	2	6	3521 ►	5	1	3	2	438 ►	8	4	3

Alternative solution

75 160 ►	5	1	6	0	7
3521 ►	1	5	3	2	438 ►

The Puzzler 231 213 or 312 132

Page 4

Looking for Patterns

9 $\xrightarrow{\times 3}$ 27 $\xrightarrow{-4}$ 23 $\xrightarrow{\times 3}$ 69 $\xrightarrow{-4}$ 65 $\xrightarrow{\times 3}$ 195 $\xrightarrow{-4}$ 191 $\xrightarrow{\times 3}$ 573

600 $\xrightarrow{\div 2}$ 300 $\xrightarrow{\times 5}$ 1500 $\xrightarrow{\div 2}$ 750 $\xrightarrow{\times 5}$ 3750 $\xrightarrow{\div 2}$ 1875 $\xrightarrow{\times 5}$ 9375 $\xrightarrow{\div 2}$ 4687.5

42 $\xrightarrow{+5}$ 47 $\xrightarrow{-2}$ 45 $\xrightarrow{+5}$ 50 $\xrightarrow{-2}$ 48 $\xrightarrow{+5}$ 53 $\xrightarrow{-2}$ 51 $\xrightarrow{+5}$ 56

8 $\xrightarrow{\times 4}$ 32 $\xrightarrow{+1}$ 33 $\xrightarrow{\times 4}$ 132 $\xrightarrow{+1}$ 133 $\xrightarrow{\times 4}$ 532 $\xrightarrow{+1}$ 533 $\xrightarrow{\times 4}$ 2132

4000 $\xrightarrow{\div 10}$ 400 $\xrightarrow{+6}$ 406 $\xrightarrow{\div 10}$ 40·6 $\xrightarrow{+6}$ 46·6 $\xrightarrow{\div 10}$ 4·66 $\xrightarrow{+6}$ 10·66 $\xrightarrow{\div 10}$ 1·066

Let's Investigate There are 20 different numbers possible: 6999, 7899, 7989, 7998, 8799, 8889, 8898, 8979, 8988, 8997, 9699, 9789, 9798, 9879, 9888, 9897, 9969, 9978, 9987, 9996.

EMU

consecutive numbers

Numbers that follow one after another in an unbroken and logical sequence.

Issue 3 Negative numbers

Prerequisites for learning

- Relate numbers to their position on a number line
- Recognise negative numbers in context, including temperature and how it is measured
- Find the difference between a positive integer and a negative integer, or two negative integers, in context
- Identify and use patterns, relationships and properties of numbers
- Construct and interpret frequency tables and line graphs
- Calculate mentally with whole numbers and decimals
- Use efficient written methods to add, subtract, multiply and divide whole numbers and decimals

Resources pencil and paper; RCM 2: My notes (optional); RCM 3: Pupil self assessment booklet (optional); RCM 12: 0·5 cm squared paper; ruler; calculator (optional); computer with internet access

Teaching support

Page 1
Around the World

- You may wish to suggest to the children that they record their findings in a table, e.g.

City / Town	Maximum temperature	Minimum temperature	Temperature range

- Ensure the children are able to find the difference between a positive number and a negative number, or two negative numbers. If necessary, suggest the children use a number line to help them.

Page 2

In the Past

- Although this activity does not deal directly with calculating with negative numbers, it does involve the notion of adding numbers either side of a point of time, i.e. Christ's birth.

Focus on Science

- Ensure the children realise that although eight-ninths of the volume of the iceberg is underwater this does not mean that eight-ninths of the height of the iceberg is underwater.

Page 3

Focus on Science

- Ensure the children are able to order a set of positive and negative numbers, and also find the difference between a positive and a negative number. If necessary, suggest the children use a number line to help them.
- Children write statements comparing the difference in temperatures between different planets. For example,

  'The maximum temperature on Mercury is nine times hotter than on Earth.'

  'The difference in the maximum temperatures between Mercury and the Moon is 340 °C. However, the difference in the minimum temperatures between Mercury and the Moon is only 2 °C.'

Looking for Patterns

- Ask the children to make up some number sequences of their own using negative numbers.

Page 4

Focus on Science

- This activity requires the children to construct a line graph. Discuss the graph with the children before setting them to work independently on the activity. Draw children's attention to the labelling of the axes. If appropriate, point out to the children that the numbering of the depth axis could be written as negative numbers, i.e. 0, $^-50$, $^-100$, $^-150$, $^-200$.
- Ask the children to write a description of the submarine's journey.

The Puzzler

- Can the children find other solutions to any of these triangles?

AfL

- What is the difference between these two numbers?
- What is the rule for finding the difference between a positive number and a negative number? What about the difference between two negative numbers?
- What about adding together a positive number and a negative number?
- How does a number line help when working with negative numbers?
- What is the rule for this number sequence? What is the next number in the sequence?
- What does this graph tell us? Is this the best way to show this? How else could you have displayed the information?
- How did you work out the answer to this problem? What calculation(s) did you do?

Answers

Page 1

Around the World Results of the investigation will vary.

Page 2

In the Past
64 years old
184 years
463 years
1163 years
1480 years

Focus on Science
27·2 m
18·19 m
22·48 m
10·5 m
111·01 m

Page 3

Focus on Science
The hottest planet is Venus.
The coldest planet is Mercury.
The planet with the greatest temperature difference is Mercury at 634 °C.
The planet with the least temperature difference is Venus at 20 °C.

Page 3 continued

Looking for Patterns

⁻7, [⁻5], ⁻3, ⁻1, 1, [3], [5]

⁻13, [⁻10], ⁻7, ⁻4, ⁻1, [2], [5]

11, 7, 3, ⁻1, [⁻5], [⁻9], [⁻13]

[⁻32], ⁻25, ⁻18, ⁻11, [⁻4], [3], 10

19, 14, 9, 4, [⁻1], [⁻6], [⁻11]

20, [11], [2], ⁻7, ⁻16, [⁻25], ⁻34

Page 4

Focus on Science

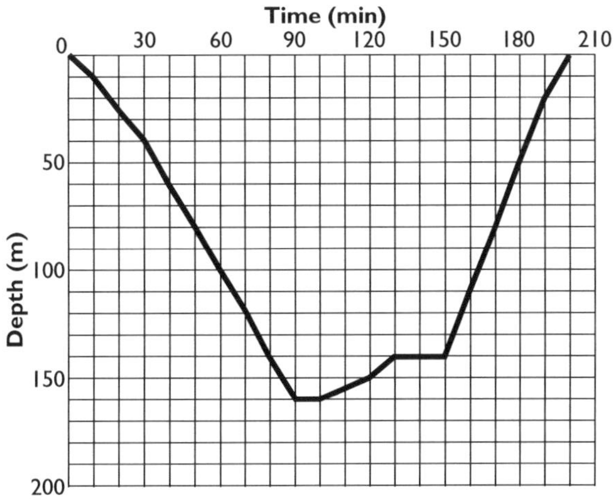

The Puzzler

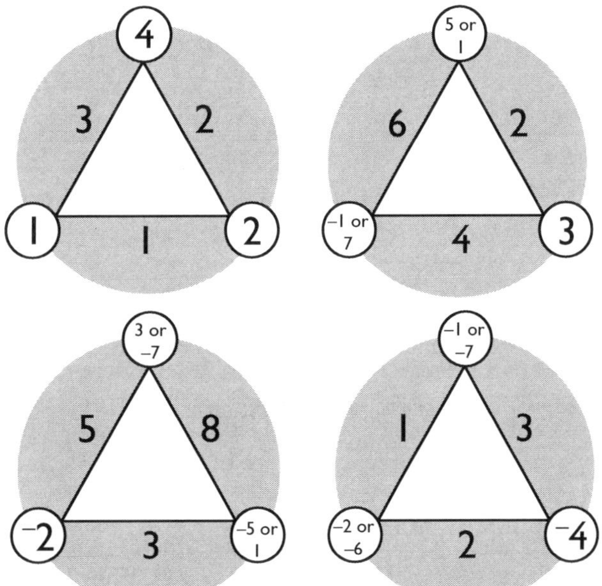

EMU temperature

The degree or intensity of heat, usually measured in degrees Celsius (°C) or degrees Fahrenheit (°F).

Issue 4 Fractions

Prerequisites for learning

- Understand the term 'lowest common multiple'
- Read and write proper fractions, e.g. $\frac{3}{7}$, $\frac{9}{10}$, interpreting the denominator as the parts of a whole and the numerator as the number of parts
- Identify and estimate fractions of shapes
- Use diagrams to compare fractions
- Find equivalent fractions
- Find fractions of numbers, quantities or shapes
- Understand simple expressions and formulae in words and symbols

Resources pencil and paper; RCM 2: My notes (optional); RCM 3: Pupil self assessment booklet (optional); RCM 10: 1 cm squared paper; RCM 11: 2 cm squared paper; RCM 13: Squared dot paper; ruler; scissors (optional); tape measure; calculator; red, blue and green counters; paper clips

Teaching support

Page 1

Construct

- Suggest the children use 2 cm squared paper to draw their diagrams.
- Children draw a diagram to show that $\frac{1}{3} \times 2$ is the same as $2 \times \frac{1}{3}$.

Let's Investigate

- Remind the children that they are only expected to find an approximate fraction.
- Once the children have worked out an approximation, ensure they spend time writing about what they did. Then hold a discussion with different pairs of children discussing their method. How could they make their approximation more accurate?

The Language of Maths

- Prior to the activity discuss the different aspects of their day that the children could describe, e.g. time spent in school; time spent eating; time spent alone; time spent playing.

Page 2

Looking for Patterns

- Ensure children realise that they need to draw lines enclosing a rectangle 6 cm × 8 cm.
- Point out to the children that $\frac{7}{16}$ is equal to $\frac{21}{48}$.

The Puzzler

- Ensure children are able to answer what fraction of each of the three squares in the issue is shaded before drawing, shading and describing their own squares.
- If children have difficulty in seeing what fractions of the squares are shaded, suggest they use 2 cm squared paper to draw a blank 2 × 2 square. They then reproduce each of the three squares on the squared paper and cut them out. Can they arrange the individual pieces onto the blank 2 × 2 square and see what fraction is shaded? For example,

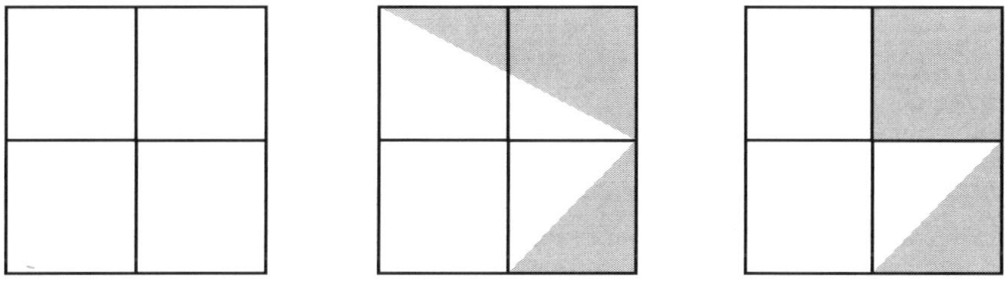

Page 3

Let's Investigate

- Ensure the children understand how to use the spinner.
- Ask the children to spin the paper clip another 20–40 times. Are the answers closer to their predictions? Why do they think this is?

Page 4

What's the Problem?

- Ask the children how the pizzas could be cut if 15 friends shared 8 pizzas?

The Puzzler

- The solution to this puzzle can be best understood through the use of a diagram, i.e.

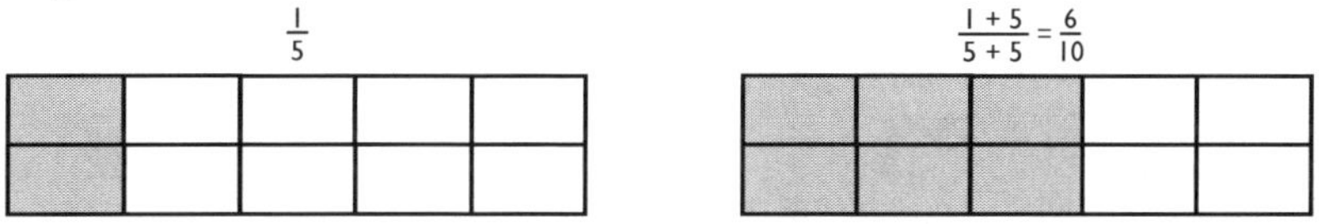

  Six parts ($\frac{6}{10}$) are three times as many as two parts ($\frac{1}{5}$).
- If seven is added to both the numerator and denominator of a fraction, it quadruples in value. What is the fraction? ($\frac{1}{7}$)

Teaching support continued

Page 4 continued

The Puzzler

- *a* is the hundreds digit of the numerator, so it must be as large as possible.

  b and *c* need to be as small as possible to keep the denominator as small as possible.

  So the largest fraction is $\frac{921}{9+2+1} = \frac{921}{12} = 76{\cdot}75$

AfL

- Explain this diagram to me. How does it show this equation / this relationship / this fraction?
- Explain to me how you worked out the answer / approximation.
- Tell me one of your statements. How else could you express this?
- What was your prediction? Was your prediction accurate?
- How did you work out the solution to this puzzle / answer to this problem?

Answers

Page 1

Construct Diagrams will vary. Possible diagrams may include:

$\frac{1}{2}$ of $\frac{1}{4}$

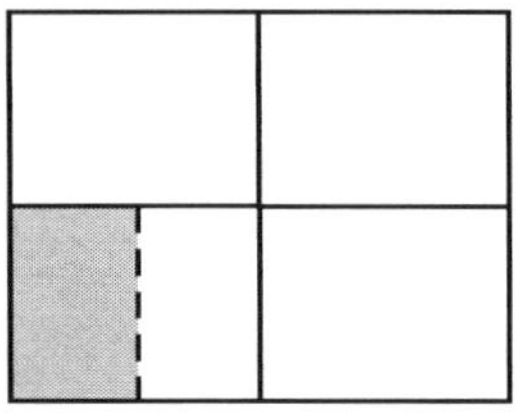

$\frac{1}{4}$ of $\frac{1}{2}$

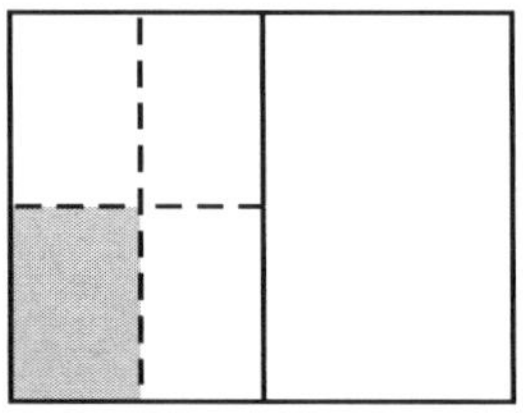

Let's Investigate Results of the investigation will vary.

The Language of Maths Statements will vary.

Page 2

Looking for Patterns

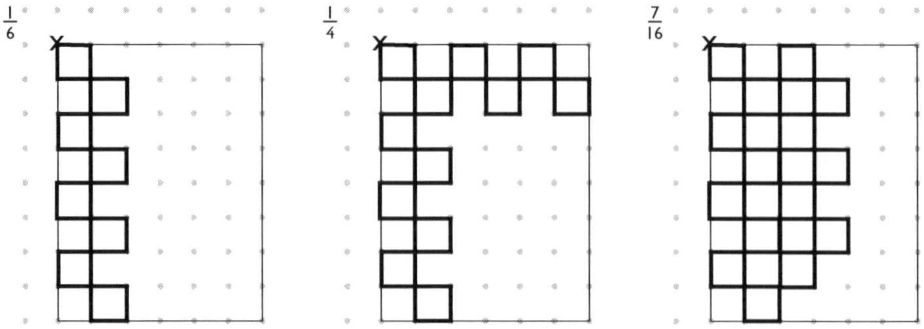

Page 2 continued

The Puzzler $\frac{3}{8}, \frac{1}{4}, \frac{1}{2}$

Fractions of other shaded 2 × 2 squares will vary.

Page 3

Let's Investigate 'Red': $\frac{1}{2}$(10 times)
'Blue': $\frac{1}{4}$(5 times)
'Green': $\frac{1}{4}$(5 times)

Page 4

What's the Problem? Four of the pizzas are cut into thirds and three pizzas into quarters. Each friend has one third and one quarter of a pizza.
($4 \times \frac{3}{3} = \frac{12}{3}$ so each friend gets $\frac{1}{3}$
$3 \times \frac{4}{4} = \frac{12}{4}$ so each friend gets $\frac{1}{4}$)

The Puzzler $\frac{1}{5}$

The Puzzler The largest fraction s $\frac{921}{9+2+1} = \frac{921}{12} = 76{\cdot}75$

EMU

proper fraction

A fraction in which the value of the numerator is less than the value of the denominator, such as $\frac{2}{3}$.

Issue 5 Decimals

Prerequisites for learning

- Use decimal notation for tenths and hundredths
- Partition, round and order decimals
- Recognise the equivalence between decimal and fraction forms
- Use understanding of place value to multiply and divide whole numbers and decimals by 10, 100 or 1000
- Calculate mentally with whole numbers and decimals
- Use efficient written methods to add, subtract, multiply and divide whole numbers and decimals

Resources pencil and paper; RCM 2: My notes (optional); RCM 3: Pupil self assessment booklet (optional); calculator; coloured pencils

Teaching support

Page 1

Focus on Science

- For this activity children need to be confident with multiplying and dividing whole numbers and decimals by 10, 100 and 1000.

Looking for Patterns

- Ensure the children realise that 0·375 is equivalent to $\frac{3}{8}$ and 0·625 is equivalent to $\frac{5}{8}$.

Page 2

Around the World

- 0·1 × 150 = 15

  0·96 × 150 = 144

  15 + 144 = 159

  So 9 people must speak both Welsh and English.

Focus on Science

- Ensure children understand the millesimal fineness system and the example provided in the issue.
- What does the word 'millesimal' mean? (relating to thousandths)

Page 3

Around the World

- Allow the children to use a calculator for this activity.

What's the Problem?

- If Samuel works for a day by himself and then Taylor joins him for two days, in three days they bag up (3 × 1·38) + (2 × 0·74) = 5·62 tonnes. The pile of sand weighs between 11 and 12 tonnes. 2 × 5·62 tonnes lies between 11 and 12 tonnes, so they must take 3 days × 2 = 6 days to bag it up.

Looking for Patterns

- One way of working out the missing numbers in these calculations is to rearrange the equations so that the unknown quantity is by itself on one side of the equation.

  i.e.

  0·5 + 0·35 + ☐ = 1

  minus 0.5 from each side of the equation to give:

  0·35 + ☐ = 1 – 0·5

  minus 0.35 from each side of the equation to give:

  ☐ = 1 – 0·5 – 0·35

  This now makes it easier to work out.

Page 4

What's the Problem?

- Suggest the children round calculations to two decimal places.

  After the second jump the frog is 0·96 m above the water.

  0·96 m + 3rd jump = 1·96 m, then slides back 1·96 × 0·4 = 0·78, so ends up 1·96 – 0·78 = 1·18 m above the water

  1·18 m + 4th jump = 2·18 m, then slides back 2·18 × 0·4 = 0·87, so ends up 2·18 – 0·87 = 1·31 m above the water

  1·31 m + 5th jump = 2·31 m, then slides back 2·31 × 0·4 = 0·92, so ends up 2·31 – 0·92 = 1·39 m above the water

  1·39 m + 6th jump = 2·39 m, then slides back 2·39 × 0·4 = 0·96, so ends up 2·39 – 0·96 = 1·43 m above the water

  1·43 m + 7th jump = 2·43 m, then slides back 2·43 × 0·4 = 0·97, so ends up 2·43 – 0·97 = 1·46 m above the water

  1·46 m + 8th jump = 2·46 m so the frog escapes.

Teaching support continued

Page 4 continued

What's the Problem? continued

- Would the frog escape if the well were more than 2·5 m deep? Why? (The frog can never get higher than 2·5 metres, so it would never escape. If the frog reaches 2·5 m after jumping 1 m, it then slips back down 0·4 of this height, i.e. it slips back down 1 m. This brings the frog to 1·5 m: it then jumps 1 m to reach 2·5 m and carries on this way forever.)

The Language of Maths

- If children are unsure of the decimal equivalents for the fractions, suggest that they use the relationship between fractions and division to work out the relevant decimal equivalent.

AfL

- What is the solution to this puzzle / answer to this problem? How did you go about finding it out?
- This activity involved calculating with decimals. How did you work it out? What strategies did you use?
- What is this fraction expressed as a decimal?

Answers

Page 1

Focus on Science Earth: 781 parts nitrogen, 210 parts oxygen and 9 parts argon
Mars: 0·29 sodium, 0·22 hydrogen, 0·42 oxygen, 0·06 helium and 0·005 potassium

Looking for Patterns

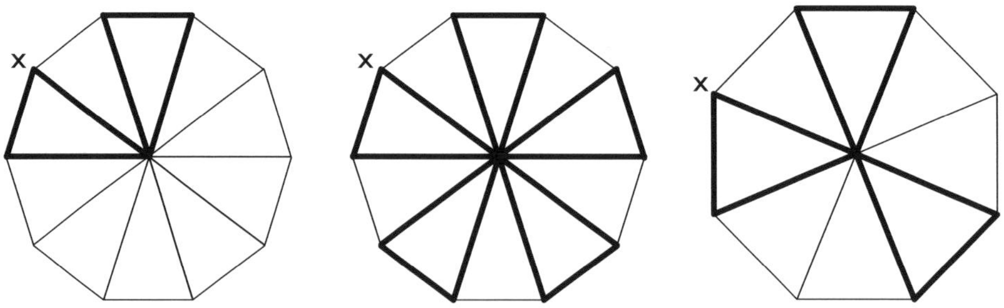

Other routes are possible.
It is not possible to draw a route around more than half of the triangles and still get back to the start.

Page 2

Around the World 9 people speak both Welsh and English.

Page 2 continued

Focus on Science
Gold pin: 60 g
Gold earrings: 169 g
Gold necklace: 207 g
Gold bracelet: 154 g
Gold box: 936 g or 0·936 kg

Page 3

Around the World
Milk: 15p
Coffee: 5p
Labour: 45p
Rent: 30p
Administration: 62·5p
Cup / sugar / lid: 10p
VAT: 50p
Profit: 32·5p

What's the Problem?
6 days
Samuel works for two days by himself, and then they work together for another four days.

Looking for Patterns

$0{\cdot}5 + 0{\cdot}35 + \boxed{0{\cdot}15} = 1$	$2{\cdot}75 + 0{\cdot}8 - \boxed{1{\cdot}43} = 2{\cdot}12$
$\boxed{0{\cdot}66} + 0{\cdot}74 + 2{\cdot}6 = 4$	$0{\cdot}2 - 3{\cdot}67 + \boxed{5{\cdot}05} = 1{\cdot}58$
$3{\cdot}2 - 1{\cdot}58 - 0{\cdot}63 = \boxed{0{\cdot}99}$	$6{\cdot}24 - 3{\cdot}79 - \boxed{2{\cdot}13} = 0{\cdot}32$

Page 4

What's the Problem?
8 jumps

The Language of Maths
0·35 is less than $\frac{1}{3}$: False
$\frac{1}{4}$ is less than 0·3: True
$\frac{2}{3}$ is more than 0·65: True
$\frac{8}{9}$ is more than 0·9: False
0·6 is less than $\frac{5}{8}$: True
$\frac{1}{4}$ is more than 0·25: False
$\frac{5}{16}$ is more than 0·3: True
$\frac{7}{9}$ is less than 0·75: False

EMU 
tonne
1 tonne is equivalent to 1000 kilograms.

Issue 6 Ratio and proportion

Prerequisites for learning

- Use the vocabulary of ratio and proportion to describe the relationship between two quantities
- Use sequences to scale numbers up or down
- Understand and use ratio notation
- Use efficient mental and written methods to multiply and divide whole numbers and decimals

Resources pencil and paper; RCM 2: My notes (optional); RCM 3: Pupil self assessment booklet (optional); calculator; child's reading book; two 1, 2, 3, 1, 2, 3 dice; computer with internet access

Teaching support

Page 1
Around the World

- Ensure children are familiar with ratio notation, e.g. 8 : 5, before attempting this activity.
- Allow the children to use a calculator for this activity.
- As this activity requires the children to use sequences to scale numbers up or down, you may wish to introduce them to the following method as a way of working out the answers.
- Take, for example, the Great Pyramid of Khufu, with a base width of 230 m. The height of the pyramid can be calculated using the following diagram:

base	height	
8	5	
↓	↓	28·75
230 m	143·75 m	

(230 m ÷ 8 = 28·75 m
28·75 m × 5 = 143·75 m)

Page 2
Money Matters

- Ensure children are familiar with ratio notation, e.g. 5 : 8, before attempting this activity.
- Allow the children to use a calculator for this activity.
- Discuss with the children the use of the inverse ratio to change back dollars into pounds, i.e. 8 : 5.

Page 2 continued

What's the Problem?

- Allow the children to record their ratios and proportions in their own way.
- Once several children have completed the activity, hold a discussion and allow individual children to present their method of recording. What are the similarities and differences?

Page 3

Let's Investigate

- Mercury is the closest planet to the Sun. What is the approximate ratio of the time that each of the other planets takes to the time that Mercury takes?

The Language of Maths

- What is the second most frequently used letter in your book?

Page 4

Let's Investigate

- What is the approximate ratio of the totals 2 to 3 to 4 to 5 to 6?

Money Matters

- The ratios give (1 × 50p) + (3 × 20p) + (2 × 10p) + (2 × 5p) = £1.40. £5.60 is four times this amount, so there are four times these numbers of coins.
- What is the ratio of 50p to 20p to 10p to 5p coins? (1 : 3 : 2 : 2)

Looking for Patterns

- Ensure children are familiar with ratio notation, e.g. 6 : 5, before attempting this activity.
- The minimum number of yellow counters there can be is 5. If this is the right number, there must be 8 blue counters (ratio 8 : 5), therefore 10 green counters (ratio 5 : 4), therefore 12 red counters (ratio 6 : 5). This makes 35 counters in total, so not enough.
- Doubling the number of each coloured counter keeps the ratios the same and gives a total of 70 counters, which fits the clues.

AfL

- What does the word 'ratio' mean? What about 'proportion'?
- How did you use ratio to work out the answer to this problem?
- How did you work out that proportion? Is it an approximation or the actual proportion?
- How do you write a ratio / proportion? How else can you express a ratio / proportion?
- What ratio / proportion is this?
- Tell me some of your statements / problems that involve ratio and proportion.

Answers

Page 1

Around the World

The Great Pyramid of Khufu: 143·75 m
The Pyramid of Khafre: 133·75 m
The Pyramid of Menkare: 65·625 m

Page 2

Money Matters

Peter received $160.
Aslan received $80.
Silvia received $224.
Tommi received $280.
Rada received $512.

Silvia returned with £45.
Tommi returned with £72.50.
Rada returned with £101.25.

What's the Problem?

The ratio of starfish to shells is 5 : 7.
$\frac{7}{12}$ of the bucket is shells.
$\frac{5}{12}$ of the contents are starfish.
The ratio of fish to starfish to shells is 3 : 5 : 7.
$\frac{1}{3}$ of the contents of the bucket are starfish now.

Page 3

Let's Investigate
Mercury : Earth 1 : 4
Venus : Earth 2 : 3
Mars : Earth 2 : 1
Jupiter : Earth 12 : 1
Saturn : Earth 30 : 1
Uranus : Earth 84 : 1
Neptune : Earth 165 : 1

The Language of Maths
3 : 1
Providing there is enough text, the ratio should be the same on any page.

Page 4

Let's Investigate
The most frequent total is 4. The least frequent totals are 2 and 6. Ratio of the most frequent total to the least frequent total is 3 : 1.

Money Matters
4 × 50p, 12 × 20p, 8 × 10p, 8 × 5p

Looking for Patterns
There are 24 red, 20 green, 16 blue and 10 yellow counters in the bag.

EMU

:
Mathematical symbol for writing a ratio.

Issue 7

Counting and understanding number – General

Prerequisites for learning

- Identify and use patterns, relationships and properties of numbers
- Recognise and continue number sequences formed by counting on or back in steps of constant size
- Solve logic puzzles
- Make estimations and approximations

Resources pencil and paper; RCM 2: My notes (optional); RCM 3: Pupil self assessment booklet (optional); selection of tariffs for different mobile phone providers; computer with internet access

Teaching support

Page 1

Technology Today

- Before investigating on the internet what each of the terms mean, can the children make any predictions? What is the relationship between a byte and a kilobyte? Why?

Money Matters

- To accurately compare postal charges across Europe, children will need to take into account exchange rates. You will probably need to spend time discussing this concept with the children.
- You may wish to modify this activity by asking the children to compare rates in the United Kingdom to one other European country. Alternatively, children can compare rates in the United Kingdom with those in the USA, Canada, Australia, South Africa …

Page 2

What's the Problem?

- Suggest the children make a list, e.g.
MM (Mr and Mrs Roach); T (Tasmin); L (Lisa); W (William).

MMTLW	TMMLW	TLMMW	TLWMM
MMTWL	TMMWL	TWMML	TWLMM
MMLWT	LMMWT	LWMMT	LWTMM
MMLTW	LMMTW	LTMMW	LTWMM
MMWTL	WMMTL	WTMML	WTLMM
MMWLT	WMMLT	WLMMT	WLTMM

Page 2 continued

What's the Problem? continued

There are 24 possibilities shown in the list at the bottom of page 126. However the total number of possibilities is double this, i.e. 48, as Mr and Mrs Roach are able to swap places.

The Puzzler

- Suggest the children draw a logic box, i.e.

	Trevor	Steven	Nigel
7 years-old	✔	✘	
9 years-old		✔	✘
10 years-old	✘	✘	✔

Page 3

The Puzzler

- Suggest children draw a table similar to the following, writing the number of each spell in order underneath the appropriate apprentice until they have reached the 100th spell.

Apprentice							
1	**2**	**3**	**4**	**5**	**6**	**7**	**8**
1	2	3	4	5	6	7	8
9	10	11	12	13	14	15	16
17	18	19					

- Discuss the following calculation with the children as a way of working out the answer:

  100 ÷ 8 = 12 R 4

  So the fourth apprentice gets the last spell.

Money Matters

- Children will need to undertake part of this investigation outside school. It is therefore advised that a discussion is held with the children before embarking on this aspect of the investigation to decide which goods children will try to find the prices of.

Teaching support continued

Page 4

Technology Today

- Almost all of the large chains of mobile phone providers publish tariffs of the different packages they offer.

Looking for Patterns

- Tell the children that apart from the first column where the rule has only one operation, i.e. × 3, the rules for all the other columns have two operations, e.g. × 2 + 1.

AfL

- Tell me what you found out about computer memory size / postal charges / mobile phone tariffs.
- What patterns / relationships do you notice? What conclusions can you draw?
- How did you solve this puzzle / find the answer to this problem?
- Can you give me a rule to describe this?
- Can you predict what the next number / the answer will be? What did you base your prediction on?
- How did you arrive at that estimate / approximation?

Answers

Page 1

Technology Today

byte = 8 binary digits or bits

kilobyte = 1024 bytes
= 2^{10} bytes
≈ 1000 bytes

megabyte = 1 048 576 bytes
= 2^{20} bytes
= 1024 kilobytes
≈ one million bytes

gigabyte = 1 073 741 824 bytes
= 2^{30} bytes
= 1024 megabytes
≈ one billion bytes

terabyte = 1 099 511 627 776 bytes
= 2^{40} bytes
= 1024 gigabytes
≈ one trillion bytes

Money Matters Results of the investigation will vary.

Page 2

What's the Problem? There are 48 different ways that the Roach family can stand in line to have their picture taken.

The Puzzler Nigel is 10 years old, Trevor is 7 years old and Steven is 9 years old.

Page 3

The Puzzler The fourth apprentice gets the last spell.
Apprentices 1, 2, 3 and 4 each get 13 spells. Apprentices 5, 6, 7 and 8 each get 12 spells.

Money Matters Results of the investigation will vary.

Page 4

Technology Today Results of the investigation will vary.

Looking for Patterns

33	25	35	78	18	16	19
39	31	43	103	24	20	24
(×3)	(× 2, + 1)	(× 4, – 1)	(× 5, + 3)	(÷ 2, – 1)	(– 1, ÷ 3)	(+ 1, ÷ 2)

EMU 

approximation
A value that is not exact. A guess or estimate of an amount or number.

Issue 8 Counting and understanding number – General

Prerequisites for learning

- Identify and use patterns, relationships and properties of numbers
- Recognise and continue number sequences formed by counting on or back in steps of constant size
- Solve logic puzzles
- Understand the use of partitioning and place value

Resources pencil and paper; RCM 2: My notes (optional); RCM 3: Pupil self assessment booklet (optional); RCM 11: 2 cm squared paper; ruler; set of dominoes (optional); computer with internet access

Teaching support

Page 1

Money Matters

- The children will be easily able to investigate on the internet the prices that individual airlines offer for each of the different classes of travel. What may be more difficult, however, is finding out about the differences in service that is offered in each class. Most airlines' websites include details about seat pitch and width, bag weight restrictions, in-flight entertainment and food.
- As the children are required to make a value judgement comparing price with service, the conclusions they draw will be highly subjective. However, insist the children are able to justify their conclusions. Allow the children to work in pairs so that they can share ideas and discuss their reasoning.

Looking for Patterns

- This activity is a simple variation on the hand-shake activity.
- Each person clinked glasses with two other people (14 × 2), but Person A clinking glasses with Person B was the same as Person B clinking glasses with Person A, so the total must be divided by two.

Page 1 continued

Looking for Patterns continued

- If children have difficulty in understanding how many times the glasses were clinked, start with four, then six people sitting round a table, using a diagram to illustrate, i.e.

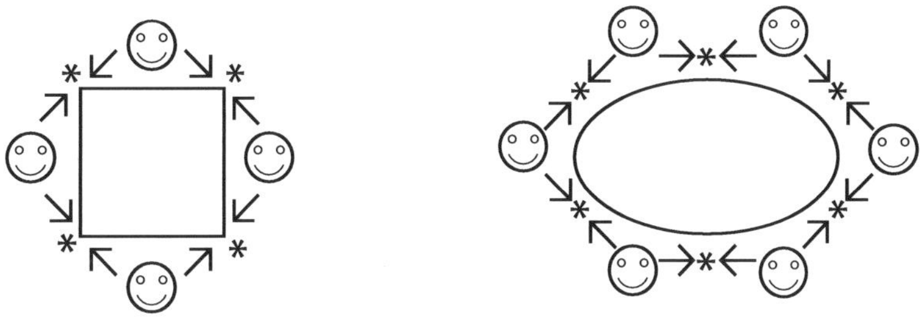

* represents 1 clink of a glass.

Page 2

The Puzzler

- If appropriate, allow the children to use a set of dominoes.
- Ask the children to create their own similar domino puzzle using 2 cm squared paper.

Looking for Patterns

- For each sequence what were the three numbers before those given, e.g. □, □, □, 4, 7, 10, 13, …

Page 3

Looking for Patterns

- Ensure the children realise that the number 1 is in the bottom right-hand corner of the grid. Also that the numbers increase in order from right to left in the first (bottom) row, then from left to right in the second (to bottom) row, and alternate in this way for all the rows of the number square.
- What if this were the pattern in the 1–100 number square?

1	20	21	40	41	60	61	80	81	100
2	19	22	39	42	59	62	79	82	99
3	18	23	38	43	58	63	78	83	98
4	17	24	37	44	57	64	77	84	97
5	16	25	36	45	56	65	76	85	96

Teaching support continued

Page 3 continued

The Language of Maths

- Ensure children are able to identify the constituent parts of two-syllable and three-syllable words.

Page 4

The Puzzler

- Ensure children have had experience with solving logic puzzles.
- Suggest the children draw a diagram to help them.

In the Past

- Ensure children understand that a numeral is a symbol or set of symbols used to represent a number, for example, the Arabic numeral 9, the equivalent Roman numeral IX, and the equivalent ancient Greek symbol ϑ.
- Work with the children to write two or three two-digit numbers using the Ancient Babylonian numeral system.

AfL

- Tell me what you found out about the cost of air travel from London to Sydney.
- How did you solve this puzzle / find the answer to this problem?
- What patterns / relationships do you notice? What conclusions can you draw?
- What is the rule to describe this number sequence? What is the next number in this sequence?
- What can you tell me about the Ancient Babylonian numeral system? How would you write the number 36 using this system? What about 58?

Answers

Page 1

Money Matters Results of the investigation will vary.

Looking for Patterns Glasses were clinked a total of 14 times.

Page 2

The Puzzler

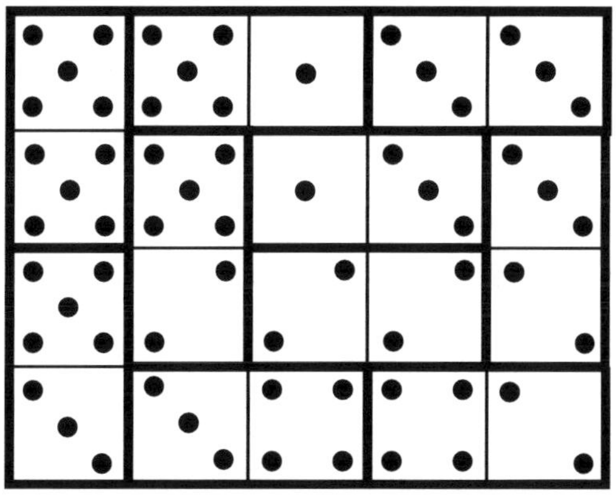

Looking for Patterns

4, 7, 10, 13, 16, 19, 22 (Rule: add 3 to the previous term)
5, 8, 12, 17, 23, 30, 38 (Rule: increase the difference between successive numbers by 1 each time)
2, 4, 8, 14, 22, 32, 44 (Rule: increase the difference between successive numbers by 2 each time)
3, 5, 9, 17, 33, 65, 129 (Rule: double the difference between successive numbers each time)
128, 64, 32, 16, 8, 4 (Rule: divide the previous term by 2)
7, 11, 19, 31, 47, 67, 91 (Rule: increase the difference between successive numbers by 4 each time)

Page 3

Looking for Patterns

	49		47	46	
31	32	33			
	29	28	27		25
11	12	13	14	15	
	9		7		

The Language of Maths

Poems will vary.

Page 4

The Puzzler

Anil is in seat 1, Firoza seat 2, Cath seat 3, Bob seat 4, Ellie seat 5 and Des seat 6.

In the Past

Numbers written in the Ancient Babylonian numeral system will vary.

EMU 

percent
Used to express a specified amount in or for every hundred.

Issue 9

Counting and understanding number – General

Prerequisites for learning

- Identify and use patterns, relationships and properties of numbers
- Recognise and continue number sequences formed by counting on or back in steps of constant size
- Identify numbers in the Fibonacci sequence
- Understand and use partitioning and place value
- Use the vocabulary of ratio and proportion to describe the relationship between two quantities
- Understand and use ratio notation
- Find fractions of numbers, quantities or shapes

Resources pencil and paper; RCM 2: My notes (optional); RCM 3: Pupil self assessment booklet (optional); RCM 10: 1 cm squared paper; ruler

Teaching support

Page 1

Focus on Science

- Before attempting this activity, ensure children have completed the Famous Mathematicians activity on page 3 and the Looking for Patterns activity on page 4 of *Enriching Maths* Volume 4 Issue 1 – Whole numbers and are familiar with the Fibonacci sequence.

The Arts Roundup

- 1 octave (from C to C) includes:

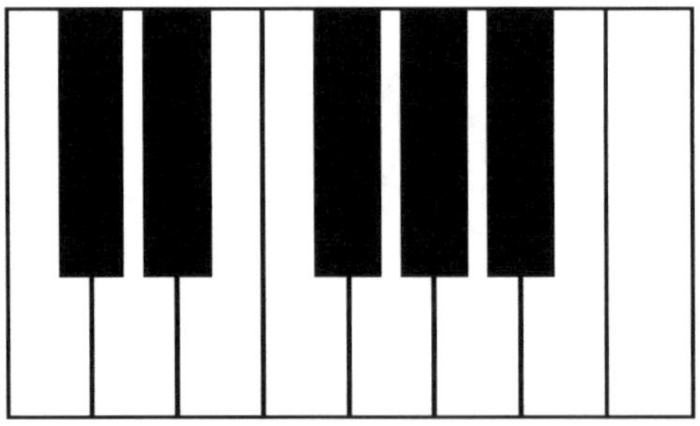

  - 2 black keys and 3 black keys – making a total of 5 black keys
  - 8 white keys
  - a total of 13 black and white keys.
- The numbers 1, 2, 3, 5, 8 and 13 are all Fibonacci numbers.

Page 2

The Puzzler

- Placing the digit '2' before the two-digit number increases the number by 200. It also makes the number 9 times larger. Therefore, 8 times the two-digit number equals 200 (8 x ☐ = 200). From this, it is possible to work out that the two-digit number is 25.
- What three-digit number is made 9 times larger when the digit '1' is placed before it? (125)

In the Past

- Ensure children understand that a numeral is a symbol or set of symbols used to represent a number, for example, the Arabic numeral 9, the equivalent Roman numeral IX, and the equivalent ancient Greek symbol ϑ.
- Work with the children to write two or three two-digit numbers using the Mayan numeral system.

Page 3

What's the Problem?

- If both tins contain 6 *l* of paint, pouring 3 *l* of red paint into 6 *l* of blue, makes 9 *l* of blue / red mixture in the blue tin.

  Pouring 3 *l* of this mixture, containing 1 *l* of red paint and 2 *l* of blue, into the red paint tin, gives 4 *l* of red paint and 2 *l* of blue in the red tin. This leaves 4 *l* of blue and 2 *l* of red paint in the blue tin. Using Sunita's method would give the same result.
- Suggest children draw the two paint tins and their contents, plus movements at each stage.

The Puzzler

- As one-quarter has been shaded, one point of the shaded triangle is exactly halfway along the long side of the rectangle. If you draw a vertical line down from the top long side to this point, and another line from the top right-hand corner to this point, the remainder of the rectangle has been divided into three equal triangles.

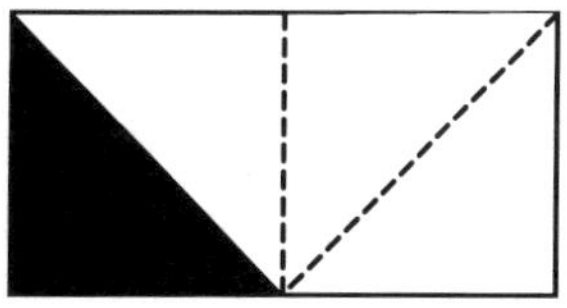

Teaching support continued

Page 3 continued

The Puzzler continued

- Now you just have to find a way of cutting off the same amount from each triangle to make a fourth shape.

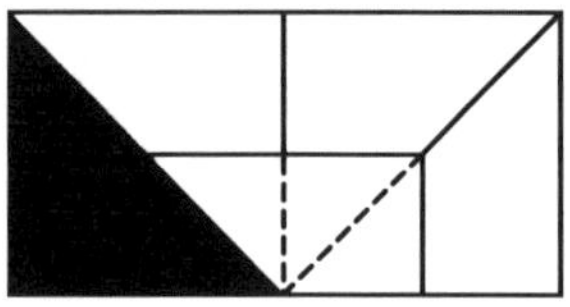

Page 4

Focus on Science

- Children make up some cogwheel puzzles of their own and give them to a friend to solve.

AfL

- What is the rule to describe this number sequence? What is the next number in this sequence?
- How does the chambered nautilus shell / keys on a piano represent numbers in the Fibonacci sequence?
- How did you solve this puzzle / find the answer to this problem?
- What can you tell me about the Central American Mayan numeral system? How would you write the number 41 using this system? What about 67?
- What patterns / relationships do you notice? What conclusions can you draw?
- How did you use ratio to work out the answer to these problems?
- How can you express this as a ratio?

Answers

Page 1

Focus on Science 21, 34, 55, 89, 144
Moving from the centre of the chambered nautilus shell, the measurements are in the ratio 1, 1, 2, 3, 5 – all Fibonacci numbers.

The Arts Roundup One octave (from C to C) has black keys in groups of 2 and 3 making a total of 5 black keys. There are 8 white keys making a total of 13 black and white keys. The numbers 1, 2, 3, 5, 8 and 13 are all Fibonacci numbers.

Page 2

The Puzzler 25

In the Past Numbers written in the Mayan numeral system will vary.

Page 3

What's the Problem? Jo is right. Whichever way the paints are mixed, they would get the same two colours.

The Puzzler

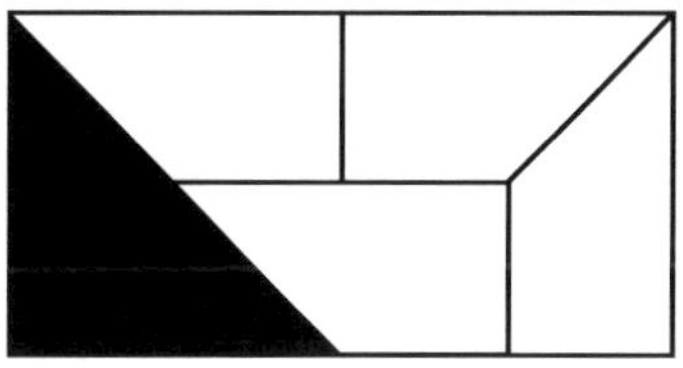

Page 4

Focus on Science Ratio of teeth – 3 : 1, number of turns – 3, ratio of turns – 1 : 3
Ratio of teeth – 3 : 1 : 3, ratio of turns – 1 : 3 : 1
Ratio of teeth – 3 : 1 : 2, ratio of turns – 2 : 6 : 3

EMU

numeral
A symbol or set of symbols used to represent a number, for example, the Arabic numeral 2 and the equivalent Roman numeral II.

Issue 10 Addition

Prerequisites for learning

- Identify and use patterns, relationships and properties of numbers
- Calculate mentally with whole numbers
- Use efficient written methods to add whole numbers

Resources pencil and paper; RCM 2: My notes (optional); RCM 3: Pupil self assessment booklet (optional); selection of supermarket advertisements / catalogues / flyers; selection of supermarket till receipts; material for making a poster; set of dominoes; computer with internet access

Teaching support

Page 1

At Home

- If it is not possible to find a selection of supermarket advertisements / catalogues / flyers, suggest the children consult the internet to plan their dinner.

Focus on Science

- If it is not possible to find a selection of supermarket till receipts, suggest the children consult the internet to find prices of different foods.

Page 2

Sports Update

- Other exercise movements may include: on the spot jogging, push-ups, crunches, stair climbing, lunges, spinning, squats and leg presses.

Page 2 continued

Sports update continued

- Children's posters may look something similar to the following:

Exercise	Difficulty rating (1: easy / 5: hard)
Toe touches	2
Star jumps	1
Sit ups	4
On the spot jogging	2
Crunches	5
Stair climbing	3
Lunges	3
Squats	5
Spinning	2
Leg presses	3

Easy workout

Exercise	Time
Star jumps	30 sec
On the spot jogging	1 min
Toe touches	30 sec
On the spot jogging	1 min
Toe touches	30 sec
On the spot jogging	1 min
Star jumps	30 sec

Let's Investigate

- For this activity children should not include their telephone number's area code.
- Children investigate separating the digits into one-digit, two-digit or three-digit numbers and finding the total each time. What is the largest / smallest total they can make?

Page 3

Looking for Patterns

- Tell the children what digit one or more of the letters represents (see Answers).

The Puzzler

- Do not provide the children with a set of dominoes.

Page 4

Looking for Patterns

- The first set of four calculations all have an even number of addends. Therefore all the addends can be made into pairs and added together without any addend remaining. Once the total of one pair of addends is calculated, this number is multiplied by the number of pairs to find the overall total.

Teaching support continued

Page 4 continued

Looking for Patterns continued

- The second set of four calculations all have an odd number of addends. Therefore the total of one pair of addends is calculated, this number is then multiplied by the number of pairs, and finally the centre addend in the calculation is added to find the overall total.

AfL

- How did you work out the solution to this puzzle? What strategies did you use? How else could you have gone about it?
- What patterns / relationships do you notice? What rules can you make? How does this help you find the total?
- How did you organise your thoughts? Did this help? What else could you have done? Why might this have been more effective?
- Have you accounted for all the different possibilities? How can you be sure?

Answers

Page 1

At Home Results of the investigation will vary.

Focus on Science Results of the investigation will vary.

Page 2

Sports Update Routines will vary.

Let's Investigate Results of the investigation will vary.

Page 3

Looking for Patterns 25 + 25 + 25 = 75

$$\begin{array}{r} 936 \\ +\ 63 \\ \hline 999 \end{array} \qquad \begin{array}{r} 147 \\ +\ 801 \\ \hline 948 \end{array}$$

Other calculations are possible.

The Puzzler

6	6	0
4		6
2	4	6

1	2	6	3
5			4
5			5
1	6	5	0

0	4	2	6	0
4				1
4				5
2				6
2	3	5	2	0

1	1	2	5	3	0
3					1
3					3
1					1
4					5
0	0	3	4	3	2

Other arrangements are possible.

Page 4

Looking for Patterns

Explanations will vary.
10 pairs of numbers that each total 21 ∴ 21 × 10 = 210
4 pairs of numbers that each total 19 ∴ 19 × 4 = 76
3 pairs of numbers that each total 35 ∴ 35 × 3 = 105
5 pairs of numbers that each total 113 ∴ 113 × 5 = 565

3 pairs of numbers that each total 8, plus number in the centre of the calculation (4) ∴ 8 × 3 + 4 = 28
4 pairs of numbers that each total 26, plus number in the centre of the calculation (13) ∴ 26 × 4 + 13 = 117
3 pairs of numbers that each total 140, plus number in the centre of the calculation (70) ∴ 140 × 3 + 70 = 490

EMU 

commutative law

Mathematical law that states that changing the order of the quantities in a calculation does not change the final result. This applies to both addition and multiplication calculations, i.e. $a + b = b + a$ and $ab = ba$.

Issue 11 Subtraction

Prerequisites for learning

- Identify and use patterns, relationships and properties of numbers
- Calculate mentally with whole numbers
- Use efficient written methods to add and subtract whole numbers
- Derive squares of numbers to 10 × 10

Resources pencil and paper; RCM 2: My notes (optional); RCM 3: Pupil self assessment booklet (optional); pack of playing cards; calculator

Teaching support

Page 1

The Puzzler

- Allow the children to use a calculator when trying out the trick on a friend.

Looking for Patterns

- Tell the children what digit one or more of the letters represents (see Answers).

Page 2

Let's Investigate

- Allow the children to use a calculator for this activity. Carrying out the calculations is the least important aspect of this activity. What's most important in this activity is the children's ability to identify patterns and relationships, and to offer a logical explanation as to why this happens.

What's the Problem?

- One method of working out the answer to this problem is to find pairs of numbers from 1 to 99 that total 100 and add the first pair, subtract the second pair, add the third pair, subtract the fourth pair and continue this pattern, i.e. (1 + 99) – (2 + 98) + (3 + 97) – (4 + 96) .... This can be written as 1 – 2 + 3 – 4 + 5 … + 95 – 96 + 97 – 98 + 99.
  As a result of pairing numbers in this way, the only unpaired number is 50, the median number.
  This is the same method described in the Looking for Patterns activity on page 4 of Issue 10. If appropriate, discuss the similarities between these two activities with the children.

Page 3

What's the Problem?

- Provide the children with either of the following:

  61 □ 55 □ 5 □ (5 □ 5) = 0

  61 – □ – □ – (□ ÷ □) = 0

The Puzzler

- Give the children one or two of the digits for each of the calculations, e.g.

  3□5 – 5□ = 282   □1□ – 13□ = 380

Let's Investigate

- This method of subtraction involves increasing both the minuend and the subtrahend by the same amount, so that the subtrahend becomes a multiple of 100 (or 10 or 1000). This then makes the subtraction easier, e.g.

1243	1243 + 52	1295
– 748	– 748 + 52	– 800
		495

- Discuss with the children how both the minuend and the subtrahend can be increased by a different amount, e.g.

1243	1243 + 252	1495
– 748	– 748 + 252	– 1000
		495

- Children use the method for subtraction calculations involving combinations of three-digit and four-digit numbers, e.g. 2436 – 857 and 3452 – 1768.

Page 4

Let's Investigate

- Ensure children understand that the number in the middle of each line is the difference between the two numbers at either end of the line.

The Puzzler

- Tell the children that there are two possible numbers for the second puzzle. Can they find them both?

AfL

- What is the answer to the problem? How did you work it out? What strategies did you use?
- What is the solution to this puzzle?
- Use your own words to explain to me this method of subtraction.
- Is this a method that you might use regularly? Why / Why not?
- How would you work out the answer to this calculation? Why would you use this method?
- Have you accounted for all the possibilities? How do you know?

Answers

Page 1

The Puzzler No answers required.

Looking for Patterns 84 – 46 = 38

$$\begin{array}{r} 510 \\ -\ 45 \\ \hline 465 \\ \hline \end{array} \qquad \begin{array}{r} 658 \\ -\ 206 \\ \hline 452 \\ \hline \end{array}$$

Other calculations are possible.

Page 2

Let's Investigate The sum of the numbers in Steps 1 to 5 is the same as the number in Step 7.
The sum of the numbers in Steps 1 and 2 is 99 999, one less than 100 000.
The sum of the numbers in Steps 3 and 4 is also 99 999.
Together, these total 2 less than 200 000.
So, to get the answer in Step 7, you add 200 000 less 2 to the number in Step 5.

What's the Problem? 1 – 2 + 3 – 4 + 5 … + 47 – 48 + 49 + 50 + 51 – 52 + 53 … + 95 – 96 + 97 – 98 + 99 = 50
Other solutions are possible.

Page 3

What's the Problem? 61 – 55 – 5 – (5 ÷ 5) = 0
Other calculations are possible.

The Puzzler 335 – 53 = 282
515 – 135 = 380
553 – 325 = 228
653 – 357 = 296

Let's Investigate 495

846 − 358 = ___	888 − 400 = 488	495 − 159 = ___	536 − 200 = 336
634 − 347 = ___	687 − 400 = 287	663 − 448 = ___	715 − 500 = 215
702 − 514 = ___	788 − 600 = 188		

Calculations and explanations will vary.

Page 4

Let's Investigate A set of three numbers (*a*, *a*, 0) is formed which repeats forever.

The Puzzler 80
25 or 36

EMU

subtrahend

A number that is to be taken away from another number, e.g. in the calculation 10 – 6 = 4, the 6 is the subtrahend.

Issue 12 Multiplication

Prerequisites for learning

- Identify and use patterns, relationships and properties of numbers
- Derive and recall multiplication facts up to 10 × 10
- Derive and recall multiples of numbers to 10 up to the tenth multiple
- Identify the doubles of two-digit numbers; use these to calculate other doubles
- Calculate mentally with whole numbers
- Use efficient written methods to multiply whole numbers
- Solve logic puzzles
- Understand simple expressions and formulae in words and symbols

Resources pencil and paper; RCM 2: My notes (optional); RCM 3: Pupil self assessment booklet (optional); RCM 4: Napier's Rods; RCM 5: Square grids; scissors; calculator (optional); computer with internet access

Teaching support

Page 1

Looking for Patterns

- Tell the children what digit one or more of the letters represents (see Answers).

Focus on Science

- Suggest the children record the information in a table, e.g.

Buttercups (5 petals)		Clovers (3 leaves)		Total number of petals and leaves (Buttercups + Clovers)
Number of flowers	Number of petals	Number of flowers	Number of leaves	
5	25	23	69	94
6	30	22	66	96
7	35	21	63	98
8	40	20	60	100
9	45	19	57	102
10	50	18	54	104
11	55	17	51	106
12	60	16	48	108
13	65	15	45	110

Page 1 continued

Money Matters

- Once children have solved the problem, discuss the strategies that different children used. Which strategies were most efficient?

Page 2

Looking for Patterns

- What patterns can be created if two different sets of multiples are shaded on the same grid?
- What if the grid numbering does not start at 1?

4	5	6	7	8	9
10	11	12			

Let's Investigate

- Children investigate what happens if you start with a multiplication fact involving decimals, e.g. 2·3 × 6.
- Children investigate what happens if you start with an addition number fact and double each of the two addends.

Page 3

Famous Mathematicians

- Before setting children off to work independently on this activity, ensure that they are confident in using Napier's Rods to solve multiplication calculations.
- Children investigate the life and work of John Napier.

Page 4

Focus on Science

- Before working out the approximations, suggest the children keep a diary for a week, noting down how long they spend each day looking at a screen, either a computer screen or a television screen.
- After the children have completed their diary, discuss with them how their viewing habits differ during holidays. This will enable the children to make a more accurate approximation.

Looking for Patterns

- As with the Looking for Patterns activity on page 3 of *Enriching Maths* Volume 4, Issue 19, this activity introduces children to the distributive law of multiplication, i.e. $a \times (b + c) = a \times b + a \times c$.

AfL

- Explain to me this method for multiplication. What do you think of this method? Is it a method that you might ever use? Why / Why not?
- What do you notice? What is the pattern? What generalisations can you make?
- What answer did you get for this problem? When you first looked at the problem how did you begin to work it out?
- Talk me through your method of working out the problem.

Answers

Page 1

Looking for Patterns $34 \times 6 = 204$ $52 \times 10 = 520$ $7 \times 100 = 700$
Other calculations are possible.

Focus on Science 13 buttercups, 15 clovers

Money Matters 20 of each value of stamp

Page 2

Looking for Patterns Patterns will vary.

Let's Investigate When you double both the numbers in the multiplication calculation, the new product is always four times (or double and double again) the previous answer.

When you double one of the numbers in the multiplication calculation, the new product is always two times (or double) the previous answer.

Page 3

Famous Mathematicians No answers required.

Page 4

Technology Today Results of the investigation will vary.

Looking for Patterns

$$42 \times 103 = (42 \times 100) + (42 \times 3) = 4200 + 126 = 4326$$

$$37 \times 106 = (37 \times 100) + (37 \times 6) = 3700 + 222 = 3922$$

$$58 \times 95 = (58 \times 100) - (58 \times 5) = 5800 - 290 = 5510$$

$$62 \times 97 = (62 \times 100) - (62 \times 3) = 6200 - 186 = 6014$$

EMU

product
The result of a multiplication of two or more quantities, e.g. in the calculation $5 \times 4 = 20$, the number 20 is the product.

Issue 13

Division

Prerequisites for learning

- Identify and use patterns, relationships and properties of numbers
- Derive and recall multiplication facts up to 10 × 10 and the corresponding division facts
- Derive and recall multiples of numbers to 10 up to the tenth multiple
- Identify pairs of factors of two-digit whole numbers
- Calculate mentally with whole numbers
- Use efficient written methods to add, subtract, multiply and divide whole numbers

Resources pencil and paper; RCM 2: My notes (optional); RCM 3: Pupil self assessment booklet (optional); calculator (optional); computer with internet access

Teaching support

Page 1

Around the World

- Children will need to consult the internet for this activity to find out both the postal charges for within the UK and abroad, and also for the distances between the UK and Europe, Australia and the USA.
- Ensure that the children realise that they don't need to be 100% accurate for the distance that each letter has to travel. An approximation will not only make calculating easier, but will also be accurate enough to evaluate which letter is the cheapest per mile / per kilometre.

Looking for Patterns

- Tell the children what digit one or more of the letters represents (see Answers).

What's the Problem?

- The original number of conkers was a multiple of 4, i.e. 8 conkers between 2 children, 12 conkers between 3, 16 conkers between 4, 20 conkers between 5, 24 conkers between 6, etc.
- When one conker and two more children were added, there were enough for each child to have exactly three conkers. Therefore, originally there must have been 20 conkers and 5 children.

Page 2

The Arts Roundup

- The average cost per episode of a television programme is £250 000.

Teaching support continued

Page 2 continued

Let's Investigate

- Ensure children understand what a palindromic number is.

Page 3

Let's Investigate

- Ask the children to investigate what happens if you start with a two-digit or a four-digit number. If you start with a four-digit number there are 12 different two-digit numbers. (The final result for a two-digit number is always 11. The final result for a four-digit number is always 33.)

Looking for Patterns

- The important aspect of this activity is not performing the calculations, but rather in being able to predict what will happen, and then once the calculations have been completed, in being able to explain why this happens.
- Allow the children to use a calculator once they have made their predictions.

Page 4

Looking for Patterns

- You may need to draw children's attention to the most and least significant digits in each of the dividends of the four seven-digit numbers, i.e. **1** 999 99**8**, **2** 999 99**7**, **3** 999 99**6**, **4** 999 99**5**. What do the children notice about the total of these two digits in each of the seven-digit numbers? (They total 9.) Does this help them identify the special relationship?

Looking for Patterns

- In this activity children need to identify the pattern in both the dividend and the quotient.
- Allow the children to use a calculator.

AfL

- Tell me what you have discovered about the cost of posting a letter / television advertising.
- What generalisations can you make?
- What predictions did you make? What patterns / relationships did you notice?
- How did you work out the answer?
- Did you use trial and improvement to help you work out the answer? Where did you begin? Why did you start there?
- How did knowing about multiples / factors / divisors help you with this problem / puzzle? What about applying tests of divisibility?

Answers

Page 1

Around the World
Results of the investigation will vary.

Looking for Patterns
$45 \div 5 = 9$ $81 \div 6 = 13{\cdot}5$ $730 \div 10 = 73$
Other calculations are possible.

What's the Problem?
21 conkers between 7 children.

Page 2

The Arts Roundup
Results of the investigation will vary.

Let's Investigate
The statement is false. Only palindromic numbers with an even number of digits are divisible by 11, e.g. 66, 1661, 437 734.

Page 3

Let's Investigate
The final answer is always 22.

Looking for Patterns
The final answer is always 37. This is because the answer to any of the nine calculations, such as $444 \div 4$, is always 111; and $111 \div 3 = 37$

Page 4

Looking for Patterns
$999\,999 \div 7 = 142\,857$
$1\,999\,998 \div 14 = 142\,857$
$2\,999\,997 \div 21 = 142\,857$
$3\,999\,996 \div 28 = 142\,857$
$4\,999\,995 \div 35 = 142\,857$

Looking for Patterns
The sum of all the digits in each of the dividends is 54, i.e.
$9 + 9 + 9 + 9 + 9 + 9 = 54$
$1 + 9 + 9 + 9 + 9 + 9 + 8 = 54$
$2 + 9 + 9 + 9 + 9 + 9 + 7 = 54$
$3 + 9 + 9 + 9 + 9 + 9 + 6 = 54$
$4 + 9 + 9 + 9 + 9 + 9 + 5 = 54$

EMU

generalisation
A general statement or conclusion that is obtained from and applies to a number of cases.

Issue 14 Mixed operations

Prerequisites for learning

- Identify and use patterns, relationships and properties of numbers
- Derive and recall multiplication facts up to 10 × 10 and the corresponding division facts
- Derive and recall multiples of numbers to 10 up to the tenth multiple
- Calculate mentally with whole numbers
- Use efficient written methods to add, subtract, multiply and divide whole numbers
- Understand and use the order of operations, including brackets

Resources pencil and paper; RCM 2: My notes (optional); RCM 3: Pupil self assessment booklet (optional); RCM 6: Function machines; selection of travel / holiday brochures; calculator; data handling software; computer with internet access

Teaching support

Page 1

Money Matters

- Ask the children to create their spreadsheet on the computer using an appropriate data handling software program.
- Encourage the children to be as detailed as possible with their expenses sheet, accounting for all possible expenses.

Around the World

- This is a very open-ended investigation. You may want to leave it open for the children, or you may wish to narrow the investigation to focus on one or more of the following:
  - Difference in prices between different airlines
  - Difference in prices between different classes
  - Difference in prices at different times of the day
  - Difference in prices at different times of the year

Page 2

Looking for Patterns

- You may need to spend some time before the children start on this activity discussing with them the concept of algebra. Use known rules and formulae, such as calculating the area or perimeter of a rectangle, to illustrate the concept.

Page 2 continued

Looking for Patterns continued

- If appropriate, discuss with the children the algebraic convention for omitting the multiplication sign when writing an algebraic expression, i.e. $2 \times (n + 3) = 2(n + 3)$.
- You may also wish to discuss with the children how the cloud (☁) can be substituted with a letter such as *a*, *n* or *x*.

Page 3

The Puzzler

- Children use the function machines at the top half of the RCM to write their own, two-step puzzles.

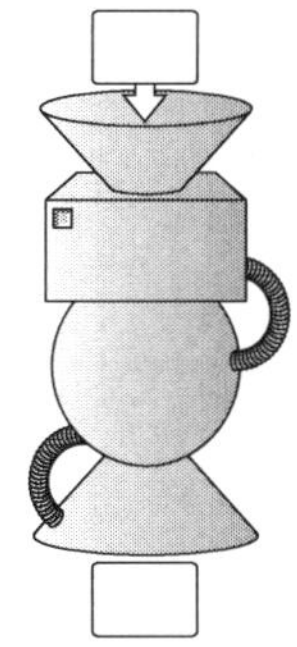

- Children use the function machines at the bottom half of the RCM to write their own, three-step puzzles.

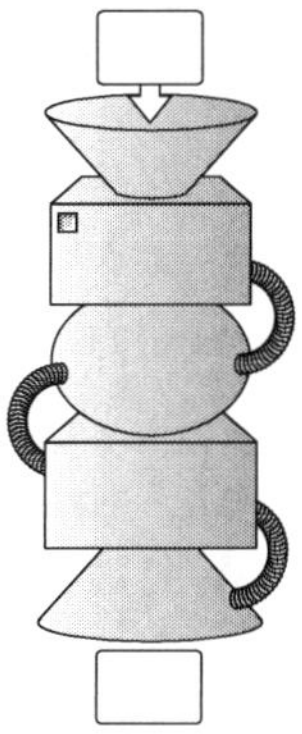

Technology Today

- When pairs of children have completed the activity, ask them to compare the different calculations they performed to get each of the answers without using the '4' key. Which is the most efficient method? Can the children work together to find an even more efficient method?
- What if the '2' and '6' keys on the calculator were broken?

Page 4

Looking for Patterns

- Once children have completed the activity, discuss and compare the strategies that the children used to solve the different grid problems. Were some easier to solve than others? Why?
- What would happen if the part of each of the grids in the issue were not the top of the grid, but taken from the middle of the grid?
- What happens if you shade two different sets of multiples on the same grid?

Teaching support continued

Page 4 continued

Let's Investigate

- Can the children find more than one way to make some of the numbers?
- Can the children find three digits that will make all the odd numbers from 1 to 29 using any of the four operations?

AfL

- How did you spend your £2000?
- How did you work out the answer to this problem? How did you begin?
- What patterns did you notice? Can you explain this in words / using symbols?
- How can you explain this using letters and symbols?
- Without using the number four, what calculations did you have to do to work out the answer?
- What is the correct answer? Why is it correct?

Answers

Page 1

Money Matters Expenses sheets will vary.

Around the World Results of the investigation will vary.

Page 2

Looking for Patterns Algebraic expressions will vary. However, may be similar to either of the following:

Think of a number.	☁	a
Multiply it by 2.	☁ × 2	$a \times 2$
Add 4.	(☁ × 2) + 4	$(a \times 2) + 4$
Halve it.	☁ + 2	$a + 2$
Subtract 2.	☁	a

Page 3

The Puzzler 3 6 27 24

Technology Today Calculations will vary.

Page 4

Looking for Patterns

Large complete grid: Multiples of 4 are shaded.
1st partial grid: Multiples of 5 are shaded. The width of the grid could be 8, 13, 18, …
2nd partial grid: Multiples of 7 are shaded. The width of the grid could be 10, 17, 24, …
3rd partial grid: Multiples of 6 are shaded. The width of the grid could be 11, 17, 23, …
4th partial grid: Multiples of 3 are shaded. The width of the grid could be 8, 11, 14 …

Let's Investigate

6 = 1 + 9 – 4
8 = 9 – 1
10 = 9 + 1
12 = 9 + 4 – 1
14 = 9 + 4 + 1
16 = 4 × 4
18 = 14 + 4
20 = (9 – 4) × 4
22 = 41 – 19
24 = 19 + 4 + 1
26 = (9 × 4) – (9 + 1)
28 = (9 × 4) – 9 + 1
30 = 49 – 19
Other answers are possible.

EMU

formula

A rule or principle represented in symbols, numbers, or letters, often written in the form of an equation.

Issue 15 Mixed operations

Prerequisites for learning

- Identify and use patterns, relationships and properties of numbers
- Recall quickly multiplication facts up to 10 × 10 and use them to multiply pairs of multiples of 10 and 100; derive quickly corresponding division facts
- Derive squares of numbers to at least 10 × 10
- Calculate mentally with whole numbers
- Use efficient written methods to add, subtract, multiply and divide whole numbers
- Understand and use the order of operations, including brackets
- Understand simple expressions and formulae in words and symbols
- Make estimations and approximations.

Resources pencil and paper; RCM 2: My notes (optional); RCM 3: Pupil self assessment booklet (optional); set of dominoes; calculator; school's electricity bill (optional); data handling software; computer with internet access

Teaching support

Page 1

What's the Problem?

- You may need to spend some time before the children start on this activity discussing with them the concept of algebra. Use known rules and formulae, such as calculating the area or perimeter of a rectangle, to illustrate the concept.
- Ensure children realise that the values of *a* and *b* are the same for both the addition and the multiplication calculation.

Let's Investigate

- Ask the children to use a calculator to check that the short-cut method for finding the square of a number ending in 5 works.

Page 2

Technology Today

- Ask the children to write a calculation that illustrates the problem, i.e. (7 × 10) – (5 × 2) = 60.

The Puzzler

- Ensure children are familiar with how a magic square works.
- Do not provide the children with a set of dominoes.

Page 3

Money Matters

- This activity will probably take the children some time to complete. Not only are they required to find out about the cost of growing their own fruit and vegetables, they also need to find out about the cost of similar fruit and vegetables from a supermarket, and compare the difference.
- Another important aspect of this activity is the justifications that children offer to support their conclusions.

Focus on Science

- A watt is a unit for measuring electrical power.

  1 kW (kilowatt) = 1000 watts

  1 kWh (kilowatt hour) = 1000 watts of electricity used for one hour
- Approximately 20% of all electrical consumption is from lighting.
- If possible, show the children the school's electricity bill and talk about it with them. Discuss how there are many different appliances and devices in the school that use electricity, but that lighting accounts for almost one-fifth of the total electricity bill.

Page 4

Money Matters

- Ask the children to create a spreadsheet of the expenses on the computer using an appropriate data handling software.

The Puzzler

- Provide the children with one number in each calculation, e.g. ◇ + 3 − ◇ = 0 (see Answers).

What's the Problem?

- Once the children have completed the activity, provide an opportunity for children to talk about, and compare, their methods for working out the answer to the problem. Which were the most effective strategies?

AfL

- What are the values of *a* and *b*? How did you work this out?
- What can you tell me about square numbers?
- How did you work out the answer to this problem / puzzle? Where did you start?
- What did you discover about 'growing your own' / the amount of electricity used by the lights in your classroom in a year / the cost of a wedding?

Answers

Page 1

What's the Problem? The values of *a* and *b* (and *b* and *a*) are 7 and 16.

Let's Investigate The method works for any number ending in 5.

Page 2

Technology Today Lakshmi hit 7 flying saucers.

The Puzzler Many solutions are possible. Here is one:

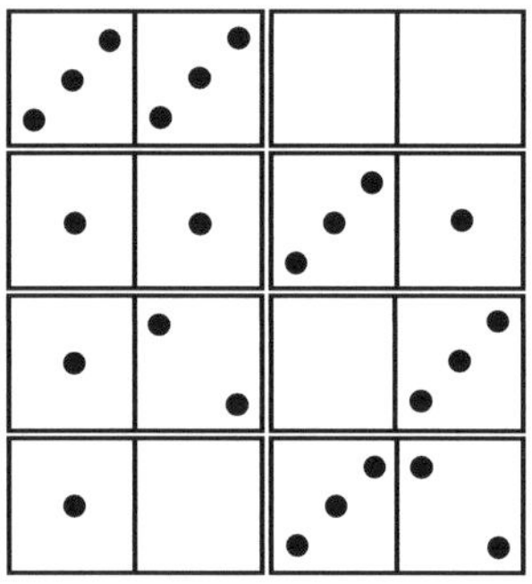

The magic number is 6.

Page 3

Money Matters Results of the investigation will vary.

Focus on Science Results of the investigation will vary.

Page 4

Money Matters Results of the investigation will vary.

The Puzzler

5 + 3 − 8 = 0
16 − 3 × 5 = 1
16 ÷ (12 − 8) = 4
16 ÷ 8 + 3 = 5
3 × 16 ÷ 8 = 6
(8 + 12) ÷ 5 = 4

Other answers are possible.

What's the Problem? Pascal has baked 18 loaves of bread by 5:00 a.m.

EMU

average

The degree to which something is typical of a group or class of people or things.

A number that can be regarded as typical of a group of numbers, calculated by adding the numbers together, then dividing the total by the amount of numbers.

Issue 16 Mixed operations

Prerequisites for learning

- Identify and use patterns, relationships and properties of numbers
- Calculate mentally with whole numbers
- Use efficient written methods to add, subtract, multiply and divide whole numbers
- Understand the term 'percent'
- Interpret pie charts
- Find fractions of numbers, quantities or shapes
- Make estimations and approximations

Resources pencil and paper; RCM 2: My notes (optional); RCM 3: Pupil self assessment booklet (optional); RCM 5: Square grids; stopwatch; 'culture / arts' section from several Sunday newspapers; calculator

Teaching support

Page 1

In the Past

- Average respiratory rate reported in a healthy adult at rest is usually given as 12 breaths per minute.

  12 breaths per minute = 720 per hour = 17 280 per day
  = 6 307 200 per year.

Focus on Science

- Average respiratory rates vary by age, but for most children this is 16 – 25 breaths per minute.

Page 2

Looking for Patterns

- Ask the children to look for other arrangements of numbers on the grid, e.g.

  5 × 15 = 75
  7 × 13 = 91
  91 – 75 = 16

1	2	3	4
5	6	7	8
9	10	11	12
13	14	15	16

Teaching support continued

Page 2 continued

Money Matters

- This activity includes two mathematical concepts that the children may not yet have been formally taught – percentages and pie charts. If this is the case, before setting the children to work on the activity independently, spend time introducing and discussing these two concepts.

Page 3

Money Matters

- Ensure children realise that:
  - 10% is equivalent to $\frac{10}{100}$ or $\frac{1}{10}$ and can be calculated by moving the decimal point one place to the left.
  - 20% is equivalent to $\frac{20}{100}$ or $\frac{2}{10}$ and can be calculated by finding 10%, then multiplying this amount by two.
  - 15% is equivalent to $\frac{15}{100}$ or $\frac{3}{20}$ and can be calculated by finding 10%, then adding half of this amount to the 10%.

Page 4

Looking for Patterns

- Ensure children are familiar with the terms 'consecutive numbers', 'sum' and 'product'.
- Tell the children that all the consecutive numbers, in all eight questions, are less than 40.

The Arts Roundup

- Ensure that the 'culture / arts' section from each of the Sunday newspapers contains a list of the bestselling books for the past week.

AfL

- What patterns / relationships can you tell me? What generalisations can you make?
- How did you work out what the numbers were?
- Did you use trial and improvement? Where did you start? Why did you start with that number?
- How did you arrive at your estimations / approximations?
- What does the word 'percent' mean? Where have you seen it used? Why do you think we often express fractions / proportions as a percentage?
- What can you tell me about pie charts? How do you 'read' a pie chart?

Answers

Page 1

In the Past

Queen Elizabeth I took at least 70 × 6 307 200 = 441 504 000 breaths.
Albert Einstein took at least 76 × 6 307 200 = 479 347 200 breaths.
William Shakespeare took at least 52 × 6 307 200 = 327 974 400 breaths.
Sir Isaac Newton took at least 84 × 6 307 200 = 529 804 800 breaths.

Focus on Science

Results of the investigation will vary.

Page 2

Looking for Patterns

The difference is always the same as the number of columns in the grid.

Money Matters

Housing: £4400
Food: £6600
Clothing: £2200
Savings: £3300
Other expenses: £5500

Page 3

Money Matters

Sub-total: £28
Service charge (10%): £2.80
Total: £30.80

Sub-total: £45
Service charge (10%): £4.50
Total: £49.50

Sub-total: £37
Service charge (20%): £7.40
Total: £44.40

Sub-total: £48
Service charge (15%): £7.20
Total: £55.20

Page 4

Looking for Patterns

14 and 15
12 and 13
21, 22 and 23
17, 18 and 19
36 and 38
14 and 16
18, 20, 22
17 and 19
Explanations will vary.

The Arts Roundup

Results of the investigation will vary.

EMU

income

The amount of money received on a regular basis as payment for work, goods or services.

Issue 17 Calculating with fractions

Prerequisites for learning

- Read and write proper fractions, e.g. $\frac{3}{7}$, $\frac{9}{10}$, interpreting the denominator as the parts of a whole and the numerator as the number of parts
- Identify equivalent fractions
- Interpret mixed numbers
- Simplify fractions by cancelling common factors
- Relate fractions to multiplication and division
- Find fractions of numbers, quantities or shapes
- Use mental methods of calculation with fractions
- Use understanding of place value to multiply and divide whole numbers and decimals by 10, 100 or 1000

Resources pencil and paper; RCM 2: My notes (optional); RCM 3: Pupil self assessment booklet (optional); calculator (optional)

Teaching support

Page 1

What's the Problem?

- The adults occupy $\frac{45}{60} = \frac{3}{4}$ of the viewing platform, so $\frac{1}{4}$ of it is free.
  $\frac{1}{4} \times 96$ children = 24 children

What's the Problem?

- Once the children have completed the activity, provide an opportunity for children to talk about, and compare, their methods for working out the answer to the problem. Which were the most effective strategies?

Page 2

What's the Problem?

- Suggest children work backwards, i.e.

  Sammi had £8 after giving her brother half, so £8 is half of £16.

  She had £16 after spending one-third on a CD, so £16 is two-thirds of £24.

  She had £24 after spending one-fifth on coffee and cake, so £24 is four-fifths of £30.

  She had £30 after spending one-quarter on a skirt and one-quarter on a top, so £30 is half of £60.

Page 2 continued

Focus on Science

- 'Rose gold', a pink coloured gold, is often made from $\frac{3}{4}$ gold, $\frac{1}{5}$ copper and the rest silver. If the 18 carat gold ring and chain were made from rose gold, calculate the weight of copper and silver in each of them.

Page 3

What's the Problem?

- Farmer Dobbs keeps $\frac{1}{4} \times 430 = 107{\cdot}5$ hectares.
- Ask the children to check that the youngest child receives 0 hectares by adding the fractions. If the fractions total 1, then they are correct: the youngest child receives 0 hectares.

  $\frac{1}{4} + \frac{3}{10} + \frac{1}{4} + \frac{2}{10}$
  $= \frac{5}{20} + \frac{6}{20} + \frac{5}{20} + \frac{4}{20}$
  $= \frac{20}{20}$

What's the Problem?

- The number of children around the table must be divisible by 4 ($\frac{1}{4}$) and by 3 ($\frac{1}{3}$). Therefore the lowest common multiple is 12. Using trial and improvement try 12:

  $\frac{1}{2} \times 12 = 6$ drink water, $\frac{1}{4} \times 12 = 3$ drink milk, 2 drink both: so this covers $6 + 3 - 2 = 7$ children.

  $\frac{1}{3} \times 12 = 4$ drink neither: so $7 + 4 = 11$ children altogether. This is not enough children.
- The next common multiple of 3 and 4 is 24. See if it works:

  $\frac{1}{2} \times 24 = 12$ drink water, $\frac{1}{4} \times 24 = 6$ drink milk, 2 drink both: so this covers $12 + 6 - 2 = 16$ children.

  $\frac{1}{3} \times 24 = 8$ drink neither: so $16 + 8 = 24$ children.

Page 4

Money Matters

- If the children have completed *Enriching Maths* Volume 4 Issue 15, ask them to compare their results from the Money Matters activity on page 4 with these answers.

Teaching support continued

Page 4 continued

Let's Investigate

- Ensure children can convert mixed numbers to improper fractions and vice versa.
- Pairs of fractions that total 2 can be made in the following ways: $\frac{1}{2} + 1\frac{1}{2}$, $\frac{1}{4} + 1\frac{3}{4}$, $\frac{3}{4} + 1\frac{1}{4}$, $\frac{1}{3} + 1\frac{2}{3}$, $\frac{2}{3} + 1\frac{1}{3}$, …
  For example, $\frac{2}{4} + \frac{9}{6}$, $\frac{2}{8} + \frac{7}{4}$, $\frac{6}{8} + \frac{5}{4}$, $\frac{2}{6} + \frac{5}{3}$, $\frac{2}{3} + \frac{8}{6}$, …
- Pairs of fractions that total 3 can be made in the following ways: $1\frac{1}{2} + 1\frac{1}{2}$, $\frac{1}{2} + 2\frac{1}{2}$, $\frac{3}{4} + 2\frac{1}{4}$, $\frac{1}{3} + 2\frac{2}{3}$, $\frac{2}{3} + 2\frac{1}{3}$, …
  For example, $\frac{3}{2} + \frac{9}{6}$, $\frac{4}{8} + \frac{5}{2}$, $\frac{6}{8} + \frac{9}{4}$, $\frac{2}{6} + \frac{8}{3}$, $\frac{4}{6} + \frac{7}{3}$, …
- Pairs of fractions with a difference of 1 can be made in the following ways: $1\frac{1}{2} - \frac{1}{2}$, $1\frac{2}{3} - \frac{2}{3}$, $1\frac{1}{3} - \frac{1}{3}$, $1\frac{1}{4} - \frac{1}{4}$, …
  For example, $\frac{3}{2} - \frac{4}{8}$, $\frac{5}{3} - \frac{6}{9}$, $\frac{4}{3} - \frac{2}{6}$, $\frac{5}{4} - \frac{2}{8}$, …
- Pairs of fractions with a difference of 2 can be made in the following ways: $3\frac{1}{2} - 1\frac{1}{2}$, $2\frac{2}{3} - \frac{2}{3}$, $2\frac{1}{3} - \frac{1}{3}$, $2\frac{1}{4} - \frac{1}{4}$, …
  For example, $\frac{7}{2} - \frac{6}{4}$, $\frac{8}{3} - \frac{4}{6}$, $\frac{7}{3} - \frac{2}{6}$, $\frac{9}{4} - \frac{2}{8}$, …

AfL

- When you were working out the answer to this problem / puzzle did you always think of these numbers as proper fractions or did you convert them in your mind to decimal fractions? Did this help? How?
- How did you work out the fraction of this amount?
- Did you use trial and improvement to work out the answer? How did this help?
- Explain to me how you found two fractions with a total of 2 or 3?
- What about with a difference of 1 or 2?

Answers

Page 1

What's the Problem? 24 children

What's the Problem? At the start of the game Marcus had 32 football cards.

Page 2

What's the Problem? £60

Focus on Science
18 carat gold ring: 18 g
12 carat gold brooch: 135 g
18 carat gold chain: 321 g
24 carat gold necklace: 137 g
12 carat gold bracelet: 147 g

Page 3

What's the Problem?

Farmer Dobbs: 107·5 hectares
Eldest child: 129 hectares
Second child: 107·5 hectares
Third child: 86 hectares
Youngest child: 0 hectares

What's the Problem?

24 children

Page 4

Money Matters

Wedding reception: £6475
Flowers & decoration: £925
Clothing for bride, groom and attendants: £2775
Wedding cake: £370
Photography: £1850
Honeymoon: £3700
Transport, stationary, gifts etc.: £2405

Let's Investigate

Pairs of fractions that total 2:

$\frac{2}{4} + \frac{9}{6}, \frac{4}{8} + \frac{9}{6}, \frac{6}{9} + \frac{4}{3}, \frac{2}{8} + \frac{7}{4}, \frac{6}{8} + \frac{5}{4}, \frac{2}{6} + \frac{5}{3}, \frac{2}{3} + \frac{8}{6}$

Pairs of fractions that total 3:

$\frac{3}{2} + \frac{9}{6}, \frac{4}{8} + \frac{5}{2}, \frac{6}{8} + \frac{9}{4}, \frac{2}{6} + \frac{8}{3}, \frac{4}{6} + \frac{7}{3}, \frac{3}{6} + \frac{5}{2}$

Pairs of fractions with a difference of 1:

$\frac{8}{2} - \frac{9}{3}, \frac{3}{2} - \frac{4}{8}, \frac{7}{4} - \frac{6}{8}, \frac{8}{6} - \frac{3}{9}, \frac{4}{3} - \frac{2}{6}, \frac{9}{3} - \frac{4}{2}, \frac{9}{3} - \frac{8}{4}, \frac{5}{4} - \frac{2}{8}, \frac{5}{2} - \frac{6}{4}, \frac{5}{3} - \frac{6}{9}$

Pairs of fractions with a difference of 2:

$\frac{8}{2} - \frac{6}{3}, \frac{7}{2} - \frac{6}{4}, \frac{5}{2} - \frac{4}{8}, \frac{8}{3} - \frac{4}{6}, \frac{7}{3} - \frac{2}{6}, \frac{9}{4} - \frac{2}{8}$

EMU

improper fraction

A fraction in which the numerator is equal to or greater than the denominator, such as $\frac{3}{2}$.

Issue 18

Calculating – General

Prerequisites for learning

- Identify and use patterns, relationships and properties of numbers
- Derive squares of numbers to at least 10 × 10
- Calculate mentally with whole numbers
- Use efficient written methods to add, subtract, multiply and divide whole numbers
- Find fractions of numbers, quantities or shapes
- Understand simple expressions and formulae in words and symbols
- Make estimations and approximations

Resources pencil and paper; RCM 2: My notes (optional); RCM 3: Pupil self assessment booklet (optional); calculator; computer with internet access

Teaching support

Page 1

Let's Investigate

- Ask the children to use a calculator to check that the short-cut method for finding the square of a decimal ending in 0·5 works.

Let's Investigate

- Children investigate what other numbers they can make using no more than four 9s.

Page 2

The Puzzler

- Once the children have answered the three questions to the puzzle, provide an opportunity for children to talk about, and compare, their methods for finding the solutions to the puzzle.

Money Matters

- Children could combine this activity and the Money Matters activity on page 3 into one, looking at how both debit and credit cards work and their similarities and differences.
- Imagining that the school has formed a bank, the children create a school debit card.
- Children give reasons as to why all debit and credit cards are the same shape and size.

Page 3

Money Matters

- Children could combine this activity and the Money Matters activity on page 2 into one, looking at how both credit and debit cards work and their similarities and differences.
- Imagining that the school has formed a bank, ask the children to create a school credit card.
- Children give reasons as to why all credit and debit cards are the same shape and size.

At Home

- Once the children have completed the activity, ensure that there is an opportunity in class for pairs or groups of children to discuss their results.

Page 4

The Language of Maths

- Ensure children understand that the sign '≠' means 'not equal to'.
- Before children work independently on this activity you may need to discuss with them the concept of a mathematical formula. Also ensure that the children have a good understanding of the four different laws of mathematics and the formulae for expressing these.

Focus on Science

- Suggest the children work in pairs. One method of working out an approximate number of hairs on their forearm is to measure and count the number of hairs on a small square area of their arm and then scale up.

AfL

- What can you tell me about finding the square of decimal numbers?
- This problem involved finding fractions of amounts. How did you work out the answer to this problem?
- What patterns / relationships did you notice about these numbers?
- What did you discover about debit cards / credit cards?
- Is there a big difference in price between different brands of groceries?
- How did you work out the approximation? How accurate do you think it is?
- Explain to me some of the different laws of mathematics.

Answers

Page 1

Let's Investigate It is possible to use this method for any number ending in 0·5. Results of the investigation will vary.

Let's Investigate

9 × 9 = 81	9 × 9 + 9 = 90
9 – 9 = 0	9 ÷ 9 = 1
(9 + 9) ÷ 9 = 2	99 ÷ 9 = 11
(99 ÷ 9) + 9 = 20	(9 + 9) × 9 = 162

Page 2

The Puzzler £200
£40
£32

Money Matters Results of the investigation will vary.

Page 3

Money Matters Results of the investigation will vary.

At Home Results of the investigation will vary.

Page 4

The Language of Maths

Commutative Law of Addition
When adding two numbers, the order of the addition does not matter.

Commutative Law of Multiplication
When multiplying two numbers, the order of the multiplication does not matter.

Associative law of Multiplication
When multiplying three numbers, the order of the multiplication does not matter.

Distributive Law
When multiplying the sum of two numbers by a third number, it is the same as multiplying each of the two numbers by the third number and adding together the two results.

Calculations for each of the above laws will vary.

Focus on Science Results of the investigation will vary.

EMU

coupon
A voucher that entitles somebody to a discount, refund or gift, generally issued as a promotion.

Issue 19

Calculating – General

Prerequisites for learning

- Derive and recall multiples of numbers to 10 up to the tenth multiple
- Identify pairs of factors of two-digit whole numbers
- Calculate mentally with whole numbers
- Use efficient written methods to add, subtract, multiply and divide whole numbers
- Understand and use the order of operations, including brackets
- Understand simple expressions and formulae in words and symbols
- Make estimations and approximations

Resources pencil and paper; RCM 2: My notes (optional); RCM 3: Pupil self assessment booklet (optional); stopwatch; several different bank statements (optional); calculator; computer

Teaching support

Page 1

Focus on Science

- Ensure that children realise that when calculating the total number of times they blink in one day, they must only use the number of hours that they are awake.
- The important aspect of this investigation is how children scale up their amount for one minute to work out the amounts for an hour / day / year / during their life so far, taking into consideration the fact that they don't blink when they are asleep.
- Suggest the children use a calculator to work out how many times they blink in an hour / year / during their life so far.

In the Past

- Blink rate increases with age. However, an adult blink rate of 10 times per minute = 600 per hour = 9 600 per day (based on being awake for 16 hours a day) = 3 504 000 per year.

Teaching support continued

Page 2

The Arts Roundup

- The first clue says that the number must be between 31 and 40, unless it is a multiple of 8. The third clue says that if the number is a multiple of 4, it must be less than 20. Any multiple of 8 will be a multiple of 4, so the number must be 8 or 16; or 31, 33, 34, 35, 37, 38 or 39. The second clue says that the number must be between 21 and 30 (which it can't be) or a multiple of 7. The only number that fits is 35.

What's the Problem?

- Dennis had collected three cards less than a multiple of 11, and four cards less than a multiple of 7.

Page 3

The Arts Roundup

- A possible method for working out the answer is as follows:
  When the director lays off the musicians, he has 30 days × 50 musicians' pay left, i.e. a total of 1500 days pay left. He needs 80 days × 20 musicians' pay, i.e. 1600 days pay. So he will be 100 days pay short. As he is still paying 20 musicians, this is $\frac{100}{20}$ = 5 days pay short.
- How many days early will he run out of money? (5 days)

Looking for Patterns

- As with the Looking for Patterns activity on page 4 of *Enriching Maths* Volume 4, Issue 12, this activity introduces children to the distributive law of multiplication, i.e. $a \times (b + c) = a \times b + a \times c$.

Page 4

Let's Investigate

- 111 is the smallest three-digit number in which all the digits are the same. The sum of these three digits is 3 (1 + 1 + 1).

  So, 111 ÷ 3 = 37.

  Both 222 and 6 (2 + 2 + 2) are twice 111 and 3, therefore

  222 ÷ 6 = 37 also.

  The same applies for all other three-digit numbers in which all the digits are the same: 333 ÷ 9 = 37, 444 ÷ 12 = 37;

  555 ÷ 15 = 37; …

Money Matters

- Children can create their own bank statements on the computer. However before doing this, if available, show the children several different bank statements.

AfL

- How did you work out the approximation? How accurate do you think it is?
- How did you start to solve this problem / puzzle?
- Why is this a more efficient way of working out the answer?
- What patterns / relationships did you notice about these numbers?
- What is a bank statement? What do they show? How?

Answers

Page 1

Focus on Science Results of the investigation will vary.

In the Past Queen Elizabeth I blinked approximately 70 × 3 504 000 = 245 280 000 times.
Albert Einstein blinked approximately 76 × 3 504 000 = 266 304 000 times.
William Shakespeare blinked approximately 52 × 3 504 000 = 182 208 000 times.
Sir Isaac Newton blinked approximately 84 × 3 504 000 = 294 336 000 times.

Page 2

The Arts Roundup There are 35 players in the Bomaderry Primary School orchestra.

What's the Problem? Dennis has collected 52 cards already.

Page 3

The Arts Roundup No, the director will run out of money five days early.

Looking for Patterns

7 × 8 + 7 × 5 = 7 × (8 + 5) = 7 × 13 = 91	9 × 12 + 9 × 7 = 9 × (12 + 7) = 9 × 19 = 171	6 × 8 – 6 × 2 = 6 × (8 – 2) = 6 × 6 = 36
10 × 9 – 10 × 5 = 10 × (9 – 5) = 10 × 4 = 40	14 × 6 + 14 × 7 = 14 × (6 + 7) = 14 × 13 = 182	16 × 7 – 16 × 3 = 16 × (7 – 3) = 16 × 4 = 64

Answers continued

Page 4 continued

Let's Investigate The answer is always 37.

Money Matters

Date	Transaction	Deposit	Withdrawal	Balance
1/7/2011	Salary	1562.00		1562.00
3/7/2011	Go! Supermarket		15.60	1546.40
6/7/2011	Electricity bill		69.70	1476·70
11/7/2011	Better Electrics		399.00	1077·70
14/7/2011	Go! Supermarket		27.38	1050·32
18/7/2011	Cheque from Mrs Grant	50.00		1100·32

EMU

rate

The change in one measured quantity (e.g. distance) compared to another measured quantity (e.g. time).

The frequency of something expressed as a proportion of a larger amount or in relation to a whole.

The amount of money charged per unit, e.g. per hour.

Issue 20 2-D shapes

Prerequisites for learning

- Identify and use patterns, relationships and properties of shapes
- Describe, visualise, classify, draw and make the shapes

Resources pencil and paper; RCM 2: My notes (optional); RCM 3: Pupil self assessment booklet (optional); RCM 7: Folding shapes; RCM 8: Sierpinski Triangle; RCM 10: 1 cm squared paper; RCM 11: 2 cm squared paper; RCM 12: 0·5 cm squared paper; ruler; scissors; paper squares; 10 sheets of A4 paper (per child or pair of children); geostrips and fasteners; computer with internet access

Teaching support

Page 1

The Arts Roundup

- Children can print out and make a display of the art works, as well as a brief description of how each piece uses lines, shape and geometric patterns in the work.

Construct

- With one cut the most number of sides that can be created is five (pentagon). With a second cut the maximum number of sides possible is six (hexagon). Therefore, it is not possible to make an octagon or a heptagon.
- Children draw squares and record their cuts, naming each shape, e.g.

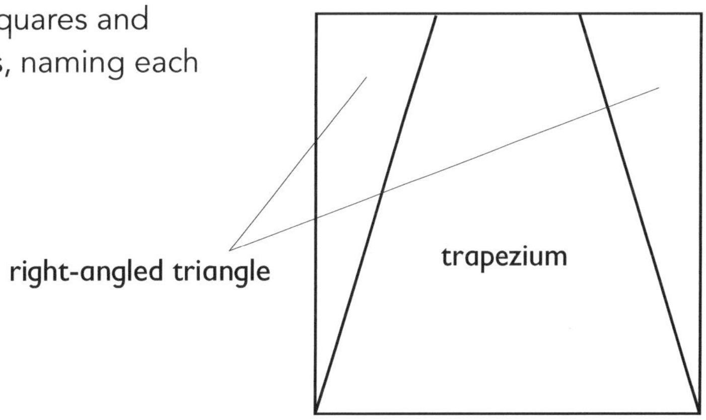

- What shapes can the children make using three cuts?

Teaching support continued

Page 2

Looking for Patterns

- When identifying the pattern, ask the children to look at the sides of the triangle opposite the vertices that have the lines crossing through the triangle. How many parts are each of these sides divided into? (Triangle 1: 2; Triangle 2: 3; Triangle 3: 4; Triangle 4: 5)

Let's Investigate

- Ensure children understand how each of the large squares in the issue has been divided into smaller squares.
- Discuss the patterns and relationships children notice.

Page 3

Looking for Patterns

- Work with the children to complete Steps 1 and 2.

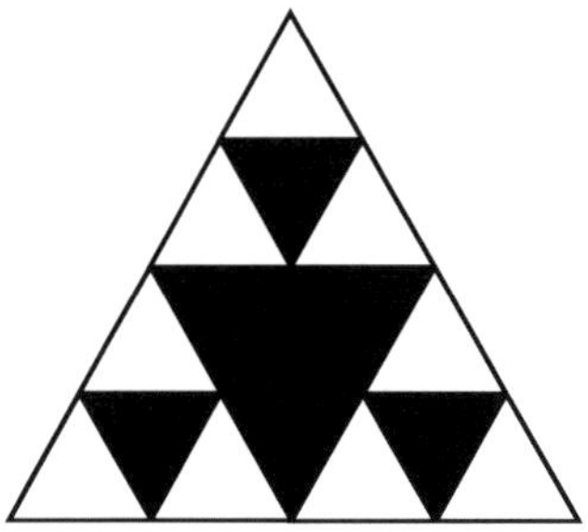

Let's Investigate

- Do the children realise that the polygons are made rigid through the use of struts to create triangles?

Page 4

Construct

- As this activity requires children to use a total of 10 sheets of A4 paper, it is advised that this activity be done in pairs. This will enable the children to share ideas and discuss their reasoning.
- Once pairs have made their first attempt at folding the paper into the five different shapes, if appropriate, join together two pairs for children to compare and discuss their shapes.
- Only once the children have made their five shapes, provide them with the RCM.
- Did any of the children make any of their shapes using the same method as on the RCM? Discuss the similarities and differences in construction.

Page 4 continued

Construct

- Children could print out and make a display of the bridges, buildings and other structures, as well as a brief description of how each of them is made rigid.

AfL

- Which abstract artists use shapes and lines in their work? How?
- When writing a set of instructions describing a picture, what words are extremely useful? Why?
- How many shapes did you find in the diagram? What methods did you use to ensure that you accounted for them all?
- What shapes were you able to make? How? Which were you not able to make? Why?
- What patterns did you notice when dividing up a large square into smaller squares?
- What can you tell me about the *Sierpinski Triangle*?

Answers

Page 1

The Arts Roundup Results of the investigation will vary.

Construct It is possible to make each of the shapes with the exception of a heptagon and an octagon.

Page 2

Looking for Patterns

Triangle 1: 8 triangles
Triangle 2: 27 triangles
Triangle 3: 64 triangles

In Triangle 1 the two sides opposite the vertices that have the lines crossing through the triangle have been divided into 2 parts ($2 \times 2 \times 2 = 8$).

In Triangle 2 the two sides opposite the vertices that have the lines crossing through the triangle have been divided into 3 parts ($3 \times 3 \times 3 = 27$).

In Triangle 3 the two sides opposite the vertices that have the lines crossing through the triangle have been divided into 4 parts ($4 \times 4 \times 4 = 64$).

Triangle 4: 125 triangles ($5 \times 5 \times 5 = 125$)

Answers continued

Page 2 continued

Let's Investigate

8 squares

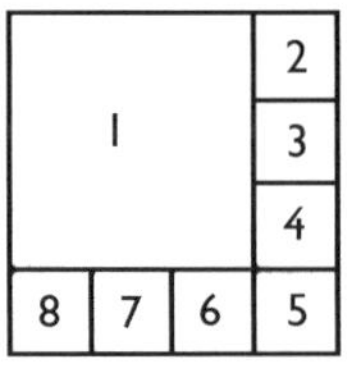

9 squares

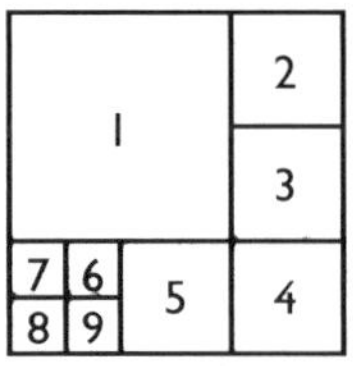

10 squares

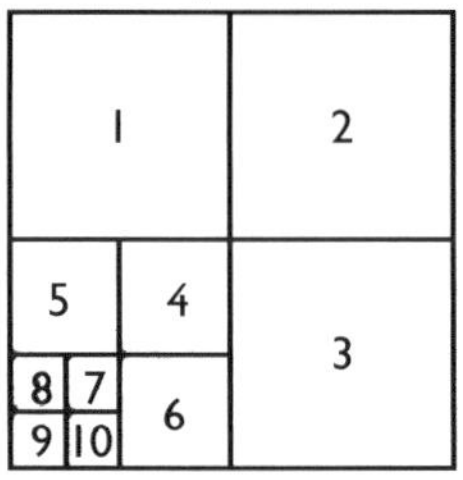

11 squares

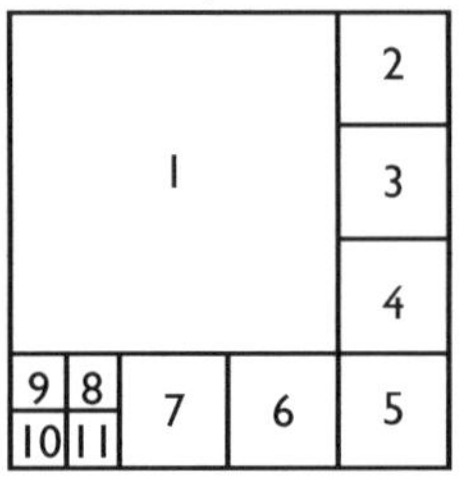

12 squares

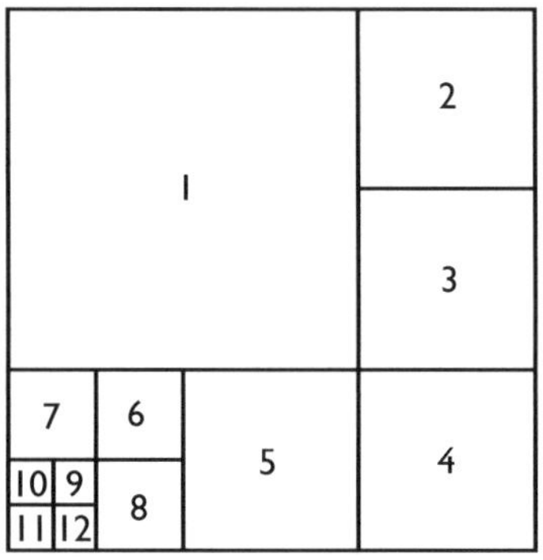

Other answers are possible.

Page 3

Looking for Patterns

Let's Investigate The following numbers of struts are needed to make the shapes rigid.
Pentagon: 2 struts, resulting in 3 triangles
Hexagon: 3 struts, resulting in 4 triangles
Heptagon: 4 struts, resulting in 5 triangles
Octagon: 5 struts, resulting in 6 triangles

Page 4

Construct The construction of the shapes will vary as will comments regarding similarities and differences.

Construct Results of the investigation will vary. However, it is triangles and circles (arcs) that are commonly used to make bridges, buildings and other structures rigid.

EMU

fractal
A geometric shape that can be repeatedly subdivided into parts, each of which is a smaller copy of the whole, e.g. the Sierpinski Triangle.

Issue 21 3-D solids

Prerequisites for learning

- Describe, classify, draw and make shapes
- Visualise 3-D objects from 2-D drawings
- Make nets of common solids

Resources pencil and paper; RCM 2: My notes (optional); RCM 3: Pupil self assessment booklet (optional); RCM 10: 1 cm squared paper; RCM 11: 2 cm squared paper; RCM 14: Isometric paper; several sheets of coloured A4 paper; several large sheets of paper; ruler; scissors; sellotape; glue; Centicubes or interlocking cubes (optional); pair of compasses

Teaching support

Page 1

Construct

- If appropriate, allow the children to work in pairs or groups to make their own origami box.
- Children can investigate other origami shapes.

Page 2

Construct

- Remind the children that the key criteria for designing and constructing their paper box are to use as few other resources as possible, while still managing to create a 'useable' box.

Construct

- To assist children in visualising each of the solid shapes, provide them with either Centicubes or interlocking cubes and ask them to use these to build the solids. This will make it easier for them when representing the solid shape on isometric paper.

Teaching support continued

Page 3

Construct

- If children are unfamiliar with how to use a pair of compasses, spend time prior to this activity showing the children how it works.
- Some children may need help in drawing the body (as opposed to the base) of the cone. Point out that the point of the cone is the same distance from the bottom all the way around, so the body of the cone is part of a circle with a radius of 10 cm.

Looking for Patterns

- Ask the children to explain why shapes 2, 4 and 6 are not nets of a triangular prism.

Page 4

The Puzzler

- Provide children with Centicubes or interlocking cubes if they are having difficulty visualising the shapes.

Construct

- If children have difficulty, suggest they draw the net of the cube, cut it out and fold it to shape, then draw arrows on the sides they want to make longer. They should then open it up again and make the changes to the net.
- Children draw different nets of a cuboid.

AfL

- Were you able to visualise what the solid shapes were? Did you need to use anything to help you?
- Was your net successful? What would you do next time to improve your net?
- How did you know what shape the net needed to be?

Answers

Page 1

Construct No answer required.

Page 2

Construct Boxes will vary.

Page 2 continued

Construct

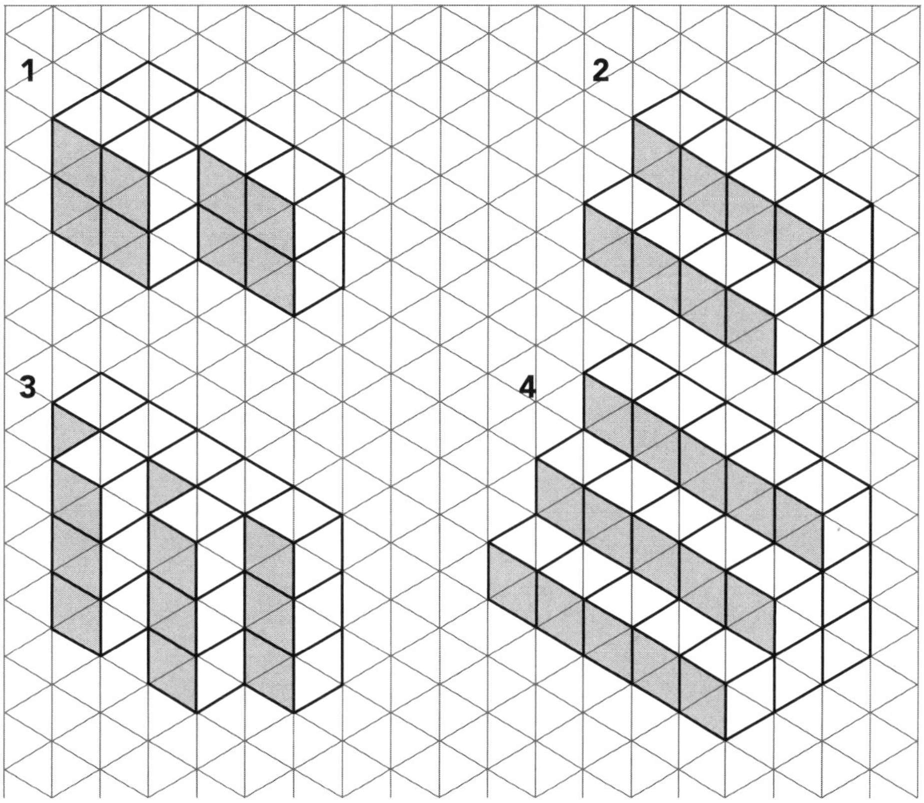

Page 3

Construct

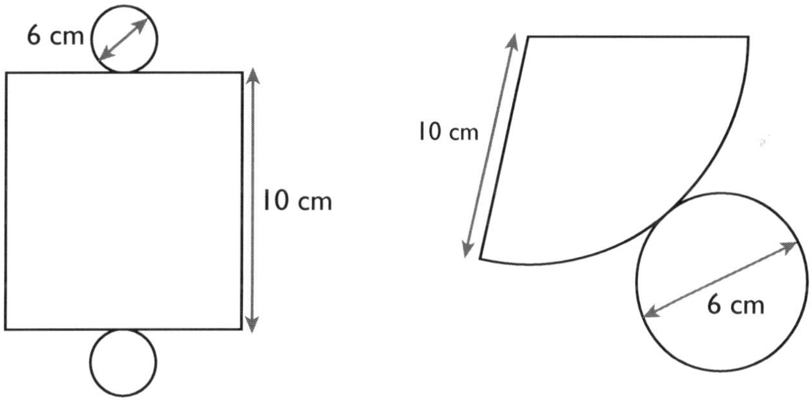

Looking for Patterns Nets 1, 3 and 5

Page 4

The Puzzler

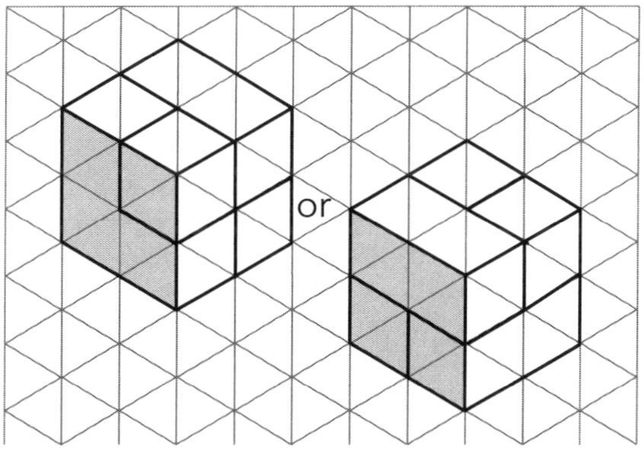

Answers continued

Page 4 continued

The Puzzler continued

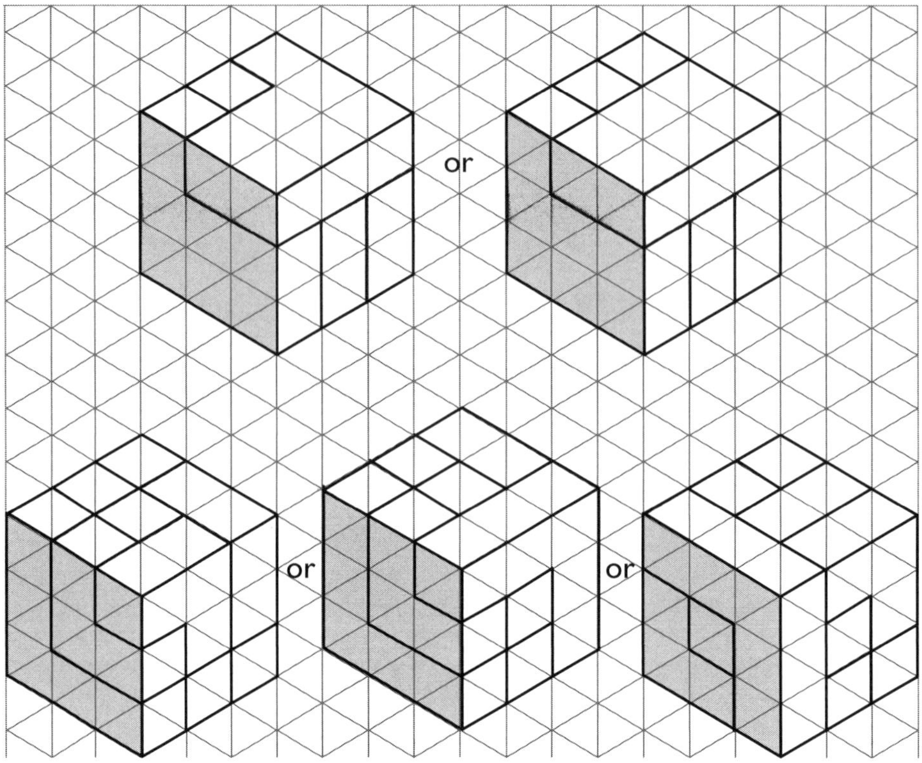

Construct

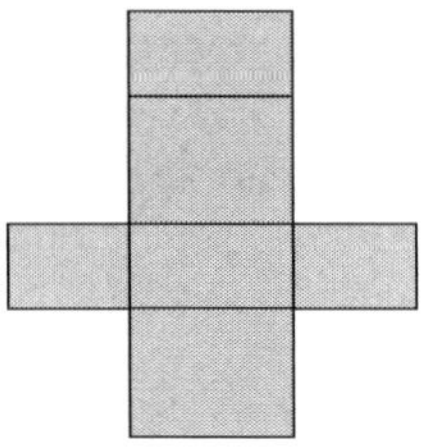

Other nets are possible.

EMU

net

A diagram of a hollow solid consisting of the plane shapes of the faces so that when arranged the diagram can be folded to form the solid.

Issue 22 Symmetry and reflection

Prerequisites for learning

- Identify and use patterns, relationships and properties of shapes
- Draw and complete shapes with reflective symmetry
- Understand the difference between rotational and reflective symmetry

Resources pencil and paper; RCM 2: My notes (optional); RCM 3: Pupil self assessment booklet (optional); RCM 9: Analogue clocks; RCM 10: 1 cm squared paper; ruler; four different coloured pencils; paper square; scissors; selection of different fruit; knife; two sheets of A4 paper; two paper clips; computer with internet access

Teaching support

Page 1

Focus on Science

- Prior to the activity, cut each fruit crosswise, i.e. to produce a slice of each.
- Ensure the children understand the difference between rotational and reflective symmetry. Discuss with the children how the plane of the cut can change a fruits' symmetry from reflective to rotational.
- Children use the internet to investigate this activity further.

Looking for Patterns

- Children draw a diagonal line of symmetry and use colours to make a pattern that shows reflective symmetry about this line.

Page 2

Construct

- Children may have difficulty folding the paper into a concertina. If appropriate, go through it with them. The main focus of this activity is not in creating the concertina, but in predicting what the patterns they make will look like when opened up.

Page 3

Looking for Patterns

- To make the pattern symmetrical about the two diagonal axes, the square sheet of paper needs to be folded diagonally, corner to corner, to make a triangle and then corner to corner again to make another triangle half the size. All cuts on each of the four overlapping sheets of paper need to be made through all the other sheets.

Teaching support continued

Page 3 continued

Focus on Science

- Ensure children do not spend too much time making elaborate drawings. The focus of this activity is for them to realise that almost all forms of transport have lines of symmetry from top to bottom and from front to back to facilitate forward movement in a straight line.
- Children may benefit from using the internet for this activity to get ideas for suitable transportation.

Page 4

Focus on Science

- Ensure children do not spend too much time making elaborate drawings. The focus of this activity is for them to realise that almost all animals have lines of symmetry from top to bottom and from front to back to facilitate forward movement in a straight line.
- Children may benefit from using the internet for this activity to get ideas for suitable animals.

Let's Investigate

- Remind children that the hour hand moves in relation to the minute hand, and encourage them to be as accurate as possible.
- Tell the children that apart from 6 o'clock there are 10 other times when the hands of an analogue clock are directly opposite each other. Can they find them all?

Around the World

- Children should have little or no difficulty in drawing the lines of symmetry on each of the three buildings. The main focus of this activity is for the children to find and comment on the floor plans of other buildings that show reflective symmetry.
- Children can print out and make a display of the floor plans of the buildings they find, drawing in all the lines of reflective symmetry.
- Do any of the floor plans show rotational symmetry?

AfL

- Describe to me the symmetry in your pattern?
- How does this show reflective symmetry?
- Describe to me the symmetry in these fruit / buildings / clock times.
- How does each of these objects show reflective symmetry?
- How do these different types of transport show symmetry? Why do they have symmetry?
- How do these animals show symmetry? Why do you think they have this symmetry?

Answers

Page 1

Focus on Science Results of the investigation will vary.

Looking for Patterns Symmetrical designs will vary.

Page 2

Construct Symmetrical designs will vary.

Page 3

Looking for Patterns Symmetrical designs will vary.

Focus on Science Results of the investigation will vary. However, most types of transportation have symmetry as they are required to move in a straight line and symmetrical form is the most energy efficient shape. Transport that travels along the surface of the Earth and water, i.e. cars and boats, exhibits vertical symmetry but has no need for horizontal symmetry as it cannot burrow into the ground or take off into the air. Aeroplanes and submarines on the other hand, exhibit both vertical and, to a limited extent, horizontal symmetry as they can travel up and down as well as left and right.

Page 4

Focus on Science Results of the investigation will vary. However, the same reasoning applies for animals as for transportation.

Let's Investigate As well as 6 o'clock, there are 10 other times when the hands of an analogue clock are directly opposite each other (to the nearest minute). These are: 1:38, 2:44, 3:49, 4:55, 7:05, 8:11, 9:16, 10:22, 11:27, 12:33.

Around the World

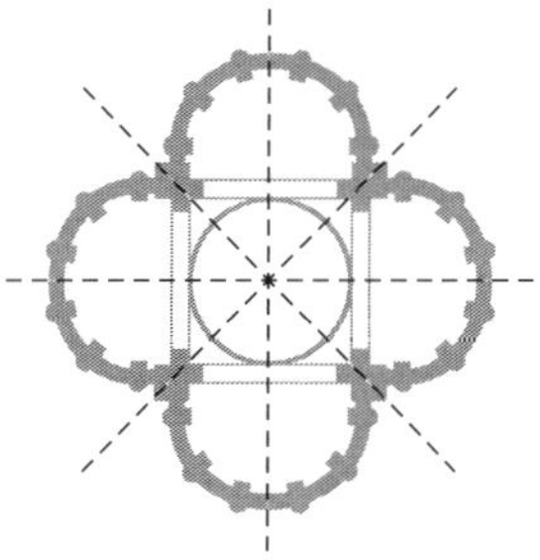

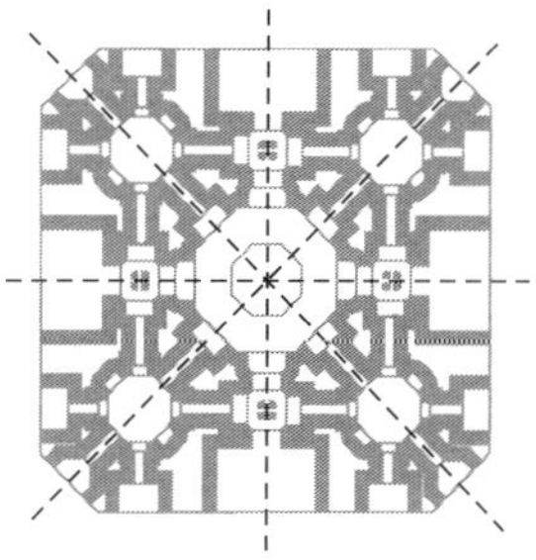

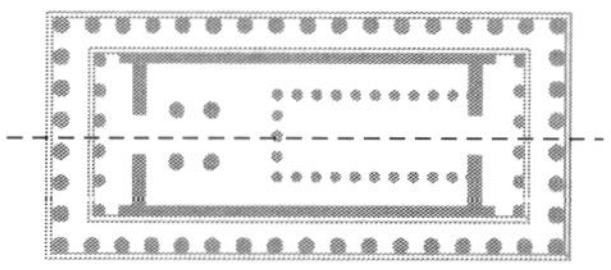

Results of the investigation will vary.

EMU

rotational symmetry
The property of being the same or corresponding around an axis.

Issue 23

Position and direction

Prerequisites for learning

- Use the eight compass points to describe direction
- Describe and identify the position of a square on a grid of squares
- Read time using 24-hour clock notation
- Solve logic puzzles

Resources pencil and paper; RCM 2: My notes (optional); RCM 3: Pupil self assessment booklet (optional); RCM 10: 1 cm squared paper; RCM 11: 2 cm squared paper; tape recorder, or similar (optional); road map or street directory that shows distances between points; compass; analogue watch; computer with internet access

Teaching support

Page 1

Construct

- Discuss with the children how they need to place each piece of furniture in a suitable position in the sitting room and that they need to be able to justify their decisions.
- Ensure the children realise that they can either translate or rotate the pieces of furniture.
- Once the children have completed the activity, discuss with them how they either translated or rotated each piece of furniture.

Page 2

Around the World

- Children can write their instructions for the Sat Nav using a computer.
- Children can record their set of instructions on to a tape recorder (or similar).

Construct

- Encourage the children to be as accurate as possible in the drawing up the plan of the school building, taking into account both position and scale.
- Suggest the children just draw a plan for their class showing the best, and an alternative, escape route in case of a fire.
- Children mark on the map the best position to place fire extinguishers / blankets. What about fire alarms?

Page 3

Construct

- The important aspect of this activity is not the detail of the map, but rather the labelling of the distances between the three towns and the position of Hugh and the sign.

Around the World

- For this activity you will need to provide children with a road map or street directory that shows distances between points. Tourist maps generally include such information. Tell the children that they should focus on one particular page (or double-page spread), or a specific section of the road map.
- If it is not possible to find an appropriate road map or street directory, the children can use the map that is included in the issue.

Page 4

Around the World

- Allow the children an opportunity to have free play with a compass, perhaps going into the playground and describing the position of certain features.
- Children investigate what the numbers around the circumference of the compass refer to.

Around the World

- Ensure children have completed the Around the World activity above before starting on this activity as they need to be able to use a compass to check the accuracy of their watch compass.

AfL

- What words did you use when writing your set of instructions?
- What 'landmarks' did you use when drawing your plan?
- Tell me the grid references for a piece of your furniture. Why did you decide to place this piece of furniture in this location?
- How did you go about working out the solution to this problem?
- How do you read a map in a street directory?
- What can you tell me about a compass?
- How accurate is the compass you made?

Answers

Page 1

Construct Grids and grid references will vary.

Page 2

Around the World Maps and instructions will vary.

Construct Plans will vary.

Page 3

Construct It is 81 miles from Luxton to Longridge.
It is 36 miles from Luxton to Elfton.
It is 45 miles from Elfton to Longridge.

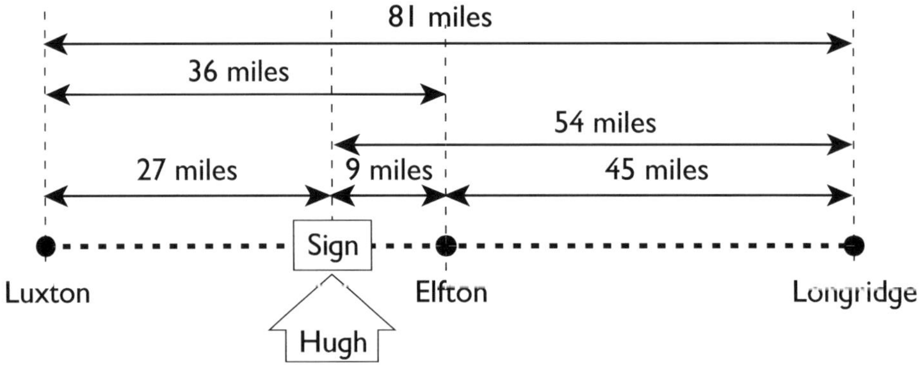

Maps will vary.

Around the World Descriptions and distances will vary.

Page 4

Around the World A compass is an instrument for finding directions, usually with a magnetized arrow that automatically points to the direction of magnetic north.

Around the World Results of the experiment will vary.

EMU route
A way of travelling from one place to another.

Issue 24

Movement and angle

Prerequisites for learning

- Draw and measure acute and obtuse angles using an angle measurer or protractor to a suitable degree of accuracy
- Know that angles are measured in degrees and that one whole turn is 360°
- Compare and order angles less than 180°
- Read and record the vocabulary of position, direction and movement
- Read time to the nearest minute; use a.m., p.m. and 12-hour clock notation

Resources pencil and paper; RCM 2: My notes (optional); RCM 3: Pupil self assessment booklet (optional); RCM 13: Squared dot paper; ruler; protractor

Teaching support

Page 1

At Home

- Ensure children are familiar with the terms 'acute angle' and 'obtuse angle'.
- Once the children have completed the activity, ensure that there is an opportunity in class for pairs or groups of children to discuss their results.

Focus on Science

- Discuss with the children how many degrees the Earth spins in 12 hours (180°), 6 hours (90°) …

Page 2

Looking for Patterns

- Ensure the children fully understand how the two linear spiral patterns in the issue have been constructed.
- Discuss with the children how, before they start to draw each of the spiral patterns, they need to first think about where to start the pattern on the squared dot paper. This requires the children creating a mental image of the pattern to ensure that the pattern fits onto the paper.

Teaching support continued

Page 3
Around the World

- Ensure children are familiar with a protractor and how to use it.
- If necessary, work with the children to measure one or two of the angles and write the instructions.

Page 4
In the Past

- As this activity requires the children to consider possible methods of construction for the Pyramids at Giza, it is advised that this activity be done in pairs. This will enable the children to share ideas and discuss their reasoning.

AfL

- Tell me some examples of different angles. Is this an example of a right angle, an acute angle or an obtuse angle?
- What is the difference between a right angle, an acute angle and an obtuse angle?
- What can you tell me about the angles formed by the Earth turning?
- How good is your set of instructions for getting around the island? Can you improve on them? How?
- What can you tell me about a linear spiral? How can you tell whether the spiral will be a closed spiral or an open spiral?

Answers

Page 1

At Home Results of the investigation will vary.

Focus on Science 180°, 90°, 180°, 90°, 90°
Accept any two times 4 hours apart.
Accept any two times 2 hours apart.

Page 2

Looking for Patterns

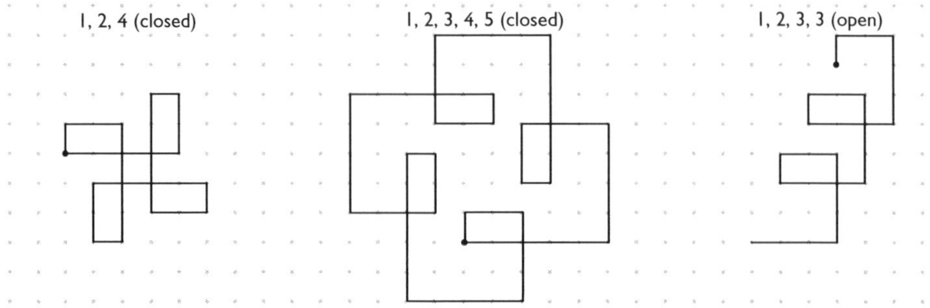

Page 2 continued

Looking for Patterns continued

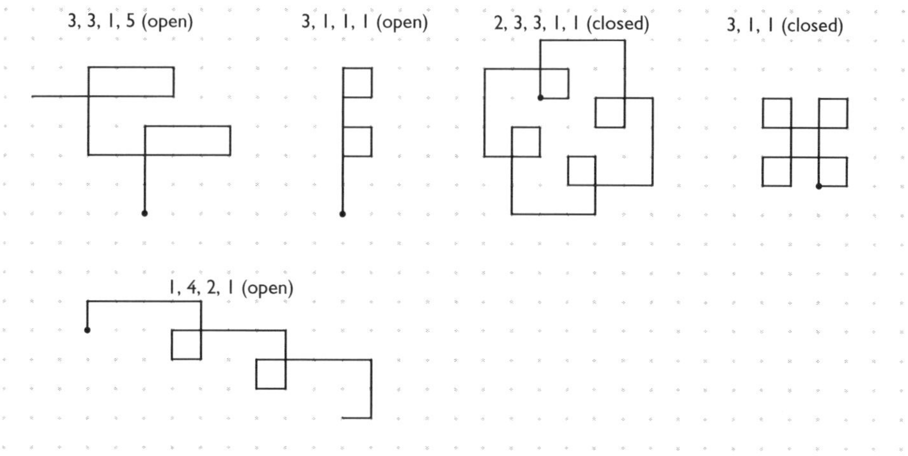

All patterns with an odd number of terms will form a closed linear spiral.
All patterns with an even number of terms will form an open linear spiral.

Page 3

Around the World

Day 1: We sail on a route 20° clockwise from north.
Day 2: We sail on a route 60° clockwise from north.
Day 3: We sail on a route 110° clockwise from north.
Day 4: We sail on a route 100° clockwise from north.
Day 5: We sail on a route 90° clockwise from north.
Day 6: We sail on a route 130° anticlockwise from north.
OR: We sail on a route 230° clockwise from north.

Page 4

In the Past

The steepest, and shortest route, is from the mid-point of one the sides of the base directly up to the top.
The least steep, and longest, direct route is from one of the corners of the base up to the top.

Using a zig-zag path to raise the stone blocks means that the angle of the path could be made smaller, and the path less steep, making it easier to raise the stones up the sides of the pyramids.

EMU 

reflex angle
An angle between 180° and 360°.

Understanding shape – General

Issue 25

Prerequisites for learning

- Visualise 3-D objects from 2-D drawings
- Describe, visualise, classify, draw and make the shapes
- Use the eight compass points to describe direction
- Know that angles are measured in degrees and that one whole turn is 360°
- Solve logic puzzles

Resources pencil and paper; RCM 2: My notes (optional); RCM 3: Pupil self assessment booklet (optional); RCM 10: 1 cm squared paper; RCM 11: 2 cm squared paper; RCM 14: Isometric paper; ruler; tape measure; interlocking cubes; compass

Teaching support

Page 1

Construct

- Encourage the children to be as detailed as possible in their plan.
- Ask the children to draw their ideal classroom to scale.
- Children design the ideal playground.

The Puzzler

- This puzzle is similar to Sudoku. However, it involves shapes rather than digits, and is only a 4 × 4 grid.

Page 2

The Puzzler

- Draw a simple diagram for each crossing, showing who is on which bank during the crossing (see Answers).

Construct

- These are the 12 different five-cube shapes.

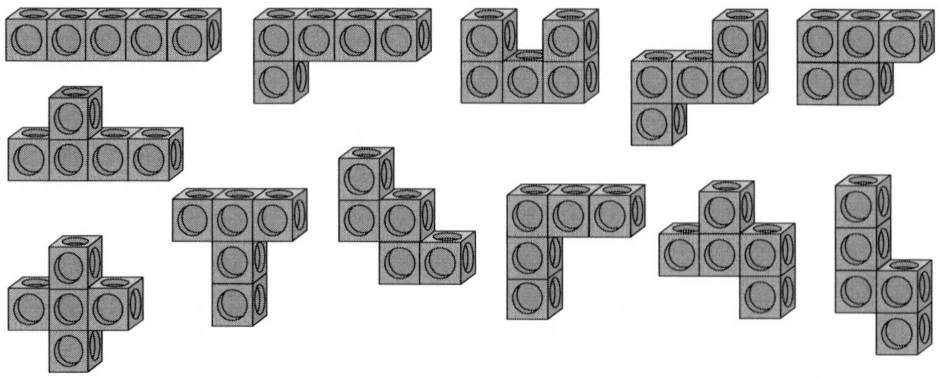

Page 2 continued

Construct continued

- If the children have completed the Let's Investigate activity on page 4 of *Enriching Maths* Volume 4, Issue 26, ask them to comment on what they notice about the similarities between these two activities.

Looking for Patterns

- When recording which shapes, when replicated five times, will fit together to make a 5 × 5 square, suggest the children use colour. For example,

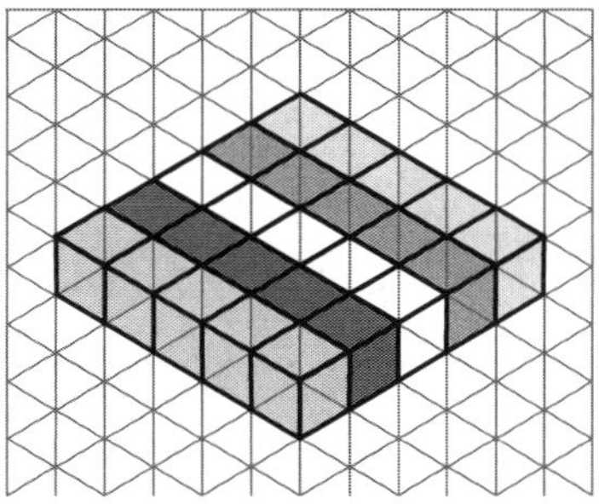

Page 3

The Language of Maths

- Ensure that children are familiar with the concept that a 'turn to the left' (or right) means a 90° turn to the left (or right) and covers two of the eight points of a compass.
- It will help if the children have a compass when describing how to get to their classroom. Therefore it is recommended that children have completed the first Around the World activity on page 4 of *Enriching Maths* Volume 4, Issue 23, before starting on this activity.

The Language of Maths

- Remind the children that 2-D shapes have sides and corners (or vertices); and that 3-D solids have faces, edges and corners (or vertices).
- Tell the children the names of the eight shapes. Can they match the name to the description?

Teaching support continued

Page 4

Let's Investigate

- What if the 4 × 4 square was divided into four congruent parts?

Looking for Patterns

- Ensure that children realise that each question is referring to the position of the baskets in the illustration.

AfL

- Why is the classroom you designed better than your current classroom?
- How did you start to solve this puzzle? What strategies did you use?
- How did you go about constructing your cube shapes? How did you make sure that you didn't make duplicate shapes?
- Which clues were tricky when trying to identify the different solids? Why was this?

Answers

Page 1

Construct Plans will vary.

The Puzzler

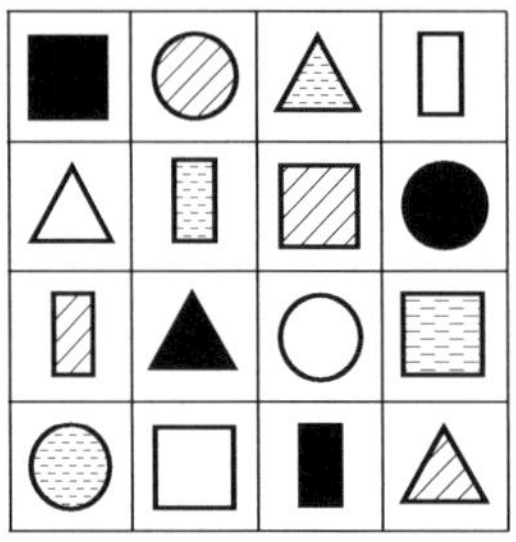

Other solutions are possible.

Page 2

The Puzzler First the two children row across to the other side. One stays behind on the far bank and the other rows back to the parents. The first parent then rows across by themselves and gets out on the far bank. The child on the far bank then rows back alone, picks up the child on the near bank, and they both row to the far bank. One child gets out on the far bank and the other rows back to the second parent on the near bank. The second parent then rows to the far bank alone and gets out. The child on the far bank rows back to pick up the other child from the near bank, and both children then row across to the far bank.

Page 2 continued

Construct These are the 12 different five-cube shapes.

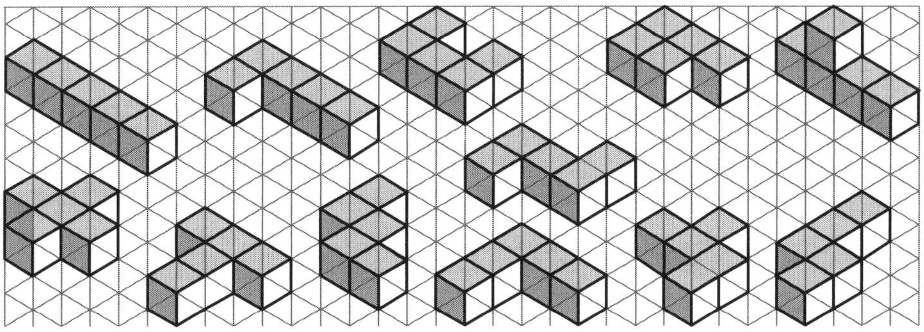

Looking for Patterns The first shape above (i.e. Shape I) will fit together to make a 5 × 5 square when replicated. None of the other shapes will do this.

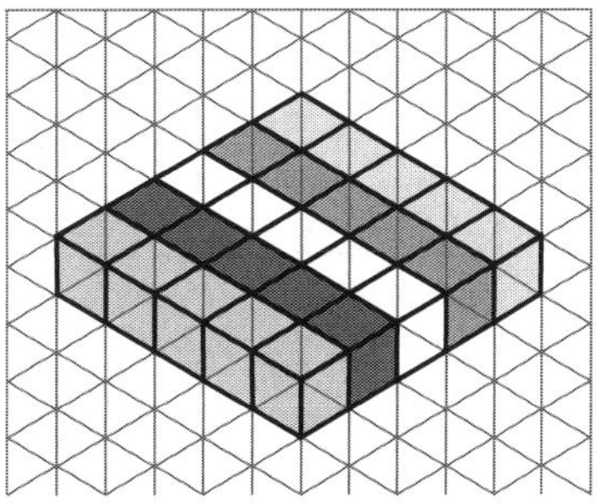

Page 3

The Language of Maths Descriptions will vary.

The Language of Maths

1 Semi-circle
2 Circle
3 Cylinder
4 Cone
5 Cube
6 Sphere
7 Square-based pyramid
8 Pentagonal prism

Page 4

Let's Investigate Results of the investigation will vary.

Looking for Patterns 90°, 180°, 45°, 135°, position 6, position 7

EMU 

isometric paper
Paper used for drawing a figure in three dimensions.

Issue 26

Understanding shape – General

Prerequisites for learning

- Draw polygons and classify them by identifying their properties, including their line symmetry
- Describe, visualise and make shapes
- Know that angles are measured in degrees and that one whole turn is 360°

Resources pencil and paper; RCM 2: My notes (optional); RCM 3: Pupil self assessment booklet (optional); RCM 11: 2 cm squared paper; A4 paper; scissors; glue; sellotape; cardboard

Teaching support

Page 1

Let's Investigate

- The five different tetrominoes are:

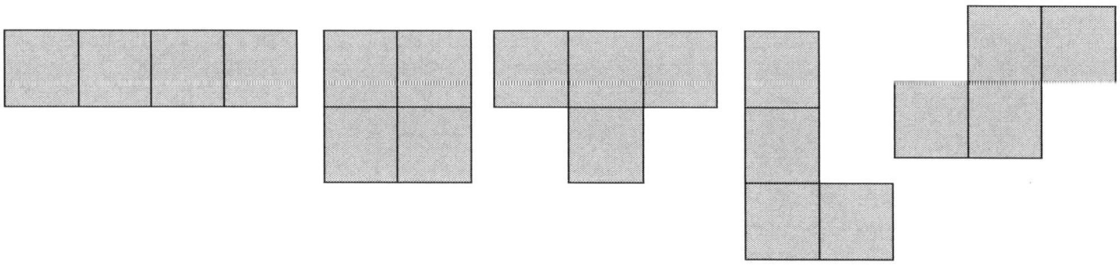

- Remind the children that 10 tetrominoes are made from 40 squares, so the rectangles must have dimensions of 5 × 8 or 4 × 10.
- Can children make both the 5 × 8 and 4 × 10 rectangles?
- If the children have completed the Construct activity on page 2 of *Enriching Maths* Volume 4, Issue 25, ask them to comment on what they notice about the similarities between these two activities.

Page 2 / Page 3

Famous Mathematicians

- Ask the children to investigate the life and work of August Ferdinand Möbius.

Page 3

Construct

- Suggest children draw small triangles and quadrilaterals, around 5 cm long, so that they use only one or two sheets of cardboard for each shape.
- Remind children that angles on a straight line total 180°, and one whole turn is 360°.

Page 4

Let's Investigate

- The 12 different pentominoes are:

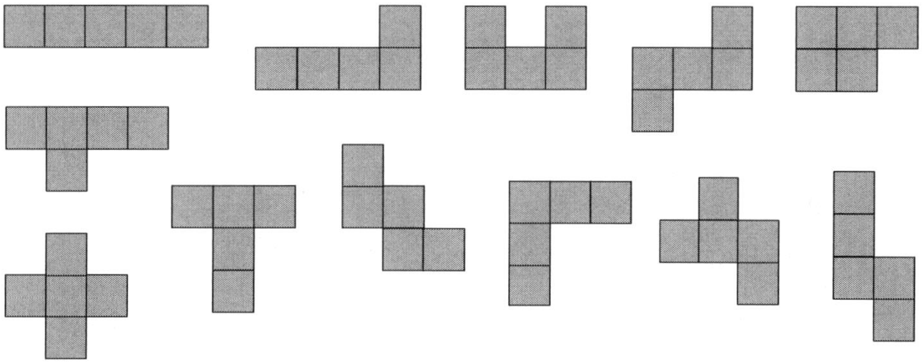

- Remind the children that 12 pentominoes are made from 60 squares, so the rectangles must have dimensions of 6 × 10, 5 × 12, 4 × 15 or 3 × 20.
- Can children make all four rectangles (i.e. 6 × 10, 5 × 12, 4 × 15 or 3 × 20)?
- If the children have completed the Construct activity on page 2 of *Enriching Maths* Volume 4, Issue 25, ask them to comment on what they notice about the similarities between these two activities.

Looking for Patterns

- Tell the children the following:
  - There are 4 pentominoes with 1 line of symmetry.
  - There is 1 pentomino with 2 lines of symmetry.
  - There is 1 pentomino with 4 lines of symmetry.
  - There are 6 pentominoes with 0 lines of symmetry.

The Language of Maths

- Explain to the children that they may need to flip or rotate the pentominoes to better see which letter a pentomino represents.
- Tell the children the letters: F (or R), I (or O), L (or Q), N (or S), P, T, U, V, W, X, Y, Z. Can they match the letters with the pentominoes?

AfL

- What can you tell me about a Möbius strip? Why does this happen?
- What do you notice about the way the triangles / quadrilaterals fit together?
- Did you find all the different tetrominoes / pentominoes? Which were difficult to find? Why? How did you make sure that you didn't keep getting duplicates of the same shape?
- What did you visualise as you were arranging your tetrominoes / pentominoes into a rectangle?

Answers

Page 1

Let's Investigate It is possible to make a 4 × 10 rectangle and a 5 × 8 rectangle.

Page 2 / Page 3

Famous Mathematicians Check Möbius strips.

Page 3

Construct The triangles will fit together in bands with parallel edges, because when three triangles are put together, with a different point on each one touching, the three angles, A + B + C, will total 180° and make a straight line.

The quadrilaterals will fit together as long as four different points are touching, W + X + Y + Z, so that the sum of the four angles is 360°, and similar sides are put together, e.g. WX next to XW.

Page 4

Let's Investigate It is possible to make 6 × 10, 5 × 12, 4 × 15 and 3 × 20 rectangles.

Looking for Patterns

1 line of symmetry

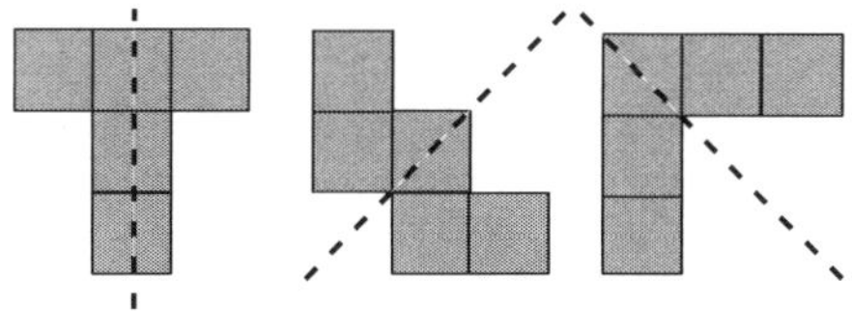

2 lines of symmetry

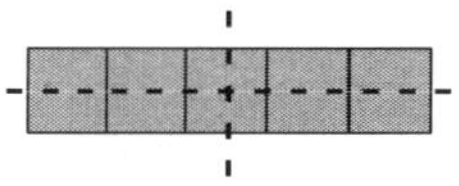

4 lines of symmetry

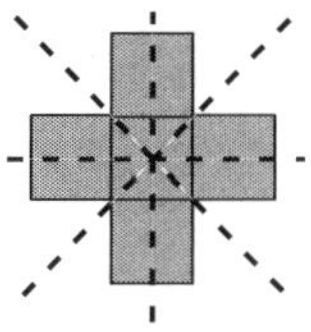

No lines of symmetry

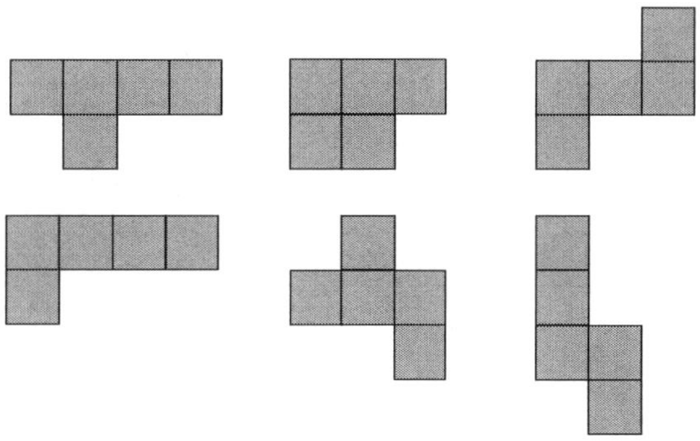

The Language of Maths

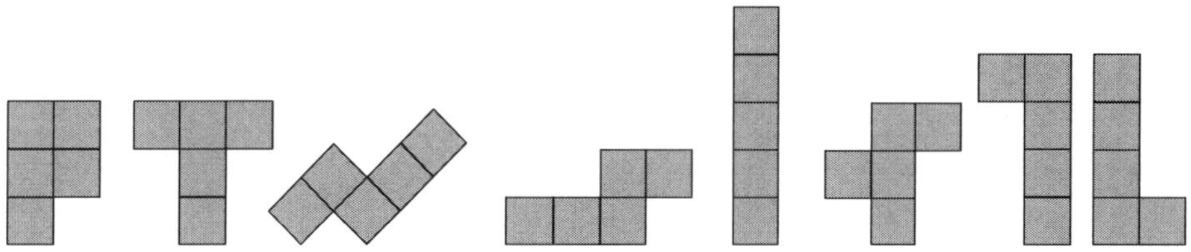

P T N or S I or O F or R Q or L

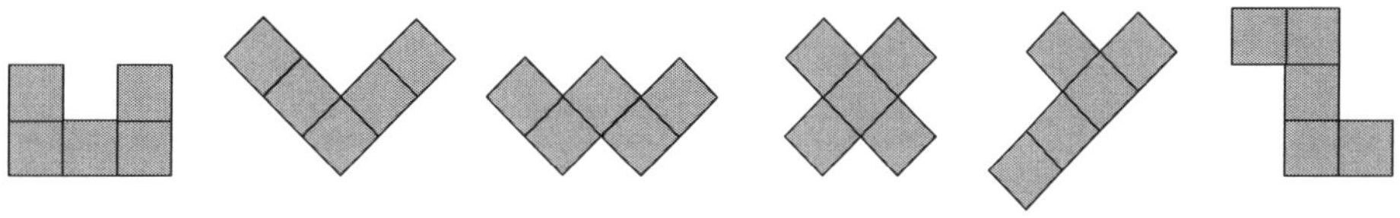

U V W X Y Z

EMU

tessellate

To cover a plane surface by repeated use of the same shape without overlapping or leaving any gaps.

Issue 27 Length

Prerequisites for learning

- Choose and use standard metric units and their abbreviations when estimating, measuring and recording length
- Use sequences to scale numbers up or down
- Round four-digit whole numbers
- Calculate mentally with whole numbers
- Use efficient written methods to add, subtract, multiply and divide whole numbers
- Make estimations and approximations

Resources pencil and paper; RCM 2: My notes (optional); RCM 3: Pupil self assessment booklet (optional); RCM 10: 1 cm squared paper; RCM 11: 2 cm squared paper; labels from a collection of supermarket fruit and vegetables showing country of origin; atlas with a scale; road map; ruler; 5p and 10p coins; computer with internet access

Teaching support

Page 1

Around the World

- You may wish to provide the children with labels from a collection of supermarket fruit and vegetables showing country of origin.
- Alternatively, ask the children to visit a supermarket and investigate the country of origin for a selection of fruit and vegetables. They can then complete the rest of the activity back in school.
- If the children do visit a supermarket, provide an opportunity for pairs or groups of children to pool their lists before working on the rest of the activity.

Around the World

- You may wish the children to do this activity alongside the first Around the World activity on page 3, as both these activities deal with locating places that are a given distance apart.

Around the World

- Before starting work on this activity, draw children's attention to the second Around the World activity on page 3. Explain to them that they must leave enough room on the diagram to mark four more buildings.

Page 2

In the Past

- The important aspect of this activity is in the children comparing car journeys of today with those in the early 1900s. As a result, allow the children to work in pairs so that they can share ideas and discuss their reasoning.

Around the World

- Ensure children are able to round four-digit numbers to the nearest multiple of 100.
- Before children start constructing their scale drawing, discuss with them that the scale does not need to start at zero. What might be a good starting number for the river scale drawing? What about the mountain range scale drawing?

Page 3

Money Matters

- A 5p coin is 18 mm in diameter, so you would get 33 of them in 60 cm, making £1.65.
- A 10p coin is 24·5 mm in diameter, so you would get 16 of them in 40 cm, making £1.60.

Around the World

- You may wish the children to do this activity alongside the second Around the World activity on page 1, as both these activities deal with locating places that are a given distance apart.

Around the World

- Children draw another diagram similar to that in the last Around the World activity on page 1 to show the approximate heights of other structures they find during their investigation.

Page 4

Around the World

- Referring to the illustration in the Around the World activity that follows, ask the children to calculate the latitude of Paris (5439 km ÷ 111 = 49°).

Around the World

- Many websites provide precise latitudes for specific locations. However, to start with, you may need to spend some time with the children helping them to interpret the readings.

AfL

- What did you discover about the 'food miles' different fruit and vegetables have travelled?
- Can you tell me two places that are approximately 4000 miles / 50 km apart?
- What is the scale of this diagram? What does this mean?
- What is the approximate difference in height between these two buildings?
- What statements can you make about the world's longest rivers / mountain ranges?
- How did you arrive at your approximation? How accurate is it?
- How far from the equator is London? What about Sydney? Can you tell me the distance from the equator for another city? How did you arrive at that answer?

Answers

Page 1

Around the World Results of the investigation will vary.

Around the World Results of the investigation will vary. However, examples may include:
London, England to Chicago, USA
London, England to Karachi, Pakistan
Sydney, Australia to Singapore
Mumbai, India to Munich, Germany

Around the World

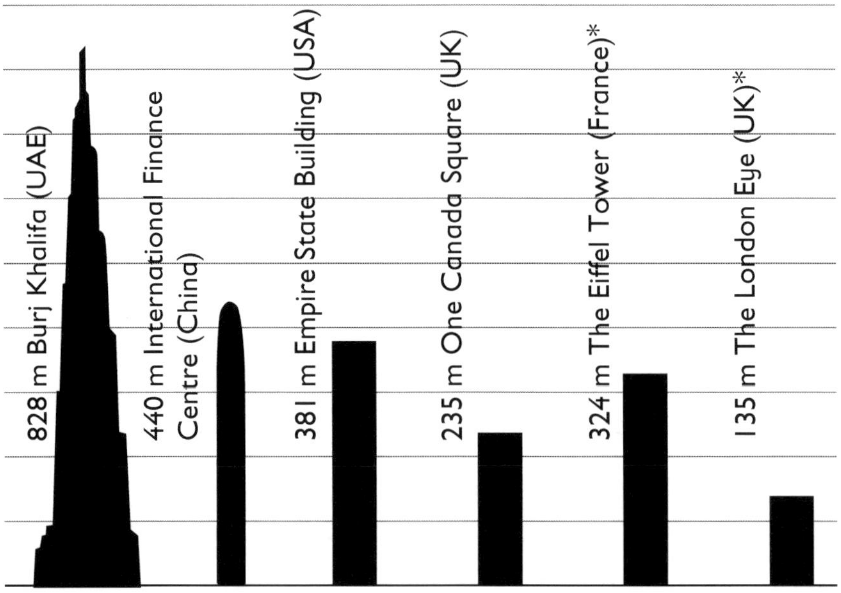

* These two buildings form part of the second Around the World activity on page 3.

Page 2

In the Past

Travelling from London to Brighton:
1900s: 5 hours
Today: 1·5 hours (averaging just over 30 mph)

Explanations concerning time to travel will vary, however, may include:

- cars are much faster now, but traffic congestion makes travelling times longer
- early cars often had mechanical problems.

Similarities and differences between now and 1900 include:

- quality of roads
- traffic congestion
- encroachment of town on countryside.

Around the World

River	Length (rounded to 100 km)
Nile	6700
Amazon	6500
Yangtze	6300
Mississippi	6000
Huang He	5500

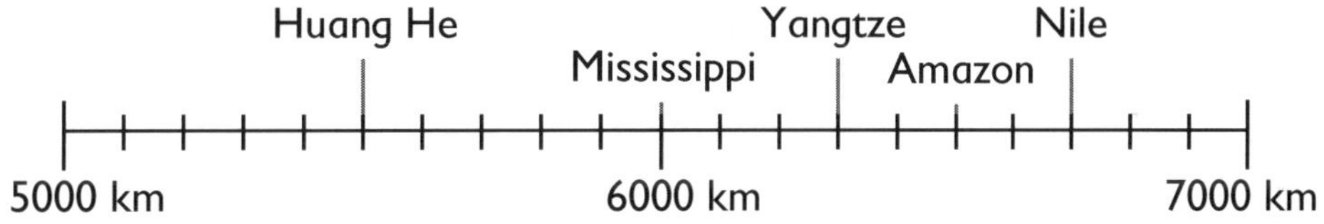

Scale drawings will vary.

Mountain range	Length (rounded to 100 km)
Andes	7200
Rocky Mountains	6000
Himalayas	3900
Great Dividing Range	3600
Transantarctic Mountains	3500

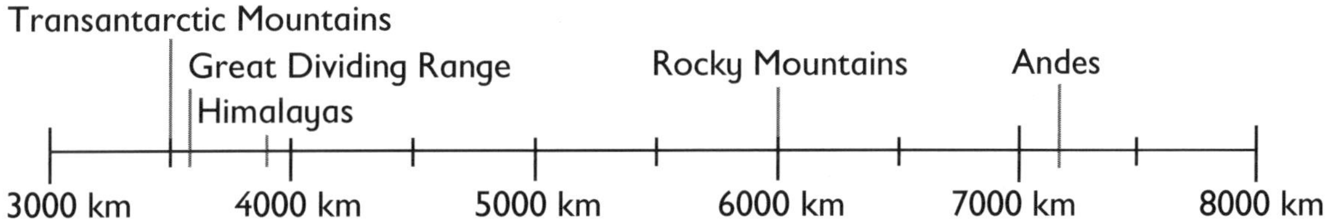

Scale drawings will vary.

Answers continued

Page 3

Money Matters
60 centimetres of 5-pence coins placed side by side is worth £1.65.
40 centimetres of 10-pence coins placed side by side is worth £1.60.
So 60 centimetres of 5-pence coins is worth 5p more than 40 centimetres of 10-pence coins.

Around the World
Results of the investigation will vary.

Around the World
Results of the investigation will vary.

Page 4

Around the World
London, UK 5661 km
Sydney, Australia 3774 km
Bangkok, Thailand 1554 km
Edinburgh, UK 6216 km
Hong Kong, China 2442 km
Washington DC, USA 4329 km

Around the World
Results of the investigation will vary.

EMU

longitude
The measurement (in degrees) of how far east or west a place is from the prime meridian in Greenwich, London.

Issue 28

Weight

Prerequisites for learning

- Choose and use standard metric units and their abbreviations when estimating, measuring and recording weight
- Calculate mentally with whole numbers and decimals
- Use efficient written methods to add, subtract, multiply and divide whole numbers and decimals
- Solve logic puzzles

Resources pencil and paper; RCM 2: My notes (optional); RCM 3: Pupil self assessment booklet (optional); ruler; scissors; collection of different sized weights up to a total of 5 kg, including 1 kg, 500 g and 100 g weights; spring balance; different types of fabric and material; scale balance; computer with internet access

Teaching support

Page 1

Focus on Science

- Children will need to spend some time considering the strength of different materials, and their appropriateness for use as a carrier bag. They will need to give careful consideration as to how they will test the strength of the different materials.
- Children are not necessarily expected to construct the shopping bag, although if time and resources allow, this would be ideal. Designing, making a mock-up, and testing the design is sufficient, as long as the children are able to draw justifiable conclusions about the suitability of their chosen material as a carrier bag.

In the Past

- Children investigate different solutions for the weights from 1 oz to 32 oz.

Teaching support continued

Page 2

What's the Problem?

- One method of working out the answer is through trial and improvement.
- A correct solution might be:
  - Wheat Puffs: 500 g – 300 g = 200 g
  - Muesli: 900 g – 300 g = 600 g

  600 g is three times as heavy as 200 g.

At Home

- It is recommended that children undertake this activity over several weeks to ensure that they investigate a variety of different cooked and uncooked foods.
- Once the children have completed the activity, ensure that there is an opportunity in class for pairs or groups of children to discuss their results.

Page 3

What's the Problem?

- A + B = 13

  A + C = 21

  ∴ C is 8 more than B.

  B + C = 16

  Use trial and improvement knowing that C is 8 more than B, e.g.
  If B = 0, then C = 8 (total 8 which is too small)

  If B = 1, then C = 9 (total 10 which is too small)

  If B = 2, then C = 10 (total 12 which is too small)

  If B = 3, then C = 11 (total 14 which is too small)

  If B = 4, then C = 12 (total 16)

  ∴ B = 4 and C = 12

  So, if A + B = 13, then ☐ + 4 = 13

  OR

  if A + C = 21, then ☐ + 12 = 21

  ∴ A = 9
- Suggest the children draw a diagram, e.g.

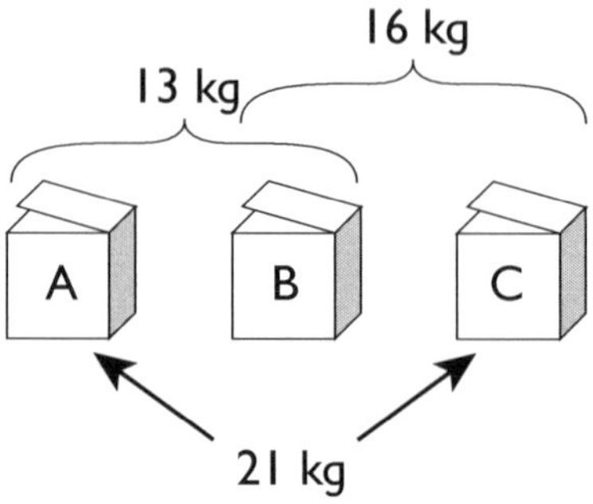

Page 3 continued

The Puzzler

- These logic problems can be solved in various ways. However, all methods are based on identifying patterns and relationships. One way of solving such problems is to assign values to the shapes. For example, in the first problem:

  By looking at the first set of scales, we can see that:

  2 × ♥ = 1 × ♣

  ∴ ♥ = 1 and ♣ = 2

  By looking at the second set of scales, we can work out using what we have discovered above that:

  ♣♣♥ = ♦

  ∴ ♦ = 5

  So, ♦♣ = 5 + 2

  ∴ 7 × ♥ balance the third scale.

- Possible values for the other puzzles are:

Puzzle 2:	Puzzle 3:	Puzzle 4:
♢ = 3	♦ = 2	♢ = 2
♧ = 2	♣ = 4	♧ or ♤ = 1·5
∴ 7 × ♡ balance the third scale.	♠ = 6	♤ or ♧ = 2·5
	∴ 6 × ♥ balance the third scale.	∴ 6 × ♡ balance the third scale.

Page 4

Focus on Science

www

- If the average 10-year-old could pull a weight that is 100 000 times their own weight they would be able to pull an object weighing 3 200 000 kg or 3200 tonnes.

What's the Problem?

- A dragon weighs $1\frac{1}{5}$ the weight of a giant. So $\frac{1}{5}$ × the weight of a giant is 1200 kg. Therefore a giant weighs 6000 kg (5 × 1200 kg) and a dragon weighs 7200 kg (6000 kg + 1200 kg).

The Puzzler

- Work with the children through the first, and possibly second weighing (see Answers).

AfL

- What did you find out? How did you record your results? Why did you decide to present them in this way?
- What conclusions can you draw from your investigation / experiment?
- How did you work out the problem / puzzle? What strategies did you use? What calculations did you do?
- What relationships can you see in the different measures?

Answers

Page 1

Focus on Science Tests and results will vary.

In the Past

Weight	Solution	Weight	Solution
1 oz	1	17 oz	16 + 1
2 oz	2	18 oz	16 + 2
3 oz	2 + 1 or 4 – 1	19 oz	16 + 2 + 1
4 oz	4	20 oz	16 + 4
5 oz	4 + 1	21 oz	16 + 4 + 1
6 oz	4 + 2 or 8 – 2	22 oz	16 + 4 + 2
7 oz	4 + 2 + 1 or 8 – 1	23 oz	16 + 4 + 2 + 1
8 oz	8	24 oz	16 + 8
9 oz	8 + 1	25 oz	16 + 8 + 1
10 oz	8 + 2	26 oz	16 + 8 + 2
11 oz	8 + 2 + 1 or 8 + 4 – 1 or 16 – 4 – 1	27 oz	16 + 8 + 2 + 1
12 oz	8 + 4 or 16 – 4	28 oz	16 + 8 + 4
13 oz	8 + 4 + 1 or 16 – 2 – 1	29 oz	16 + 8 + 4 + 1
14 oz	8 + 4 + 2 or 16 – 2	30 oz	16 + 8 + 4 + 2
15 oz	8 + 4 + 2 + 1 or 16 – 1	31 oz	16 + 8 + 4 + 2 + 1
16 oz	16	32 oz	not possible

Other solutions are possible.

Page 2

What's the Problem? The weight of the cereal box is 300 g.

At Home Results of the investigation will vary.

Page 3

What's the Problem? Parcel A weighs 9 kg.
Parcel B weighs 4 kg.
Parcel C weighs 12 kg.

The Puzzler 7♥, 7♡, 6♥, 6♡,

Page 4

Focus on Science Results of the investigation will vary. However, given that the weight of an average 10-year-old is 32 kilograms, if the average 10-year-old could pull a weight 100 000 times their own weight this would total 3200 tonnes (32 kg × 100 000). This is equivalent to ten 747 jumbo jets, 400 double-decker buses or 7 average size houses.

What's the Problem? A dragon weighs 7200 kg.

The Puzzler Yes it is possible to find the lighter coin.
Divide the 60 coins into 3 piles, each of 20 coins.
1st weighing: Weigh two of the piles; if one side is lighter than the other, it contains the light coin; if both sides balance, the light coin is in the third pile.
2nd weighing: Take the pile with the light coin in it and divide it into three piles – 7, 7 and 6 coins. Weigh the two piles of 7; if one side is lighter than the other, it contains the light coin; if both sides balance, the light coin is in the pile of 6.
3rd weighing: Take the pile with the light coin in it and divide it into three piles – 2, 2, 2 coins or 2, 2, 3 coins. Weigh two piles with 2 coins in each. If one is lighter than the other it contains the light coin; if they balance, the light coin is in the third pile.
4th weighing: If the pile contains 2 coins, weigh them to find the light coin. If the pile contains 3 coins, weigh two of them; if one is lighter than the other, it is the light coin; if they balance, the third coin is the light coin.

EMU

mass

The property of an object that is a measure of the amount of matter it contains, and its influence in a gravitational field.

Issue 29 Capacity

Prerequisites for learning

- Choose and use standard metric units and their abbreviations when estimating, measuring and recording capacity
- Round decimals to two decimal places
- Understand that capacity can be measured in both metric and imperial units
- Calculate mentally with whole numbers and decimals
- Use efficient written methods to add, subtract, multiply and divide whole numbers and decimals

Resources pencil and paper; RCM 2: My notes (optional); RCM 3: Pupil self assessment booklet (optional); calculator (optional); computer with internet access

Teaching support

Page 1

Focus on Science

- The most important aspect of this activity is in the design of the test to find out how much water children drink in a day. Encourage the children to spend time thinking about the following:
  - How they will conduct the experiment
  - How they will keep a record of their findings
  - How they will record their results

Focus on Science

- Children need to be able to convert gallons to litres for this activity (1 gallon = 4·55 litres). They also need to be able to round decimals to two decimal places.
- Ensure children understand the concept of miles per gallon.

Page 2

Around the World

- Children need to be able to convert miles to kilometres for this activity (1 mile = 1·61 kilometres). They also need to be able to round decimals to two decimal places.
- Ensure children understand the concept of miles per gallon and litres per 100 kilometre.

Page 2 continued

Money Matters

- Suggest the children draw a table to help them organise their work, e.g.

2 litre cartons at £2.90 each	5 litre cartons at £7.30 each	Total capacity	Total cost
0	3	15 litres	£21.90
3	2	16 litres	£23.30
5	1	15 litres	£21.80
8	0	16 litres	£23.20

What's the Problem?

- 1 million litres is 1000 cubic metres. It would fill a pond approximately 33 m × 30 m to 1 m depth.
- An Olympic swimming pool, 50 m × 25 m, holds 2500 m^3.

Page 3

What's the Problem?

- Each week during summer, the Moneypenny family use (7 × 750 *l*) + (3 × 1250 *l*) = 9000 *l*. Each week 7 × 1200 *l* = 8400 *l* of water flows into the well. So, each week during summer the level in the well drops by 600 *l*. The well holds a maximum of 4000 *l*, so after 6 weeks there is only 400 *l* + the daily inflow into the well. Sometime during the seventh week the well will run dry.
- Exactly when will the well run dry?

What's the Problem?

- Sonia's irrigation system uses (4 × 2·5 *l*) + (4 × 4·5 *l*) + (1 × 8·5 *l*) = 36·5 *l* per minute, or 2190 *l* per hour. The 2000 *l* pump would not be strong enough and the 4000 *l* pump would be more powerful than needed.

The Language of Maths

- For this activity children will need to have some understanding of the imperial units 'pint', 'quart' and 'gallon' and their metric equivalents, i.e.

  1 *l* = 1·76 pints

  1 gallon = 8 pints

  1 quart = 2 pints
- Children also need to understand that cl is the abbreviation for centilitre and is equivalent to 10 ml.

Teaching support continued

Page 4

What's the Problem?

- The two extra people drank 2 × 350 ml = 700 ml. If they hadn't come, all the other people could have had exactly an extra 400 – 350 ml = 50 ml of juice.

  700 ml ÷ 50 ml = 14, so 14 people were originally going to come on the picnic.

What's the Problem?

- Sandeep says that if he had twice as much he would have less than 5 *l*, so he has less than 2·5 *l*. He also says that if he had a quarter as much, he would have more than 600 ml, so he has more than 2·4 *l*.

AfL

- How did you start to solve this puzzle / answer this problem?
- What calculation strategies did you use to answer this question?
- What can you tell me about imperial units? What are their metric equivalents?
- How did you find out what a million litres looks like?

Answers

Page 1

Focus on Science Health experts and nutritionists recommend that a child should drink between 1·5 and 2 litres of water per day, and that an adult should drink around 2·5 litres of water per day.

Focus on Science For a car that does 55 miles per gallon, it will travel 12·09 miles on 1 litre of fuel and 568·23 miles on a full tank of fuel if the tank holds 47 litres. (Answers will vary depending on conversion rates used.)

Page 2

Around the World For a car that does 55 miles per gallon, it will use 5·14 litres per 100 kilometres. (Answers will vary depending on conversion rates used.)

Money Matters Five 2-litre cartons and one 5-litre carton give 15 litres exactly at a total cost of £21.80. This combination offers the best value for money.

What's the Problem? Answers will vary.

Page 3

What's the Problem? If the Moneypenny family water their garden for more than 6 weeks, the well will run dry.

What's the Problem? The 3000 *l* per hour pump

The Language of Maths 6·5 cl, $\frac{1}{2}$ pint, 350 ml, 1 pint, 0·75 ml, 1 quart, 3 pints, 1·75 *l*, 4·5 *l*, 1 gallon

Page 4

What's the Problem? 16 people came on the picnic.

What's the Problem? Sandeep has between 2·4 *l* and 2·5 *l* of petrol.

EMU 

dl

One decilitre is one-tenth of a litre or 100 ml.

Issue 30 Time

Prerequisites for learning

- Use a.m., p.m. and 12-hour clock notation
- Read time using 24-hour clock notation
- Calculate mentally with whole numbers
- Use efficient written methods to add, subtract, multiply and divide whole numbers
- Make estimations and approximations

Resources pencil and paper; RCM 2: My notes (optional); RCM 3: Pupil self assessment booklet (optional); metre rule; piece of dowel or stick about 1 m long; piece of string about 0·5 m long; small stick; computer with internet access

Teaching support

Page 1

Construct

- It is recommended that this activity be conducted over two consecutive days. On the first day, introduce the activity to the children. Provide them will all the necessary resources and, if possible, allow them to construct the sundial, leaving it in the playground overnight. On the second day, the children are then ready to use their sundial.

In the Past

- Children draw a time-line showing the major developments in transportation from 1700 to 1900.

Page 2

What's the Problem?

- Suggest the children draw a table to work out the answer, e.g.

Chiming clock 1	Chiming clock 2
12:00 noon	12:00 noon
12:55 p.m.	12:50 p.m.
1:50 p.m.	1:40 p.m.
2:45 p.m.	2:30 p.m.
3:40 p.m.	3:20 p.m.
4:35 p.m.	4:10 p.m.
5:30 p.m.	5:00 p.m.
6:25 p.m.	5:50 p.m.
7:20 p.m.	6:40 p.m.
8:15 p.m.	7:30 p.m.
9:10 p.m.	8:20 p.m.
10:05 p.m.	9:10 p.m.

Page 2 continued

The Puzzler

- To work out how old James will be in 2015: subtract the year James was born, i.e. 2001, from 2015. So James will be 14 in 2015.
- To work out how old James's mother will be in 2015: multiply 14 by 3. So James's mother will be 42 in 2015.
- To work out the year that James's mother was born: subtract 42 from 2015. So James's mother was born in 1973.
- To work out how old James's mother was when she gave birth to James: subtract 1973 from 2001. So James's mother was 28 when she gave birth to James.

In the Past

www

- Queen Victoria was queen from 20 June 1837 until her death on 22 January 1901.

Page 3

What's the Problem?

- There are generally 190 pupil days in a school year.
- When calculating the total number of days a child has been at school so far, children should take into account the number of years they have been at school in previous years, plus the number of school days to date in the current academic year.

What's the Problem?

- Each day that Caen works alone he does $\frac{1}{40}$ of the job. Each day that Able works alone he does $\frac{1}{60}$ of the job. Together they do $\frac{1}{40} + \frac{1}{60} = \frac{5}{120} = \frac{1}{24}$ of the job each day. Caen has already done $\frac{10}{40} = \frac{1}{4}$ of the job, so $\frac{3}{4}$ or $\frac{18}{24}$ of the job is left. Together Caen and Able will take 18 days to finish the job.

Page 4

The Language of Maths

- Ensure the children complete the time-line before writing the eight times in both 12-hour and 24-hour notation.
- If all the times that children write in both 12-hour and 24-hour notation are either o'clock or half past times, give them some other times, e.g. 16 minutes past 4 in the afternoon, or quarter past 9 in the morning and ask them to write these times in both 12-hour and 24-hour notation.

Teaching support continued

Page 4 continued
The Arts Roundup

- Paul and Simon together write $\frac{1}{10}$ of a song in an hour. Simon alone writes $\frac{1}{30}$ of a song in an hour. Therefore Paul writes $\frac{1}{10} - \frac{1}{30} = \frac{2}{30} = \frac{1}{15}$ of a song in an hour. It would therefore take Paul 15 hours to write a song alone.

AfL

- How accurate do you think your sundial was? What happened to the length of the shadow throughout the day?
- Talk me through your time-line.
- How did you work out the answer to the problem / puzzle? Talk me through your calculation(s). How did you work that out?
- How many days have you been at school? How did you arrive at your approximation? What about for Christopher Clever-Clogs?
- Explain to me how 24-hour time notation works. What are the benefits of using 24-hour notation rather than 12-hour notation? What are the disadvantages?

Answers

Page 1

Construct Results of the experiment will vary.

In the Past Time-lines will vary, however may include some of the following developments:
1903: first powered plane flight
1914: first passenger plane flight
1939: first jet plane
1949: first passenger jet airliner
1976: first supersonic passenger jet airliner

Page 2

What's the Problem? Both clocks will chime together again at 9:10 p.m.

The Puzzler James's mother was born in 1973.
James's mother was 28 years old when she gave birth to James.

In the Past This is four generations older than the child. Allowing 25 to 35 years between generations, this gives the great-great grandfather's birthdate between 100 to 140 years, plus the age of child in the past. So it is possible.

Page 3

What's the Problem? There are generally 190 pupil days in a school year.

Answers will vary depending on the number of years children have been at school.

Answers will vary depending on the type of school.

What's the Problem? Together it will take Caen and Able 18 more days to finish building the tree house.

Page 4

The Language of Maths

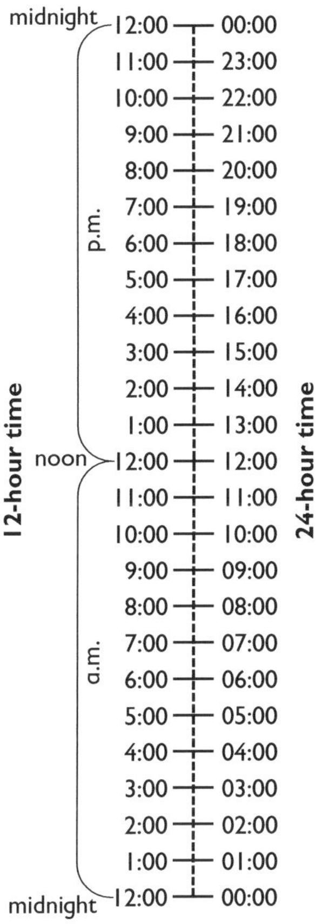

12-hour and 24-hour times will vary.

The Arts Roundup It would take Paul 15 hours to write a song alone.

EMU

GMT

GMT is the abbreviation for Greenwich Mean Time. The Earth is divided into 24 time zones. The base time zone (GMT) is at 0° longitude and passes through the Royal Greenwich Observatory in London. All the remaining time zones are measured from GMT by adding or subtracting a set number of hours.

Issue 31 Area

Prerequisites for learning

- Find the area of rectilinear shapes drawn on a square grid by counting squares
- Use the formula for the area of a rectangle to calculate its area
- Calculate mentally with whole numbers
- Use efficient written methods to add, subtract, multiply and divide whole numbers

Resources pencil and paper; RCM 2: My notes (optional); RCM 3: Pupil self assessment booklet (optional); RCM 10: 1 cm squared paper; RCM 13: Squared dot paper; coloured pencils; ruler; tape measure; computer with internet access

Teaching support

Page 1

Around the World

- Remind the children that although you want them to find out everything that they can about allotments, one of the most important aspects of this activity is about the size of the average allotment.
- If available, children can also comment on the total land area of a particular allotment association.

Construct

- If children have difficulty measuring the circumference of the cylinder, suggest they wrap a strip of paper around it and mark the measurement with a pencil.

Page 2

Looking for Patterns

- All the triangles have an area equal to half the area of the rectangle. This can be shown by drawing a perpendicular line from the side of the triangle that is adjacent to the side of the rectangle, to the opposite point of the triangle:

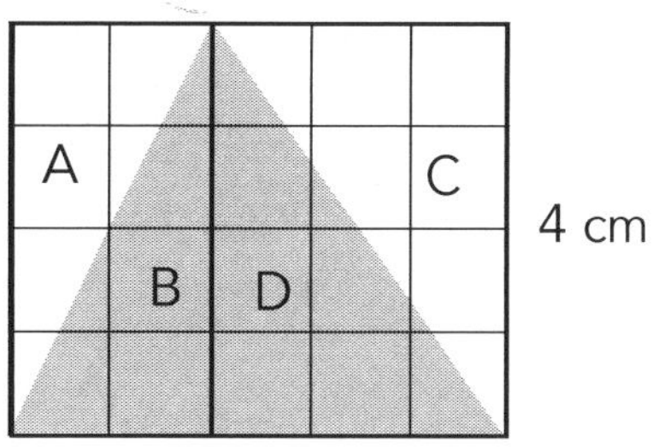

This line then divides the rectangle in two. Each of the two smaller rectangles formed is exactly bisected by a side of the triangle. Thus half the area of each of the smaller rectangles is shaded, and so half the area of the large rectangle is shaded, i.e.

The area of triangle B is half the area of rectangle A, i.e.

area of rectangle A = $4 \times 2 = 8$ cm^2

area of triangle B = $8 \div 2 = 4$ cm^2

The area of triangle D is half the area of rectangle C, i.e.

area of rectangle C = $4 \times 3 = 12$ cm^2

area of triangle D = $12 \div 2 = 6$ cm^2

$\therefore$ Total area of shaded triangle is 4 cm^2 + 6 cm^2 = 10 cm^2

Let's Investigate

- The most important aspect of this activity is how the children justify their conclusions by drawing appropriate diagrams.

Page 3

What's the Problem?

- The four extra triangles together make up a square of the same area as the original play area (see Answers).

Sports Update

- Ensure children know how to use the formula for the area of a rectangle.
- As the children are required to comment on the relationship between area, the number of players and the way the game is played, allow the children to work in pairs so that they can share ideas and discuss their reasoning.

Teaching support continued

Page 4

Construct

- Ensure children accurately draw a 4 × 4 square on the squared dot paper.
- Children work out the areas of all the squares.

Construct

- You may wish to extend this activity by asking children to design their allotment for a particular season. While this may not affect the design of their allotment space, it will obviously affect the different fruit and vegetables they choose to grow.

AfL

- What can you tell me about allotments? Talk me through your allotment.
- Talk me through how you made your label. How well does it fit? Could you improve on your design? How?
- How did you work out the areas of these triangles?
- How did you solve this problem? Did a diagram help? How?
- What can you tell me about the relationship between the size of different pitches and courts and the type of games that are played on them?
- How did you arrive at your estimate?

Answers

Page 1

Around the World Results of the investigation will vary.

Construct Labels will vary.

Page 2

Looking for Patterns
1 10 cm^2 **2** 16 cm^2 **3** 10·5 cm^2 **4** 12 cm^2
5 7·5 cm^2 **6** 9 cm^2 **7** 4 cm^2

Let's Investigate If the length of each side is doubled, the area of the rectangle will be 4 times larger.
If the length of each side is multiplied by 3, the area of the rectangle will be 9 times larger.
If the length of each side is multiplied by 4, the area of the rectangle will be 16 times larger.
If the length of each side is multiplied by 5, the area of the rectangle will be 25 times larger.

Page 3

What's the Problem?

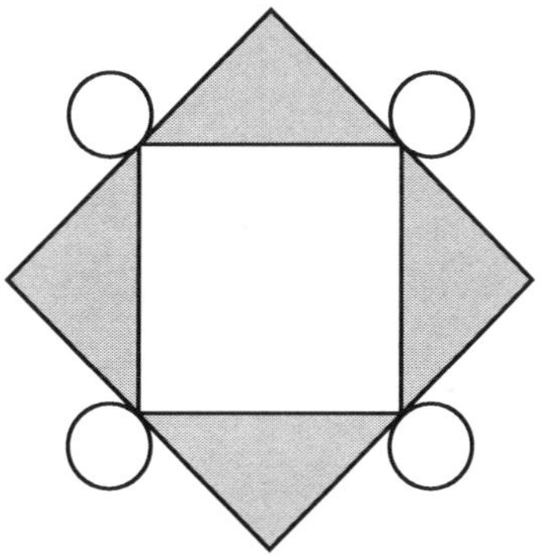

Sports Update Answers will vary depending on the sports chosen, e.g.
Football: 120 m × 90 m maximum
Rubgy: 100 m × 70 m maximum
Volleyball: 18 m × 9 m
Hockey: 91·4 m × 55 m

Page 4

Construct

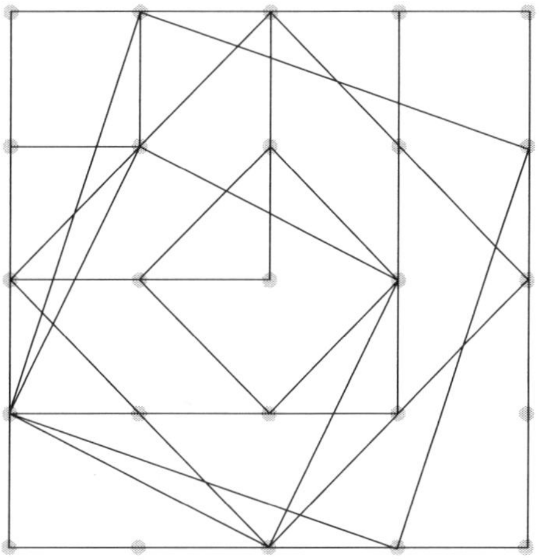

Construct Plans will vary.

EMU dimensions

The measurement of something in one or more directions, for example, its length, width or height.

Issue 32 Perimeter

Prerequisites for learning

- Draw rectangles and measure and calculate their perimeters
- Measure and calculate the perimeter of regular and irregular polygons
- Find the area of rectilinear shapes drawn on a square grid by counting squares
- Use the formula for the area of a rectangle to calculate its area
- Know that one whole turn is 360°
- Identify, visualise and describe properties of regular polygons
- Calculate mentally with whole numbers
- Use efficient written methods to add, subtract, multiply and divide whole numbers

Resources pencil and paper; RCM 2: My notes (optional); RCM 3: Pupil self assessment booklet (optional); RCM 10: 1 cm squared paper; RCM 13: Squared dot paper; ruler; tape measure; 2 large sheets of paper; scissors; glue; sellotape; selection of commercially produced paper bags (optional); two 10p coins; two £2 coins; matchsticks, interlocking cubes

Teaching support

Page 1

Construct

- If available, provide the children with a selection of commercially produced paper bags. Allow them to carefully cut open the bags to reveal the net of the bag. Discuss with the children how this may help them design and construct their own bags.

Let's Investigate

- Ensure children fully understand the terms 'diameter' and 'circumference'.
- Discuss with the children what is meant by 'vehicle size'. How are they going to measure this?

Page 2

The Puzzler

- The perimeter of the whole chessboard is 32 'square' units.
- Ensure children realise that a line of squares may be vertical, horizontal or diagonal.

Page 2 continued

What's the Problem?

- The common border between Sam and Toni forms one side of each of their gardens, so this border must be the long side of Sam's garden and the short side of Toni's.

- The sides of Toni's garden are 20 m and 40 m longer than Sam's. Toni's perimeter is twice Sam's, so 2 × 20 m by 2 × 40 m is the size of Toni's garden, i.e. 40 m × 80 m. The common border is 40 m long, and we are told that Sam's other border is 20 m less than this, so Sam's other border is 20 m long.
- Draw the diagram of Sam's and Toni's gardens showing the common border.

The Puzzler

- There are a total of 35 hexominoes altogether. Can the children find them all? Which has the smallest / largest perimeter / area?

Page 3

Let's Investigate

- Once the children have drawn the triangle and line from the top corner to the mid-point of the opposite side, ensure they make a prediction before carrying out the rest of the investigation.

The Puzzler

- Ensure children fully understand the problem, i.e.

- Also ensure children make a prediction before trying it out.

Teaching support continued

Page 4

What's the Problem?

- Ensure children are familiar with the term 'square metres (m^2)'.

Let's Investigate

- Ensure children are able to identify, visualise and describe properties of regular polygons, including triangle, quadrilateral, pentagon, hexagon, heptagon, octagon, nonagon, decagon and dodecagon. However, the shapes they create using the 12 matchsticks do not need to be regular.

AfL

- Talk me through your design. How could you have improved it?
- How did you solve this puzzle / problem? Did a diagram help? How?
- How did you work out the area?
- What strategies did you use to find a solution to this puzzle / answer to this problem?

Answers

Page 1

Construct Children's bags will vary.

Let's Investigate Results of the investigations will vary. However, there is a correlation between car tyre size and vehicle size.

Page 2

The Puzzler 32 'square' units
The squares on the black diagonal from corner to corner, or the squares on the white diagonal from corner to corner have the same perimeter as the complete chessboard.

What's the Problem? Sam's garden is 20 m × 40 m, Toni's is 40 m × 80 m.

The Puzzler There are 27 hexominoes with a perimeter of 14 units.

Page 3

Let's Investigate The rectangle has the same area as the triangle, but a smaller perimeter.

The Puzzler Two revolutions.

Page 4

What's the Problem? 16 square beds with sides of 1 m and corners touching would give a maximum perimeter of 64 m, i.e.

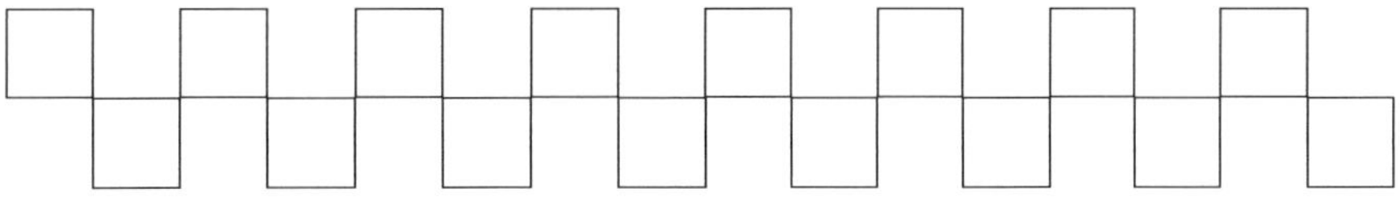

Triangular beds would give a larger perimeter, but children are not expected to be able to calculate the maximum number of beds possible.

Let's Investigate The shape that fits the most cubes inside it will depend upon the ratio of the size of the cubes to the length of the matchsticks. However, generally speaking, a regular dodecagon will probably hold the most interlocking cubes.

EMU

radius

A straight line extending from the centre of a circle to its edge. The length of a radius is half the length of the diameter.

Issue 33 Measuring – General

Prerequisites for learning

- Choose and use standard metric units and their abbreviations when estimating, measuring and recording length
- Understand simple expressions and formulae in words and symbols
- Draw rectangles and measure and calculate their perimeters
- Find the area of rectilinear shapes drawn on a square grid by counting squares
- Calculate time intervals
- Use sequences to scale numbers up or down
- Calculate mentally with whole numbers and decimals
- Use efficient written methods to add, subtract, multiply and divide whole numbers and decimals
- Make estimations and approximations
- Answer a question by identifying what data to collect; organise, present, analyse and interpret the data in tables, diagrams, tally charts, pictograms and bar charts, using ICT where appropriate

Resources pencil and paper; RCM 2: My notes (optional); RCM 3: Pupil self assessment booklet (optional); RCM 10: 1 cm squared paper; RCM 12: 0·5 cm squared paper; ruler; selection of newspapers; sheets of A4 paper; scissors; sellotape; glue; stopwatch; metre rule; tape measure; computer with internet access

Teaching support

Page 1

Focus on Science

- You may need to work with the children to identify the formula, i.e. $1{\cdot}2t^2$.
- If children are not confident with writing a mathematical rule or formula, discuss with them possible ways of writing this, including the use of the symbol *t* (to represent time).
- If appropriate, discuss with the children the algebraic convention for omitting the multiplication sign when writing an algebraic expression, i.e. $1{\cdot}2t^2$ rather than $1{\cdot}2 \times (t^2)$.
- Children investigate further the life and work of Galileo.

Page 1 continued

Around the World

- Before drawing a scale map, suggest the children first draw a quick sketch of what their school might look like from a hot air balloon. This will allow them to concentrate first on getting the position of the school's features in the correct place, before then working on making sure that their map is to scale.

Page 2

Construct

- This activity focuses on two aspects of measuring – length (distance) and time. Ensure the children realise that they are required to find ways of measuring both the distance their paper planes travel, as well as the time they take to travel this distance.
- When deciding upon which of their paper planes travelled the fastest over the longest distance, children will need to use their own criteria for making this decision. However, insist the children are able to justify their conclusions. Therefore it is important that the children work in pairs so that they can share ideas and discuss their reasoning.

Sports Update

- Ensure children understand which lines on a tennis court make up the perimeter of a singles court, i.e.

- How many rectangles are there on a tennis court?

Page 3

At Home

- Once the children have completed the activity, ensure that there is an opportunity in class for pairs or groups of children to discuss their reports and conclusions.

Focus on Science

- Suggest the children find their pulse either at the neck or at the wrist.
- The normal pulse rate for children aged 6 to 12 years is between 75 and 110 beats per minute (bpm).

Teaching support continued

Page 4

Focus on Science

- Ensure children understand the *Sun Protection Factor* (SPF) system and how to calculate how long a particular sunscreen will protect you from the sun.
- The most common SPFs are: 5, 10, 15, 20 and 30.
- Remind children that even though high SPF sunscreens provide protection for a longer time, you still need to reapply them every 2 hours.

Sports Update

- Ensure children understand the terms 'average speed' and 'kilometres per hour'.

AfL

- Tell me about Galileo's discovery. What is the formula? How did you work that out? What patterns / relationship did you notice?
- What do you need to think about when drawing a scale drawing?
- What special features did your paper plane have to make it travel the fastest over the longest distance? How did you record the results of your experiment? What makes you say that this plane in particular travelled the fastest over the longest distance?
- How do prices vary between different brands? What conclusions did you make?
- How does your pulse rate change in different situations? How did you record your results? How did this method of recording make it easy for you to make these judgements?
- Tell me about sunscreen protection. How does it work?

Answers

Page 1

Focus on Science Formula: $1{\cdot}2 \times (t^2)$ or $1{\cdot}2t^2$

Around the World Maps will vary.

Page 2

Construct Paper planes and results will vary.

Sports Update

Doubles
Perimeter: 69·6 m
Area: 261·8 m^2

Singles
Perimeter: 64 m
Area: 195·16 m^2

Page 3

At Home Results of the investigation will vary.

Focus on Science Results of the investigation will vary.

Page 4

Focus on Science Results of the investigation will vary. However, results for common SPF products include:

SPF 30:
30 × 15 = 450 minutes or 7 hours 30 minutes of protection

SPF 20:
20 × 15 = 300 minutes or 5 hours of protection

SPF 15:
15 × 15 = 225 minutes or 3 hours 45 minutes of protection

SPF 10:
10 × 15 = 150 minutes or 2 hours 30 minutes of protection

SPF 5:
5 ×15 = 75 minutes or 1 hour 15 minutes of protection

Sports Update Total distance = (1 × 18 km) + (2 × 12 km) = 42 km
Average speed = 42 km ÷ 3 h = 14 km per hour

EMU 

speed
The rate at which someone or something is able to move or function.

Issue 34

Measuring – General

Prerequisites for learning

- Choose and use standard metric units and their abbreviations when estimating, measuring and recording length and weight
- Interpret intervals and divisions on partially numbered scales and record readings accurately
- Calculate mentally with whole numbers and decimals
- Use efficient written methods to add, subtract, multiply and divide whole numbers and decimals
- Solve logic puzzles
- Make estimations and approximations

Resources pencil and paper; RCM 2: My notes (optional); RCM 3: Pupil self assessment booklet (optional); different material and fabric, including plastic and tissue paper; string or wool; glue; scissors; sellotape; modelling clay or similar (for weight of parachute); stopwatch; tape measure; selection of newspapers; computer with internet access

Teaching support

Page 1

Construct

- Be aware of health and safety issues when asking the children to drop their parachutes.

What's the Problem?

- Remind children that the snakes leave 10 cm between each other, so the total length of all five snakes is 3·1 m.
- Use trial and improvement techniques and increase from 3 snakes at 10 cm + 2 snakes at 40 cm, or (3 × 10 cm) + (2 × 40 cm). The only numbers that fit the criteria are 2 × 80 cm and 3 × 50 cm.

Page 2

Focus on Science

- Ensure children have successfully completed and understood this activity before starting on the Around the World activity below.

Page 2 continued

Around the World

- For this activity children need to understand *knot* as a unit of measuring speed, and know and understand its equivalence in kilometres per hour and miles per hour. Therefore, ensure the children have successfully completed and understood the Focus on Science activity above before starting on this activity.

The Puzzler

- Travelling at 120 km per hour, the train would take 30 seconds to travel 1 km and therefore 1 minute to travel 2 km, plus 6 seconds for the complete train to pass any point, making a total of 1 minute 6 seconds.

Page 3

Sports Update

- After the first x (it can be any number) seconds, Sam runs 200 m and Alex runs 300 m; they pass one another. Alex is therefore the faster runner and will win the race. After the next x seconds, Sam has run 400 m in total, so is 100 m from Alex's base; Alex has run a total of 600 m, so has reached Sam's base, turned around and is 100 m on the return journey.
- After 3x seconds, Sam has run 600 m, so has reached Alex's base and is 100 m on the return journey; Alex has run 900 m, so has run 400 m of the return journey. They cross again here.
- Suggest children draw a diagram similar to the following:

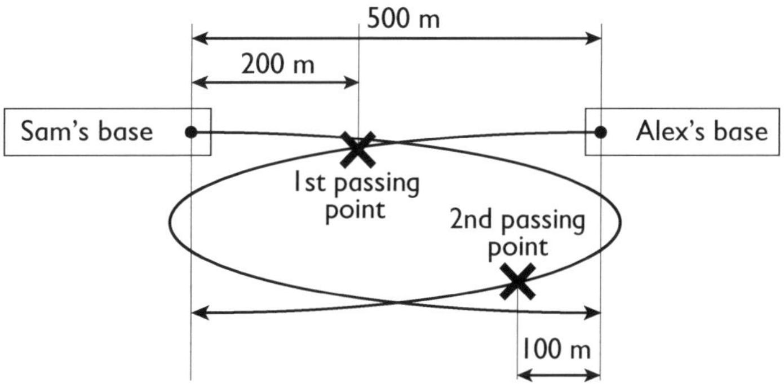

- Children work out how many times faster Alex is than Sam.

In the Past

- A Roman mile is 1480 m and is divided into 1000 paces. Therefore one Roman pace is 1480 ÷ 1000 = 1·48 m.
- A Roman pace is equal to 5 Roman feet.

  Therefore one foot is 1·48 m ÷ 5 = 29·6 cm.

Teaching support continued

Page 4

Let's Investigate

- Discuss with the children the difference between a Roman mile and a statute mile.
- Remind the children that a pace is measured from the front of the right (or left) foot to the front of the same foot. Suggest they might measure five of their paces and then divide by five to get a more accurate measurement of their pace.

Let's Investigate

- Children should understand that weather forecasting is not an exact science, and that forecasts are sometimes contradictory and often wrong.
- Children comment on the similarities and differences between how each of the different newspapers displays rainfall. Do all newspapers forecast the same likelihood of rainfall?

What's the Problem?

- What small weight would you need to measure 1 lb of sugar from a 1 kg bag using a scale balance only twice? Clue: 1 lb = 455 g.

AfL

- How did you measure the length of time each of your parachutes was airborne for?
- Explain to me how you worked out the answer to this problem / puzzle?
- What did you discover about the world's most powerful cyclones?
- What can you tell me about a Roman mile, pace and foot?
- How does this compare with your 'mille' / mile?
- What can you tell me about temperature and how it is forecast?

Answers

Page 1

Construct Designs and results will vary.

What's the Problem? Two snakes are 80 cm and three are 50 cm.

Page 2

Focus on Science 118·4 km per hour
73·6 miles per hour

Page 2 continued

Around the World Results of the investigation will vary. However, they may include some of the following:

1958: Hurricane Ida. Atlantic.
Maximum wind speed 165 knots, 190 mph, 305 kph
1973: Hurricane Nora. Pacific.
Maximum wind speed 161 knots, 185 mph, 298 kph
1979: Typhoon Tip. Pacific.
Maximum wind speed 165 knots, 190 mph, 305 kph
2005: Hurricane Wilma. Atlantic.
Maximum wind speed 161 knots, 185 mph, 298 kph
2011: Hurricane Yasi. Australia.
Maximum wind speed 161 knots, 185 mph, 298 kph

The Puzzler 1 minute 6 seconds

Page 3

Sports Update Alex wins.
They pass each other 100 m from Alex's base (which is the same as 400 m from Sam's base).

In the Past A Roman pace is 1·48 m.
A Roman foot is 29·6 cm.

Page 4

Let's Investigate Results of the investigation will vary.

Let's Investigate Answers will vary.

What's the Problem? Put the weight on one side of the balance and divide the sugar between the two sides until they balance. The side with the weight will have 480 g of sugar, the other side will have 520 g of sugar. Now transfer the 40 g weight to the other side of the balance (the one with 520 g of sugar) and remove sugar from this side until the scale balances. On one side there will be 480 g of sugar and on the other side, the 40 g weight and 440 g of sugar.

EMU

per
For each or everything mentioned.

Issue 35

Organising and interpreting data

Prerequisites for learning

- Answer a question by identifying what data to collect; organise, present, analyse and interpret the data in tables, diagrams, tally charts, pictograms and bar charts, using ICT where appropriate
- Write a short report of a statistical enquiry, justifying choices and conclusions
- Use Venn diagrams or Carroll diagrams to sort data and objects using more than one criterion
- Describe the occurrence of familiar events using the language of chance or likelihood

Resources pencil and paper; RCM 2: My notes (optional); RCM 3: Pupil self assessment booklet (optional); RCM 10: 1 cm squared paper; RCM 12: 0·5 cm squared paper; ruler; calculator; data handling software; computer with internet access

Teaching support

Page 1

Let's Investigate

- Discuss with the children the meaning of the word 'average' in the context of this problem, i.e. the most common age.
- This activity is designed to enable children to develop for themselves a method for working out the average. If appropriate, discuss with the children that the average, or *mean*, can be calculated by adding together all the ages of the children in the class (in months), then dividing the total by the number of children in the class before finally converting this into years and months.
- If appropriate, children represent their data using ICT.

At Home

- Children complete Venn diagrams similar to this, involving themselves, a parent and a sibling:

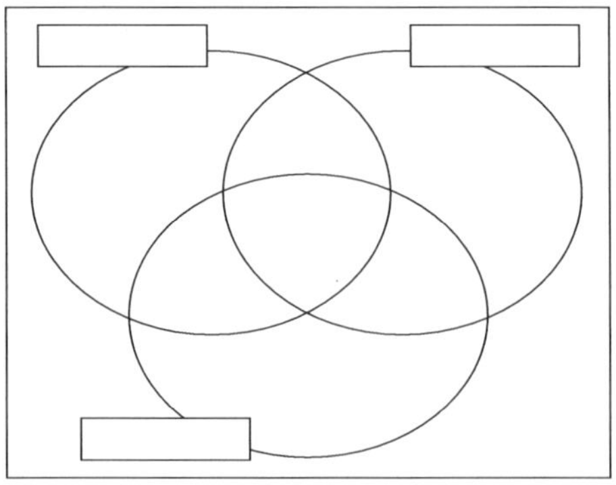

- Once the children have completed the activity, ensure that there is an opportunity in class for pairs or groups of children to share and discuss their Venn diagrams.

Page 2

Sports Update

- This activity concerns reading and interpreting results presented in a table and a Knock-out (tournament) Results diagram.
- If appropriate, children write their statements using ICT.

Page 3

Let's Investigate

- Ensure that children understand that a sample represents a subset of manageable size which can then be used to make inferences about the whole group.

Around the World

- Children could investigate this topic either on the internet or by visiting a supermarket.
- If the children do undertake this investigation out of school, once they have completed the activity, ensure that there is an opportunity in class for pairs or groups of children to discuss their results.

Page 4

Let's Investigate

- This activity is concerned with the children being able to sort in a variety of ways, choosing their own criteria, and then representing the data in a variety of ways including in a table, Venn diagram and Carroll diagram.

In the Past

- Refer children to the five aspects of the data handling cycle on page 1 of the issue:
  Step 1: Plan
  Step 2: Collect data
  Step 3: Process the data
  Step 4: Represent the data
  Step 5: Interpret and discuss the data
- If appropriate, children represent their data using ICT.

The Language of Maths

- Children write events for the following terms: 'unlikely', 'equally likely', 'likely', 'uncertain', 'probable', 'possible', 'impossible', 'good chance', 'poor chance', 'no chance', 'equal chance' and 'even chance'.

AfL

- Explain to me the results of your investigation.
- What conclusions can you draw?
- What can you tell me about the information displayed in the graph / chart / table?
- Why did you decide to present your data in this way? How else could you have displayed the data?
- How are you and a member of your family the same? How are you different? How does your Venn diagram show this?
- Tell me some interesting facts about the results of the 2010 World Cup.
- Tell me something that you are sure of seeing through the classroom window? What about something that is not very likely?

Answers

Page 1

Let's Investigate Results of the investigation will vary.

At Home Venn diagrams will vary.

Page 2

Sports Update Statements will vary.

Page 3

Let's Investigate Results of the investigation will vary.

Around the World Organic food is grown or reared without the use of synthetic chemicals in favour of naturally occurring pesticides, fertilisers, and other growing aids.
Results of the investigation will vary.

Page 4

Let's Investigate Tables, Venn diagrams and Carroll diagrams will vary.

In the Past Results of the investigation will vary.

The Language of Maths Descriptions will vary.

EMU 

probability
The likelihood of something happening.

Issue 36

Organising and interpreting data

Prerequisites for learning

- Use Venn diagrams to sort data and objects using more than one criterion.
- Answer a question by identifying what data to collect; organise, present, analyse and interpret the data in tables, diagrams, tally charts, pictograms and bar charts, using ICT where appropriate
- Write a short report of a statistical enquiry, justifying choices and conclusions

Resources pencil and paper; RCM 2: My notes (optional); RCM 3: Pupil self assessment booklet (optional); RCM 10: 1 cm squared paper; RCM 11: 2 cm squared paper; RCM 12: 0·5 cm squared paper; ruler; business section of a newspaper for 10 days; tape measure; child's skipping rope; data handling software; computer

Teaching support

Page 1
Famous Mathematicians

- Ensure children understand how to use an eight region Venn diagram.
- Children investigate the life and work of John Venn.

Page 2
Money Matters

- This activity needs to be undertaken over a two week period.
- You may need to assist children in choosing an appropriate company whose share price to follow.
- Discuss with the children that when the value of shares goes up, people sell them for more than they paid. If the value of shares goes down, investors can lose money.
- If appropriate, children represent their data using ICT.

Let's Investigate

- Discuss with the children how they are going to find out what the average height is of all the children in each of the year groups in the school. What is the least disruptive way of collecting the data? Perhaps taking a sample?
- If appropriate, children represent their data using ICT.

Teaching support continued

Page 3

The Language of Maths

- Before setting the children to work independently on this activity, discuss with them the best way to go about conducting the survey, including the things to consider mentioned in the issue.
- If appropriate, children represent their data using ICT.

Focus on Science

- Refer children to the five aspects of the data handling cycle on page 4 of the issue:
  Step 1: Plan
  Step 2: Collect data
  Step 3: Process the data
  Step 4: Represent the data
  Step 5: Interpret and discuss the data
- If appropriate, children represent their data using ICT.

Page 4

Sports Update

- Before setting the children to work independently on this activity, discuss with them the best way to go about designing their experiment, including the things to think about mentioned in the issue.
- If appropriate, children represent their data using ICT.

AfL

- Explain to me the results of your investigation.
- What conclusions can you draw?
- What can you tell me about the information displayed in the graph / chart / table?
- What do you think this chart represents? Why do you think this?
- What relationships / connections / trends do you notice?
- Tell me about your experiment.
- Why did you decide to present your data in this way? How else could you have displayed the data?

Answers

Page 1

Famous Mathematicians

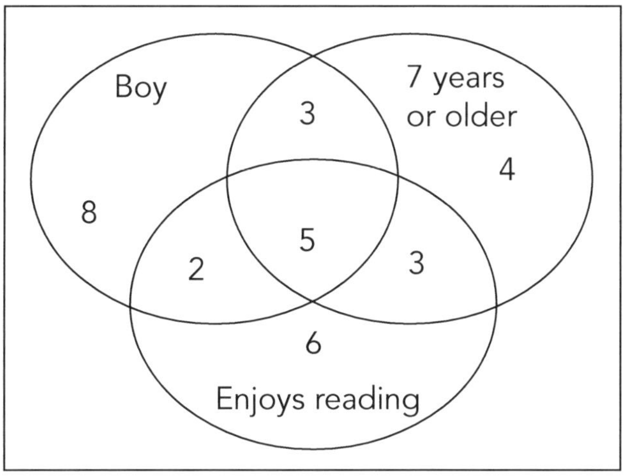

31

Page 2

Money Matters Results of the investigation will vary.

Let's Investigate Results of the investigation will vary.

Page 3

The Language of Maths Results of the investigation will vary.

Focus on Science Results of the investigation will vary. However, there is a correlation between handspan and height, and between handspan and foot length.

Page 4

Sports Update Results of the investigation will vary.

EMU

survey

To investigate the opinions, preferences and experiences of a group of people by asking them questions.

Enriching Maths 4
Record of completion

Class/Teacher ____________________

Strand	Topic	Issue	Names									
Counting and understanding number	Whole numbers	1										
	Whole numbers	2										
	Negative numbers	3										
	Fractions	4										
	Decimals	5										
	Ratio and proportion	6										
	General	7										
	General	8										
	General	9										
Calculating	Addition	10										
	Subtraction	11										
	Multiplication	12										
	Division	13										
	Mixed operations	14										
	Mixed operations	15										
	Mixed operations	16										

Strand	Topic	Issue	Names									
Calculating	Calculating with fractions	17										
	General	18										
	General	19										
Understanding shape	2-D shapes	20										
	3-D solids	21										
	Symmetry and reflection	22										
	Position and direction	23										
	Movement and angle	24										
	General	25										
	General	26										
Measuring	Length	27										
	Weight	28										
	Capacity	29										
	Time	30										
	Area	31										
	Perimeter	32										
	General	33										
	General	34										
Handling data	Organising and interpreting data	35										
	Organising and interpreting data	36										

My notes

EMU

Name: ____________ Issue: ____________

The Maths Herald

Volume 4

Date of starting issue: ____________ Date of finishing issue: ____________

My notes

My notes

My notes

Any other comments?

Your teacher's comments

Name: ____________ Issue: ____________

The Maths Herald

Volume 4

Date of starting issue: ____________ Date of finishing issue: ____________

What have you learned?

What did you use to help you?

What did you enjoy the most?

What did you enjoy the least?

Did you find the work:

too easy? ☐

just about right? ☐

too hard? ☐

What would you like to learn next about this topic and why?

Napier's Rods

×	1	2	3	4	5	6	7	8	9
1	0/1	0/2	0/3	0/4	0/5	0/6	0/7	0/8	0/9
2	0/2	0/4	0/6	0/8	1/0	1/2	1/4	1/6	1/8
3	0/3	0/6	0/9	1/2	1/5	1/8	2/1	2/4	2/7
4	0/4	0/8	1/2	1/6	2/0	2/4	2/8	3/2	3/6
5	0/5	1/0	1/5	2/0	2/5	3/0	3/5	4/0	4/5
6	0/6	1/2	1/8	2/4	3/0	3/6	4/2	4/8	5/4
7	0/7	1/4	2/1	2/8	3/5	4/2	4/9	5/6	6/3
8	0/8	1/6	2/4	3/2	4/0	4/8	5/6	6/4	7/2
9	0/9	1/8	2/7	3/6	4/5	5/4	6/3	7/2	8/1

Square grids

Function machines

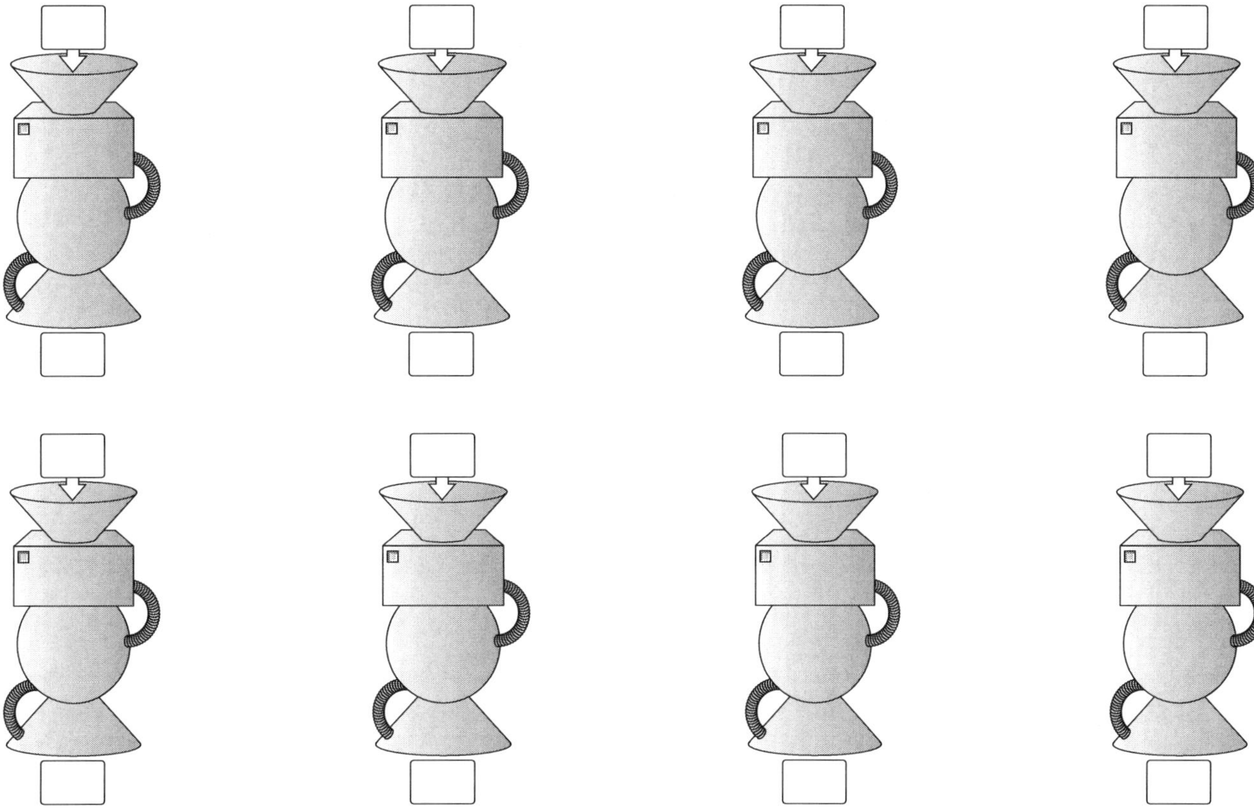

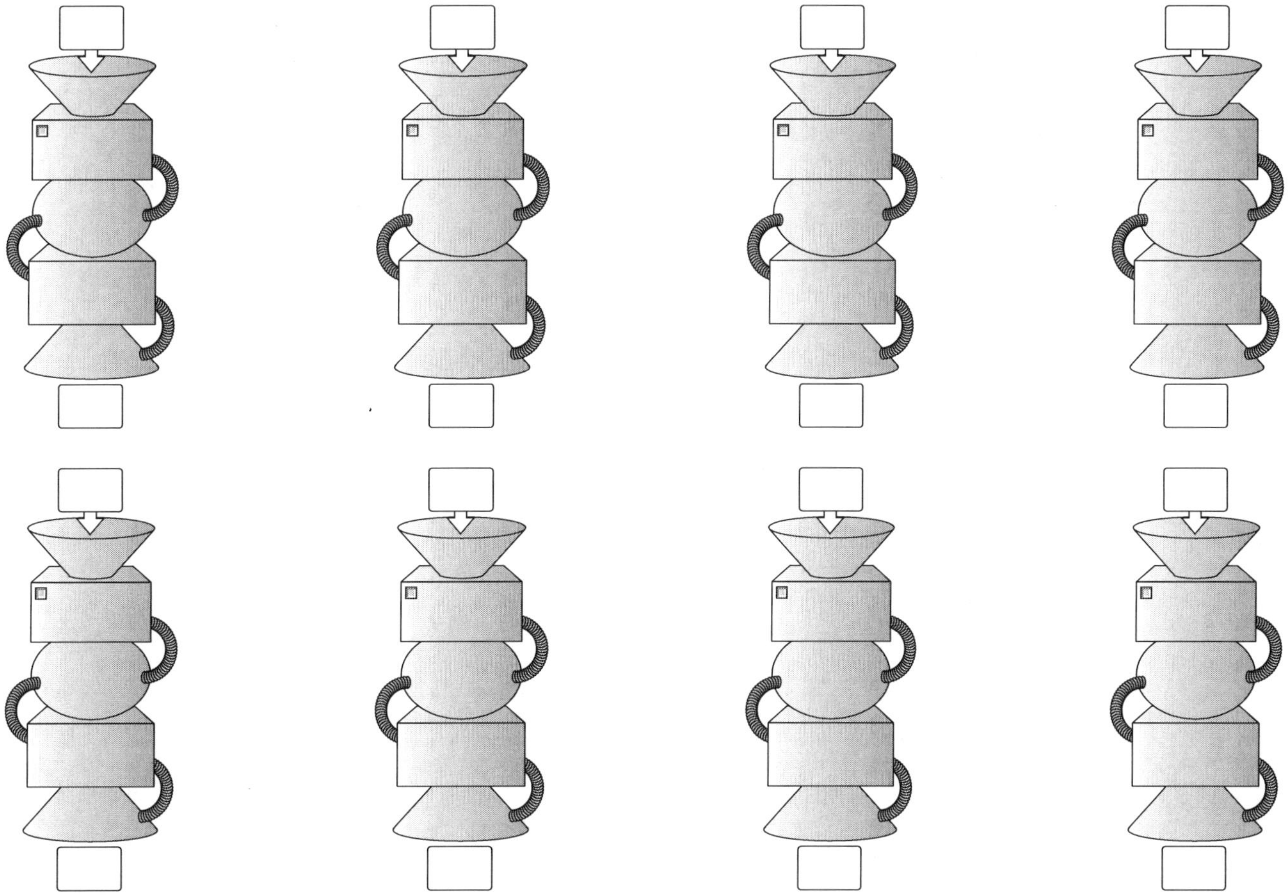

Folding shapes

Square

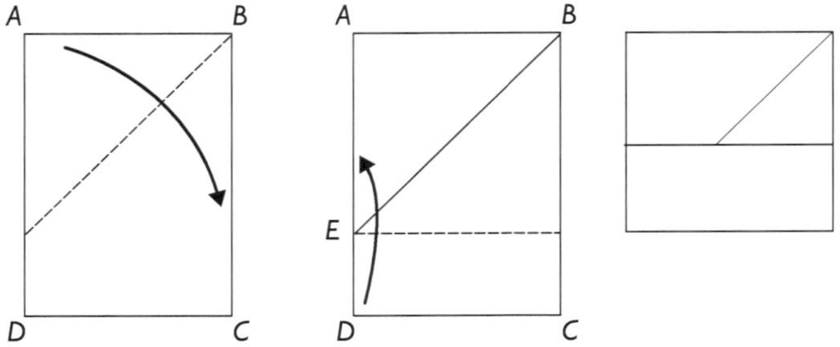

Step 1
Fold corner A onto side BC so that the crease passes through corner B, then unfold.

Step 2
Fold corner D onto side AD so that the crease passes through point E.

Equilateral triangle

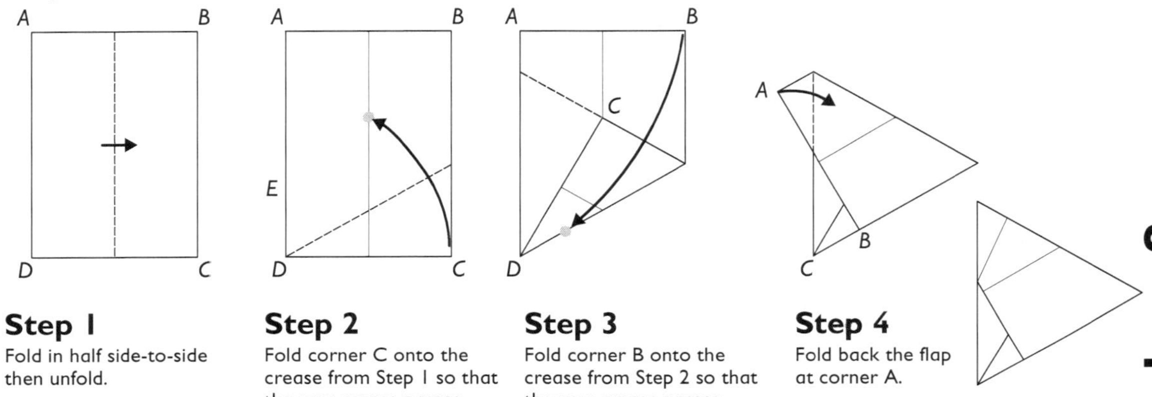

Step 1
Fold in half side-to-side then unfold.

Step 2
Fold corner C onto the crease from Step 1 so that the new crease passes through corner D.

Step 3
Fold corner B onto the crease from Step 2 so that the new crease passes through corner C.

Step 4
Fold back the flap at corner A.

Rhombus

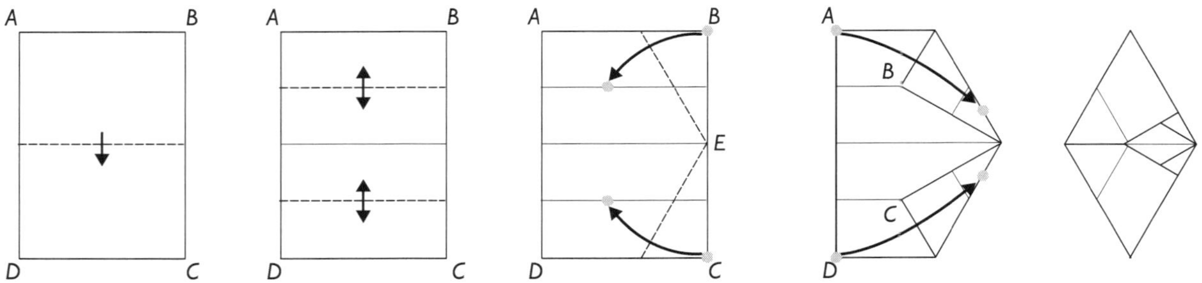

Step 1
Fold in half top-to-bottom, then unfold.

Step 2
Fold sides AB and sides CD onto the crease from Step 1, then unfold.

Step 3
Fold corner B onto the top crease from Step 2 so that the new crease passes through point E; repeat with corner C and the bottom crease.

Step 4
Fold corner A onto the top crease from Step 3 so that the new crease passes through corner B. Repeat, folding corner D onto the bottom crease from Step 3 so that the new crease passes through corner C.

Kite

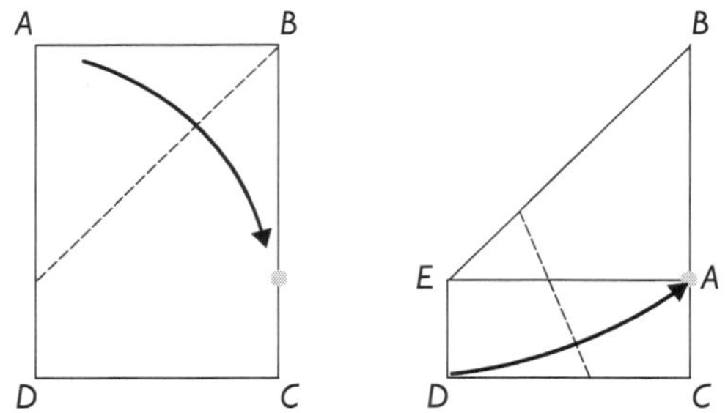

Step 1
Fold corner A onto side BC so that the crease passes through corner B.

Step 2
Fold corner D to point A.

Step 3
Fold corner C to point E.

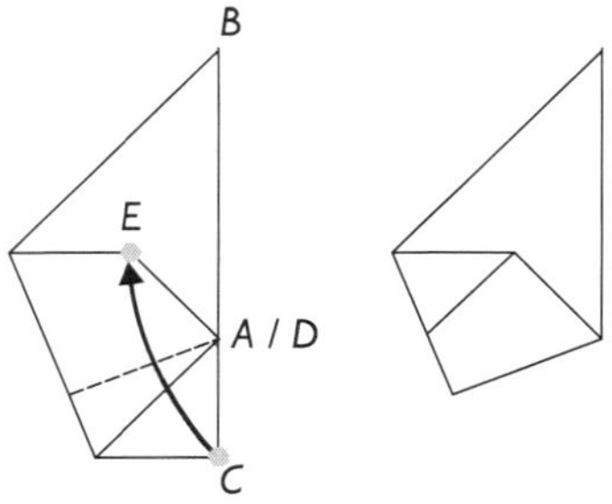

Regular hexagon

Steps 1–4
Follow the steps for the rhombus.

Step 5
Fold the top and bottom points to the centre along the creases made in the previous steps.

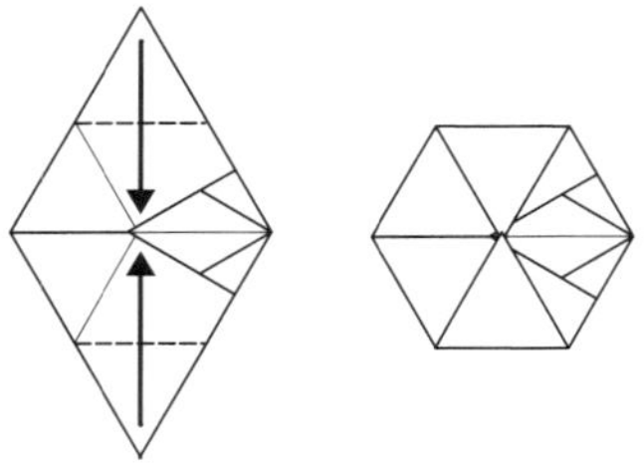

Sierpinski Triangle

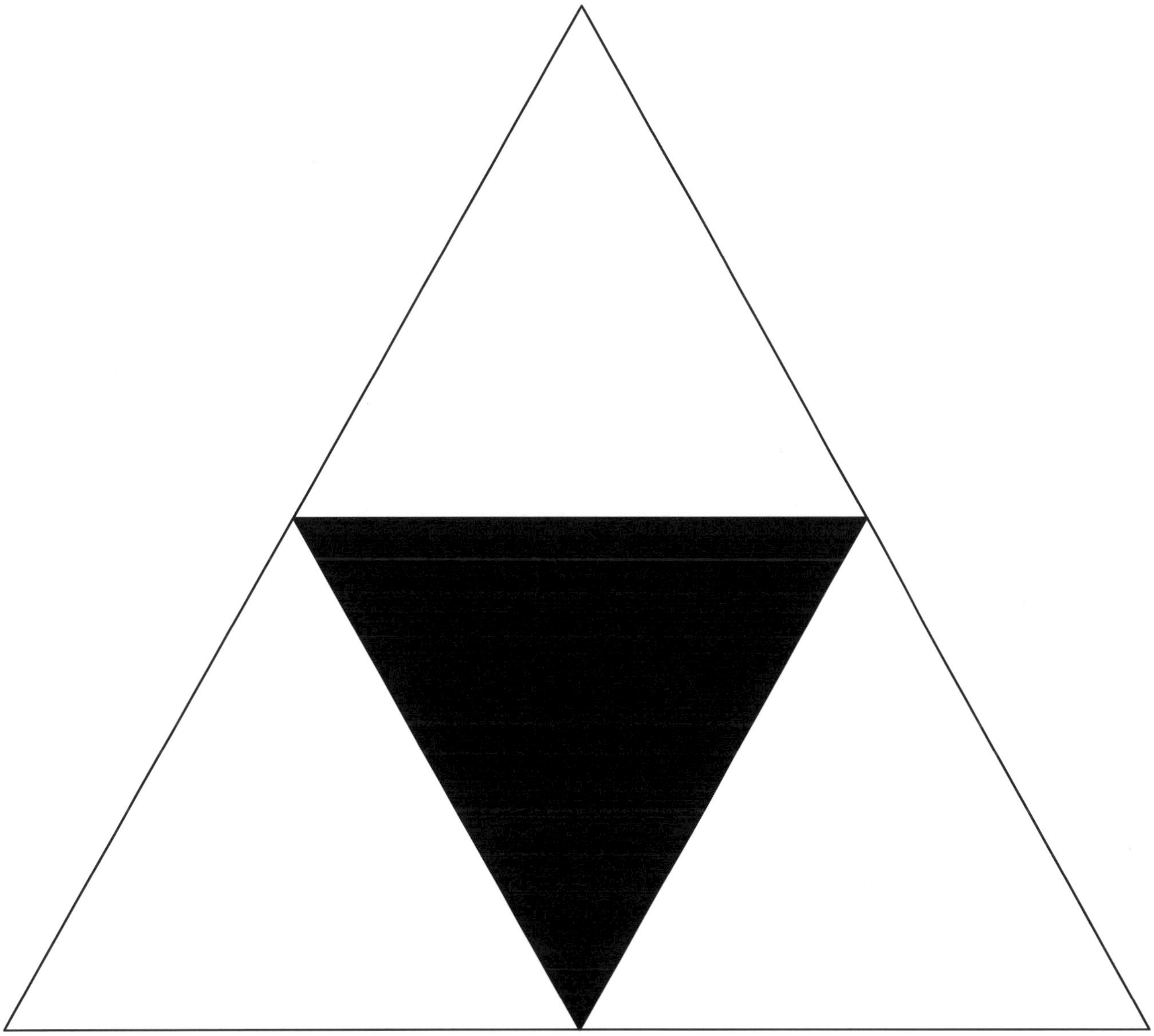

Analogue clocks

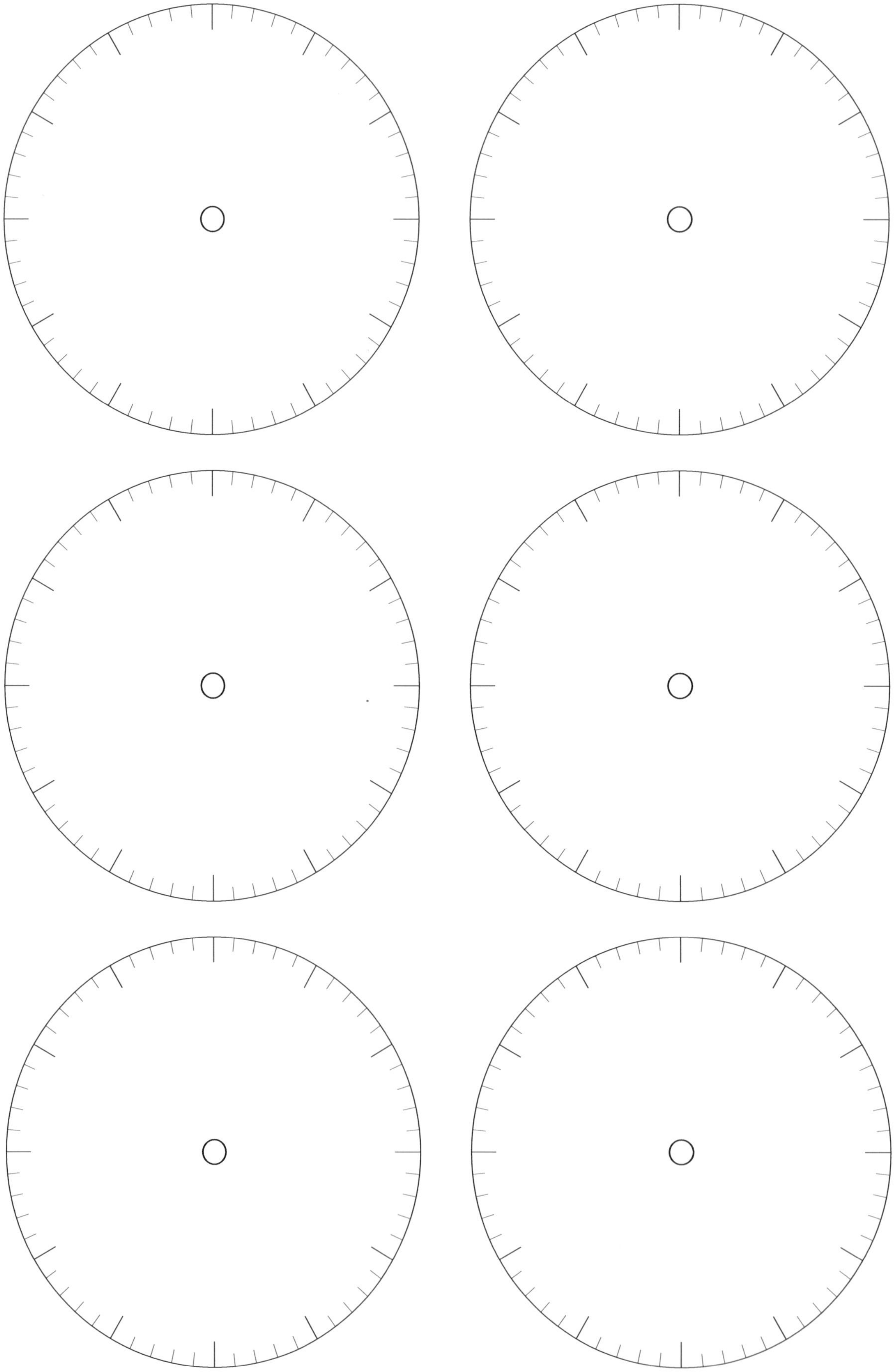

1 cm squared paper

2 cm squared paper

0·5 cm squared paper

Squared dot paper

Isometric paper